What they are saying about *Maverick Women*:

Riveting. . . and full of absolutely fascinating women.
-- *Star Trek VI* writer/director NICHOLAS MEYER

Ever since childhood, I've been inspired by rebel women, those pioneers whose courage, intelligence, and individuality sent them down untrodden paths — and lit the way for generations to come. Frances Laurence's *Maverick Women* reminds us with affection and fascinating detail how these unique ladies shaped their world, and ultimately, our nation. Spending time in their company gave me tremendous pleasure, and a fresh appreciation for their accomplishments.
-- BARBARA ALPERT, author of *No Friend Like a Sister* and *The Love of Friends*

Fina a cosy corner and a comfortable chair. With Maverick Women, you're in for a lively and enlightening series of tales about notable but little-known women that will rivet you until the very end. A fresh voice with a love of history, Laurence writes with aplomb and compelling detail — reminding us again what remarkable lives have created our world.
-- GAYLE LYNDS, author of *Masquerade*

Frances Laurence has introduced us to some remarkable women who took charge of their own lives long before such self-determination became fashionable or even acceptable!
-- *NBC Today* senior editor FRANCES WEAVER

MAVERICK WOMEN

19th Century Women
Who Kicked Over
the Traces

by Frances Laurence

Manifest Publications
Carpinteria, California
1998

Maverick Women
Nineteenth Century Women
Who Kicked Over The Traces

by Frances Laurence

Published by:
Manifest Publications
P. O. Box 429
Carpinteria, CA 93014-0429 U. S. A.

Publisher's Cataloging-in-Publication

Laurence, Frances.
    Maverick women : 19th century women who kicked over the traces / by Frances Laurence. -- 1st ed.
    p. cm.
    Includes bibliographical references.
    ISBN: 0-9627896-0-7

    1. Women--United States--19th century--Biography.   I. Title.

CT3260.L38 1998   920.72'0973'09034
                           QBI97-41302

Book Design by Valentina Laurence Pfeil

Cover Photo by George Fiske, Yosemite, California 1900
Print supplied by Leroy Radanovich

CONTENTS

To my dear husband and family

✳ ✳ ✳

There really was a Maverick. He was a prominent Texas lawyer named Samuel A. Maverick who was one of the signers of Texas' Declaration of Independence. Only once in his career was he persuaded to accept a herd of cattle in payment of a debt owed him. No cattleman, he sent his herd to a range bought for the purpose about fifty miles south of San Antonio, and left it in the care of a man who knew even less about cattle than he did, if possible. His caretaker didn't even know new calves were supposed to be branded; he let them wander far and wide over Maverick's range property.

In 1855, when a relieved Maverick sold the herd, range and all, to a neighboring stockman, his one stipulation was that the sale include — in addition to the original herd — any calves or cattle found on the range. Their new owner, watching as his riders rounded up the unbranded stock, dubbed those strays "mavericks" after their former owner.

According to Maverick's son, George, who wrote about his father in his book, *Prose and Poetry of the Live Stock Industry*, published in 1905, the term *maverick* spread throughout cattle country gaining common usage. By the time the word made its way into the dictionary, it was being used as a noun, an adverb, even an adjective. Soon applied to people, it meant anyone of either sex who strayed from the straight and narrow path to become a law unto him — or herself.

The lesser-known ladies limned in these pages were certainly mavericks. For whatever personal reasons of life experience and temperament, these fifteen women defied convention to strike out in unmarked directions. While several of them stepped from obscurity to distinguish themselves in science or social reform, others used their spirited rebellion against their society to rise above impossible odds. One woman was downright disreputable.

The true status of nineteenth century women was made perfectly clear in a speech by Carrie Chapman Catt who informed her audience that, "The common law in Great Britain and the United States held husband and wife to be one, and that one the husband. The legal existence of the wife was so merged in that of her husband that she was said to be 'dead in law.'" Most nineteenth century men considered that a reasonable premise and heartily concurred with Dr. Edward Clarke, a noted Harvard psychology professor, who maintained unequivocally that education was bad for women — it made them less manageable. Only in the movies portraying this period did women frequently demonstrate that they had minds of their own.

In simpler terms, women of the nineteenth century had no inherent rights. They could buy nothing, sell nothing, and go nowhere unless their husbands, fathers, or their brothers said so. Even their clothes reflected their restricted lives. When a proper lady of the mid-to-late nineteenth century dressed, she put on — starting from the outside and working in — a dress, usually heavily draped or ruffled; a white cambric petticoat, trimmed in *broderie anglaise;* at least two flannel petticoats under the first, with scalloped hems and handwork; a fifth petticoat lined and corded with horsehair, a straw plait in its hem to make it stand away, and lace-trimmed drawers. In hot weather, three or four starched muslin petticoats replaced the flannel ones.

Modish women used "deceivers," wheels of thick plaited horsehair tied just below the waist to make it look smaller. Beneath their dress bodices they wore a plain or embroidered camisole that was supposed to protect the fabric of their dresses from being abraded by stays — those flat narrow bones sewn into a form-fit-ting, deep-cut corset worn under the camisole — which also accen-tuated a tapered waist. The corset generally fit so snugly that they could not raise their arms much above their waists and had to be helped to dress. Remember the dressing scenes in *Gone With The Wind?*

A lady had to be careful not to stoop or bend, in fear that her stays might give way with a tremendous explosion and drop her to the ground. A father who saw this catastrophe overtake his daugh-ter cried out in alarm, "My God! I thought she'd snapped herself in two!"

But these dilemmas were for upper class women. The average nineteenth century housewife worked a sixteen-hour day in which — besides caring for her children, and her sick and elderly relatives — she did the washing and ironing (sans electricity, remember, and with nasty hot starch), cleaned up the dishes and the home; baked bread, split wood for fireplaces and stove and, in her spare time, did the necessary sewing, darning and weaving. Apart from marriage, only four careers were usually open to women. They could teach, be house servants, slave in factories or turn to prostitution.

Despite the mores of the times, each of my brave women dared to aggressively seek her chosen destiny. Many succeeded, yet the price of their success usually was a life without a home, husband or children.

I have been emotionally involved in history, mainly of the West, for more years than I can remember. Initially I gobbled up books on notable mountain men like Kit Carson and Jedediah Smith, sparked by Dale Wasserman — a frequent house guest and associate of my film producer husband — who kept me fascinated with his knowledge of Western lore. A more enduring influence has been a wonderful writer and dear friend, Jane Barry, whose historical novels deal so insightfully with the saga of native Americans at the time of the settling of the West.

When my interest narrowed to the twenty-year period of California's Gold Rush, I read all I could find on the subject and acquired an extensive library of my own. I discovered it was primarily a young man's game — the average age being twenty-four — and a self-governing but wild and woolly, polyglot society. Its most remarkabe feature was that men of that society accepted women as equals. In 1861, with the onset of the Civil War, this free and euphoric time was forever lost as the up-beat attitude of our expanding nation became one of shame, ruin and despair.

Along the way, it occurred to me that I had read almost nothing about Westering women before the era of the wagon trains. There were famous characters like Belle Starr and Calamity Jane and Annie Oakley, but most women of that earlier "golden age" were portrayed as background figures. Fortunately, the number of references available which focus upon American women from the Revolution forward have increased dramatically within the last decade, greatly benefiting my research for *Maverick Women*.

Some of my chapters are considerably longer than others because more material was available, either in autobiographies or other writings. I confess that the material on Sojourner Truth so intrigued me that my first draft on her stretched to one hundred and forty pages! It was hard to edit her down to a usable size.

I trust my profiles will tell enough about this collection of self-propelled and fascinating ladies to intrigue readers, and make them want to know a great deal more. With that in mind, I've included a brief list of references at the end of each chapter which are not alphabetized, but listed in order of their importance to each story.

ACKNOWLEDGEMENTS

The writing of a biography is an endeavor that requires several silent partners. This book is no exception. I owe thanks to many people. But first I must acknowledge the unsung heroes of book creation — the librarians — who rarely receive the recognition they deserve for the essential role they play. My sincere thanks to: Bill Slaughter, Archivist of The Church of Jesus Christ of Latter-Day Saints, who helped with Ina Coolbrith; Elaine S. Pike of Vassar College Library's Special Collections, who gave me Maria Mitchell's photograph; Dawn Rodrigues, Archivist, California State Library, who researched for me; Bill Sturm, Archivist of Oakland's Public Library, who supplied me with the memorable photograph of Ina Coolbrith; Marie Helene Gold, photograph archivist of Radcliffe College's Schlesinger Library, for the photograph of Carrie Chapman Catt; Tanya Bresinsky of the Maria Mitchell Museum, for the video about Maria; Norman Currie, Corbis-Bettmann Archives, for much help and Nellie Bly's photograph; Linda Offeney of the Yuma Territorial Prison Museum, for photos and Xerox material on Pearl Hart; Albert Schadel of the Pajaro Valley Association for the photograph of Cockeyed Charley's plaque; Nikki Pahl, for the Auburn ravine photo; Cathy and the staff of the Western Collection of the Denver Public Library for Xerox texts on two of the three "Charleys;" Leroy Radanovich, Photographer, for my cover photo, which he calls "Leaping Ladies"; Anita Skinner of Tombstone, Arizona for the menu from The Nellie Cashman Restaurant, and Ben Traywick for the fine photograph of Nellie from his collection; Peter Salmon, newsman of Victoria, British Columbia, who routed me to Tombstone; Sojourner Kincaid Rolle for introducing me to Sojourner Truth and Georgia Young, recently retired Head Librarian of the Montecito Public Library.

We all need friends for moral support, for cheer when we're sad and rejoicing when we're happy. But my friends went beyond the call of duty, encouraging me and doing me the huge favor of reading my chapters to offer suggestions as well as finding errors. I owe them much. My sincere thanks to:

Frances Halpern, Minna Calm, Harriet Ackert, Diane Billot, Jack Turley, Marsha Karpeles, Fred Klein, Joan Esposito, Warren Pattiz, Dorothy Hart, Gale Lynds, Laila Rafique, Shelly Tyson, Lucy Hilmer, Bob Hector, Barbara Alpert, Leonard Tourney and my husband, Doug Laurence, who read and re-read without complaint. My thanks also to my great proofreaders: Barbara Taylor, Blaine Patino, Laura Smith and Louise Upson.

Finally my thanks to my daughter, Valentina Laurence Pfeil, the book's designer, and to Virginia Cornell, without whose interest and good editing this book might never have been published.

Santa Barbara, California 1998

First Tourist Jane Barnes

"Another Madeira, sorr?" the young barmaid inquired.

Donald McTavish nodded morosely, shifting his middle-aged girth on the taproom stool.

She refilled his tankard. Now there's a proper gentleman, she thought, never without a fresh shirt and clean fingernails. And generous with the odd copper, too.

Her flirtatious smile was lost on the glum-faced Scotsman, preoccupied as he was with the knowledge that in his coat pocket lay a contract he'd signed reluctantly only hours earlier. While it would pay him generously, it would return him to the remote trading post where he'd spent several miserable years of his youth as a common fur trapper. It was the Northwest Fur Company's most distant trading post at the mouth of the Columbia River, taking him far from England for thirteen months. He took another swig of his wine, brooding on his weakness for money.

A man of amorous temperament, wealthy McTavish was used to surrounding himself with a bevy of "lively" blondes. Grown soft in retirement, the prospect of thirteen dismal months of enforced celibacy in a cold, rough environment — with only unwashed trappers, Flathead, Nez Perce and Chinook Indians and their fish-eating, fishy-smelling females for company — was depressing, to say the least.

He had barely glanced at the barmaid when she first served him. Now he looked more carefully.

"And what might your name be, lass?" McTavish mustered what he hoped was a charming smile.

"It be Jane Barnes, yor honor," she rattled off, glancing at him from the corners of her eyes, wondering what he was getting at.

"You're new here, aren't you, Jane?" McTavish inquired, determined to detain her long enough for the vague notion in his mind to take shape.

"Yes, sorr. I been employed these three weeks past." McTavish could tell she was proud of her use of the language. She frowned slightly. "If you please, your worship, I've done nowhat wrong, I hope?"

McTavish gave her hand a reassuring pat. "No, no, not at all. As I'm sure you know, you are an uncommonly pretty girl. That makes me want to learn more about you." It was a contrived excuse, for whatever any healthy man wanted to know of Jane was there to be seen. Blessed with a fine carriage, full breasts and a small waist, she held his gaze with her smoky blue seductive eyes. Her features were as flawless as her even white teeth and the crop of unruly golden hair that framed her creamy soap-scrubbed complexion. During Jane's three weeks as barmaid to the men who tippled here she'd become the stuff their dreams were made of.

Studying Jane as he sipped, McTavish was inspired with a new notion. Why not take this winsome barmaid with him to Fort George? Her presence would certainly help soften all the endless dull days and nights of the voyage as well as the enforced thirteen month sojourn at the fur-trapping fort. It would be a year, well into 1814 before he returned to England!

He beckoned Jane over and showed her his contract. Between attending to her other patrons he read her a paragraph or two aloud, aware she only pretended to be able to read the page. Her lovely eyes grew wide with amazement at hearing the huge sum he'd receive, more than she could earn in a lifetime as a barmaid.

In buying the *Isaac Todd*, McTavish had been given every

assurance it was the most up-to-date vessel of that year of 1812. He abhored ship travel, yet he rhapsodized to Jane about the many delights of being at sea. Warm lazy days, moonlit nights bright with stars, the water's surface shimmering with mysterious phosphorescence. Her mouth dropped open in child-like disbelief as he described the many odd and colorful sea creatures that raced alongside the ship; creatures Jane had never seen, much less heard of, waxing almost poetic about dolphins and sailfish, and huge whales surfacing for air to spew jets of water from their blowholes.

McTavish told her beguiling tales of the wonders seen in the ports at which his ship would call. To further intrigue her, he hinted at the charm of life lived in the wilderness. Seeing Jane was captivated by his stories, he suddenly assumed a despondent expression. He was a man alone, he told her, without a life's companion — a man yearning to lavish the bounty of his loving kindness on some grateful young woman. He stressed the fact that, although travel could be tremendously rewarding, for true pleasure its joys and wonders needed to be shared. At the appropriate moment, the canny Scotsman asked softly, "Mistress Jane, what would you say to coming to the New World with this lonely fellow?"

His question provoked more uneasiness than naive Jane had known in all of her tender nineteen years. She had never been beyond her Portsmouth township, and found the prospect he offered more frightening than tempting. But he could tell she was curious.

"I just don't know," she dimpled. "It's not that I wouldn't mind a bit of a change in me life, that's for sure. But," she ventured, "wouldn't I be all on my own out there, sorr, in a manner of speaking?" She waved the hand that clutched her bar cloth in the vague direction of North America.

"Not a bit of it, Mistress Jane. You would have me as your

main protector." McTavish smiled, but still Jane hesitated. In spite of the fear and uncertainty that roiled within her, part of her wanted to see and experience all the glorious sights McTavish had described.

She kept returning to add another couple of inches to his tankard as he drank its contents down. Each time McTavish embellished his invitation, and each time Jane found another excuse.

"But I would be so far from me Dad and Mum, with not even no friends to look out for poor me." Her thoughts were tumbling over themselves in rare excitement. She looked around the tavern, as if trying to see it for the last time.

"But my dear girl, I would be looking after you and taking good care of you. And believe me, it would give me great pleasure to do so," McTavish countered, his face beginning to be flushed. Each rejection made her more desirable in his eyes. He was now thoroughly resolved that, no matter what, he would take Jane with him.

"What if, upon our return to England," he proffered slyly, "I was to provide you with a lifetime annuity?"

"What's an an-newty?" she puzzled at the unfamiliar term.

"Why, an annuity is a wonderful thing. It is a sum of money you would receive once a month for the rest of your life. If you say yes, that is."

She was flabbergasted. Money for life? Provincial she might be, but even Jane understood the prettiest of barmaids must put something by for a future day when her looks would fade and age take over. Sorely tempted, Jane still managed to hold back. McTavish was forced to play his trump card.

"Mistress Jane, my ship sails in a week. Plenty of time still for a quick trip up to London to outfit you with a new wardrobe. If, that is, you decide to come along with me." What young woman could resist so fabulous an offer? But still Jane hesitated, having learned early on that men were apt to promise things they had no intention of delivering.

"Will you put everything down on paper, sorr?" she demanded, supposing herself quite shrewd. "All what you've promised?"

McTavish's smile was bland. "Certainly, my dear. I'm a man of my word. You need have no worries on that account."

McTavish stood by an uneasy-looking Jane at the rail of his ship as it plowed through the delta of Port River out into the choppy seas separating the south coast of England from the northern coast of France. To divert her, he remarked, "If the waters were calmer you might be able to see the *Mary Rose* directly below us. We are passing above its remains just about now." An unschooled small-town girl, Jane was always edified and impressed by death and sensational stories.

"What's the *Mary Rose*, sorr, if I may be so bold?"

"Henry the Eighth's favorite ship. Just remade, she led the British fleet to meet the advancing French navy. Her new design with overextended superstructures proved top-heavy. It made her founder and sink with all hands on board. She never even got a chance to fire one of her many shiny new guns."

"What a sad story," she said, frowning and shaking her head in empathy.

"Yes, isn't it?"

"And when would that'ave happened, sorr?"

"In 1543. . . mid-July, I believe. By the way, no need for you to 'sir' me, Jane. My name is Donald. Call me that."

"And all of 'em drownded? How many worr that, sorr?" She forgot her efforts at educated speech and lapsed into her own Portsmouth jargon.

"The history books say seven hundred men. . . and their captain."

Jane peered intently into the passing waters for a moment as if hoping to see all those bones on the bottom. "Gorr, really?" she gasped, the number impressing her. McTavish decided to edify her further.

"And King Henry saw it happen from up there." He pointed back at the fort on the hill. "Astride his massive stallion he watched his beautiful ship go down, powerless to save her, with the captain's poor wife on her mount by his side. A very sad story." McTavish pulled an appropriately long face. The agony of this was lost on Jane.

"Seven hundred sailors. . . coo, what a lot of sailors!" she remarked with a rakish little smile.

McTavish and his newly wardrobed companion endured what stretched into a tortuous nine-month journey, with a plentitude of gales. When the *Isaac Todd* at long last dropped anchor at the mouth of the Columbia River delta and he brought Jane ashore, her appearance caused a furor among both the white and Indian populations.

In his book, *Adventures on the Columbia River*, published in 1831, Ross Cox wrote of the pro-tem governor of Fort George, Alexander Henry the Younger, "Improbable things were always happening to Henry. Perhaps the only event in fur trade history to compete with the Orkney girl incident was the arrival of the Portsmouth barmaid Jane Barnes. . . ."

The Orkney girl provided a melodrama that took place shortly before Jane came. Henry, a prolific journal keeper, marked it as "an extraordinary affair that properly stunned." The entry read as follows:

One of the Orkney lads, apparently indisposed, requested me to allow him to remain in my house for a short time. I was surprised at the fellow's demand; however, I told him to sit down and warm himself. I returned to my own room, where I had not been for long before he sent one of my people, requesting the favor of speaking with me. Accordingly, I stepped down to him, and was much surprised to find him extended on the hearth, uttering dreadful lamentations; he stretched out his hands to me, and in piteous tones begged me to be kind to a poor, helpless, abandoned wretch, who was not of the sex I had supposed, but an unfortunate Orkney girl, pregnant and actually in childbirth. In saying this she opened her jacket and displayed a pair of beautiful, round, white breasts. . . . In about an hour she was safely delivered of a fine boy. . . .

Ross Cox labeled Jane "a flaxen-haired blue-eyed daughter of Albion who, in a temporary fit of erratic enthusiasm, had consented to become *Le campagnon du voyage* of Mr. Mac." Because of the mix of French, British and Americans who regularly trapped from and visited the various trading posts, French phrases were a commonplace. Men who normally kept their passions under control in their own homelands often lost all sense of restraint in this new amoral world.

Their rampant disregard for temperance was severely frowned on by a man named Brackenridge. During his stay as one of a party stopping overnight in an Aricara village while en route to Fort George, he recorded his impressions of what he considered the Native Americans' overt lack of morals.

The plain behind our tents was crowded and, shocking to relate, fathers brought their daughters, husbands their wives, brothers their sisters, to be offered for sale at this market of indecency and shame. Perhaps something may be attributed to the inordinate passion that seized them

(Indians) for our merchandise. The silly boatmen . . . in a short time disposed of almost every article they possessed, even their blankets and shirts. One of them actually returned to camp one morning entirely naked, having disposed of his last shirt—this might truly be called *la dernier chemise de l'amour.*

Returning to the subject of Jane Barnes' presence among them, Cox related:

The Indians daily thronged in numbers to our fort for the mere purpose of gazing on, and admiring the fair beauty, every article of whose dress was examined with the utmost scrutiny. She had rather an extravagant wardrobe, and each day exhibited her in a new dress, . . . to display her figure to the best advantage. One day, her head decorated with feather and flowers produced the greatest surprise; the next, her hair, braided and unconcealed by any covering, excited equal wonder and admiration. The young women felt almost afraid to approach her, and the old were highly gratified at being permitted to touch her person.

In truth, the sight of gorgeous Jane so fascinated the all-male population that McTavish found it necessary to keep her aboard his ship under guard until supper each day, to avert any possibility of an unpleasant incident with either Indians or trappers.

Indians had traded and bartered from tribe to tribe for centuries. The coming of white men merely heightened the stakes. In Walter O'Meara's book *Daughters of the Country*, he wrote:

In exchange for his pelts he [the Indian] received such articles of trade as twist tobacco, point-blankets, vermillion paint, Spanish beads, gun, shot and balls, brass or iron kettles, axes, knives (butcher and scalping), and printed cottons, flints and steels.

Rum was occasionally dispensed in the form of an unadulterated alcohol nick-named "high wine." This was the most highly valued of all trade goods, whether given as treat or in exchange for furs, and led to many a drunken brawl.

Jane soon began to receive marriage proposals from overeager Indian chiefs. Cox explained:

> One of them in particular, the son of Comcomly, principal chief of the Chinooks (Cassakas by name, who, because of his position as heir apparent, was known, perhaps somewhat derisively, as the "Prince of Wales") came to the fort attired in his richest dress, his face fancifully bedaubed with red paint, and his body redolent of whale oil.

Cassakas was young, and already had four wives. Yet he was so entranced by Jane's incredibly white perfection that he would peer at her tirelessly all during supper through the chinks in the fort's log walls. He desperately wanted to marry her and his outrageously extravagant dowry offer consisted of one hundred fine otter skins as bride price to her family, along with an undisclosed amount of salmon, tobacco, elk, and anchovies as dowry for her own use. In addition he promised — if only she would share his bed — that Jane would never have to dig roots, cook, tend children, gut and smoke meats, chew leathers, or perform any of the other chores required of Indian wives. Cox's account finished:

> He would make her mistress over his other wives, and permit her to sit at her ease from morning to night, and wear her own clothes. . . and be allowed to smoke as many pipes of tobacco during the day as she thought proper; together

with many other flattering inducements, the tithe of which would have shaken the constancy of a score of the chastest brown vestals that ever flourished among the tribes of the Columbia. These tempting offers, however, had no charms for Jane. Her long voyage had not yet eradicated certain Anglican predilections respecting mankind, which she had contracted in the country of her birth, and among which she did not include a flat head, a half naked body, or a copper-colored skin besmeared with whale oil.

In plainer terms, Jane's disgusted response was, "What? Me marry that smelly heathen savage? Not on yer life, sorrs! I'd as soon march myself off that mountain cliff to me death as wed the likes of him, or any of them Indian devils. A chief's son, indeed!" And she sniffed mightily in disdain.

Interpreters conveyed a polite refusal purporting to come from Jane, and the unrequited would-be lover went off to sulk and plot her abduction. To prevent such a happening, McTavish had her rowed ashore under guard each evening to preside over the post's male supper table, then promptly rowed back afterwards to the ship.

Jane was unschooled and not terribly bright, a fact which rather amused most of the men at the post. Cox reported that a clerk named Mac, however, was less than enchanted with her after the following verbal exchange:

I was coming from the main building on my way to my tent, when Mistress Jane fell into step beside me. I'd never spoken much to her heretofore, so I was taken aback. She paused to glance over at a group of Indian squaws making pemmican, the food trappers and Indians alike carried on their travels. So I stopped to watch with her.

"Ugh! Look at that," she said in revulsion. Several of

the women beat the thin strips of dried buffalo meat with stones, while others molded them into balls that, when finished, were deposited in bags of buffalo hide called taureaux.

It's a wonder to me how they manage to have those bags weigh ninety pounds exactly, I said to make pleasant conversation, although I didn't like her attitude about the Indians one bit.

"What is it they're squeezing into them balls?" she asked in a disapproving tone.

Well, I answered, it's a combination of half buffalo strips and half buffalo fat, mixed with whichever kind of berries are in season, and a handful of maple sugar to sweeten the mix.

Jane said, "Look, they're even getting dog hair and pebbles into them! Downright disgusting! It makes me sick just to think of putting such slop into my mouth. But I guess them wimmen don't know any better. After all they're heathens. Think of the way they carry on with men!"

That got my back up. As we walked on I retorted, Indian women are just as intelligent and moral as women of our race. I gave her a sudden meaningful look. More intelligent than some, I'd say. I've known plenty of white women with the morals of an alley cat! She didn't get it. Jane tried to sound learned. "Oh, Mr. Mac! I suppose you agree with Shakespeare that every women is at heart a rake?"

Pope, ma'am, if you please, I shot back at her.

"Pope! Pope!" replied Jane. "Bless me, sir! You must be wrong; rake is certainly the word. I never heard of but one female Pope."

When we reached the post building and started inside,

Jane pulled a page of an old newspaper from her dress pocket. In order to end the discussion, I suppose, she pretended to read it. I knew then she didn't know how because she held the paper upside down. I left her then, Mr. Cox, and met you.

What do you think? I have just had a conversation with that fine looking damsel there, who looks down with such contempt on our women, and may I be d___d if the b___h understands B from a buffalo!

Cox added that Mac had ". . . a wicked and malicious grin ruffling his sunburnt features."

However, having to live at a trading post, whether confined aboard ship or allowed ashore, was a trying and lonely life for Jane. As time passed and her presence became less of a distraction, McTavish let her live on shore at the post. On her daily beach walk, for want of something better to do, Jane would stop to watch the squaws making pemmican and always found it unspeakably disgusting.

Jane was a woman who tended to peevishness without constant attention. Several traders' journals cited her want of good table manners and a penchant for malapropisms that diverted the others but embarrassed her patron, Donald McTavish. As the end of his term approached, McTavish, by this time heartily sick of Jane, confided to his journal that he planned to share her favors with Alexander Henry, Jr., the man who would take his place. He also intended to leave Jane with Henry when he sailed for home.

Indians, alerted to the marvelous things traveling parties carried — necessaries like blankets, kettles, guns and knives — constantly intercepted them to trade. When the white men killed and scalped them to obtain what they wanted, the Indians reciprocated in kind. What they got, in exchange for the silly trinkets brought to enchant their squaws and children, were the curses of liquor and venereal disease. Both races grew rougher and more profane in the wilderness setting.

Alexander Henry's comment on the situation was that he dreaded and feared the routine drinking bouts that occured at the start and end of each hunt. "My hunters and other men have been drinking and rioting since yesterday; they make more d___n noise and trouble than a hundred Blackfeet," he wrote in his journal.

Two days before McTavish was to spring his unpleasant surprise on Jane before leaving, fate willed otherwise. While he and Henry were attempting to cross the Columbia River delta in a flood tide, their small skiff overturned in the churning waters and both men drowned.

When McTavish's ship, the *Isaac Todd* sailed, it carried both men's bodies home to England for burial. Jane Barnes was left behind to fend for herself, deserted and alone.

Again through diaries we learn that Jane, now stripped of her protector and no longer a novelty, was in fact regarded as something of a jinx. None of the men wanted her anymore. She spent her lonely days pacing the hard beach strand in her now bedraggled fancy gowns. Often she paused on her walks to gaze out to sea, looking in vain for a ship to rescue her. By this time, her lovely face had assumed a mask of despair, her only audience the wary Indians.

Miraculously, one day a British ship en route to Cathay, its hold full of British and American trade goods to exchange for silks and teas and Indian spices, dropped anchor at the mouth of the Columbia River. It stayed only long enough to load up on foodstuffs and other supplies for the long voyage. The captain came ashore to make the arrangements, and saw Jane. When he gave the order to up anchor and set sail, Jane and what was left of her fancy wardrobe were on board.

Three years later, a prominent firm of London solicitors received a letter from the captain, posted from an English port. He respectfully requested that they, as the firm handling the affairs of the late Donald McTavish, reimburse him for monies advanced out of pocket on behalf of a Miss Jane Barnes over the past three years. He enclosed a neatly itemized account of said expenditures. Posing as the representative of the young lady, the captain inquired after the annuity Mr. McTavish had promised her. How soon might Miss Barnes expect to receive it?

What happened to Jane isn't certain. Elliott Coues, who edited one version of her history, maintained that Jane became the mistress of an East India Company nabob. A more recent article by Mary Avery in Volume XLIV of the *Pacific Northwest Quarterly* has it that Jane Barnes came once again to the Fort George trading post, this time as the wife of a Captain Robson of the good ship *Columbia*. It is not known whether she ever received her annuity.

Ross, Nancy Wilson. *Westward The Women*. New York City: Alfred A. Knopf, Inc., 1944.

Brown, Dee. *The Gentle Tamers*. Barrie & Enkins, London, England, 1958

Coues, Elliott, Ed. *New Light on the Early History of the Greater Northwest: Manuscript Journals of Alexander Henry and David Thompson: Exploration and Adventure Among the Indians on the Red, Saskatchewan, Missouri and Columbia Rivers. 1799-1814.* F. P. Harper, New York: 1897

Ross Cox, Norman. *The Columbia River*. Edited by E. & J. Stewart. Norman, Okla.:University of Oklahoma, 1957.

Seton, Alfred. *Astorian Adventure: Journal of Alfred Seton (1811-1815)*. Edited by Robert Jones. New York City: Fordham University Press, NYC, 1993.

CHAPTER 2

Dame Shirley: '49ers Chronicler

Dame Shirley was her pen name; for pen names—as in Mark Twain, Bret Harte, Joaquin Miller—were in style on the California literary frontier. Louise Clappe chose to use it as her signature on the letters she wrote to her favorite sister Molly back in Massachusetts, in which she graphically described the many incidents that amazed and amused her during the year she and her husband Fayette spent in the mining camps of California.

Her earlier efforts before moving to the gold fields, short articles published in *The Marysville Herald*, were verbose and stiff. But the spartan life she led in the wilderness sharpened Louise's powers of observation. Even when she disapproved of the miners' cruel or capricious acts, her rendition of them evokes her readers' empathy. She somehow understood that men in the gold camps were driven to the rash things they did by sheer boredom and too much alcohol.

Several years later, when her exuberant letters had found their way into print, they caused a sensation and made her famous. Historians and experts on the period all agree that the Dame Shirley letters afford the world "a priceless window on . . . the earliest flush days of the great gold rush."

Her chronicles were exceptionally engaging because of her unique insight, vivid descriptions and lively sense of humor. Even in the process of listing for Molly the many deprivations to be endured in a mining camp, she couldn't resist including an anecdote about a merchant who imported 192 pounds of wedding cake. Packed in separate tins and sold at outrageous prices, she wrote that the miners were only too happy to pay dearly for such a rare treat. She also detailed gourmet courses served at a housewarming dinner she attended in Indian Bar: oyster soup, fried salmon fresh caught, roast beef and boiled ham, fried oysters, potatoes and onions, mince pie and pudding (without eggs or milk), Madeira, nuts and raisins, claret, champagne, and coffee.

She penned character sketches of the people she knew and observed. Of a storekeeping neighbor she wrote: "He used to be a peddler in the States, and is remarkable for an intense ambition to be thought what the Yankees call 'cute and smart;' an ambition which his true and good heart will never permit him to achieve. (I am always interested in that bizarre mixture of shrewdness and simplicity of which he is a distinguishing specimen.)"

Dame Shirley's birth name was Louisa Amelia Smith. When her father, Moses, graduated from Massachusetts' Williams College in 1817, he was already married to her mother Lois. Louisa was born and christened two years later in the town of Elizabeth, where Moses served as Master of a local academy—a post he held until Louisa turned thirteen in 1830. At that time he moved his now sizeable brood of seven children to the town of Amherst in the same state.

Sadly, soon after the move Moses fell ill and died. Within five years his grieving widow also departed this earth, leaving seven orphans to be parceled out to charitable relatives and friends.

Louise was made the ward of a prominent Massachusetts lawyer, politician and member of Congress named Osmyn Baker.

The Bakers raised her well, and provided her with the finest possible education available to a girl, first sending her to the Female Seminary in Charleston, then on to Amherst Academy.

Although there seems to be no existing photograph of Louise, all of the descriptions of her mention that she was pretty; even as a child Louisa was described as "small, fair and golden-haired." Because she detested the name Louisa, while living with the Bakers she adjusted the final letter of her first name from *a* to *e*. The separation from her siblings, especially her sister Molly, left her lonely. Perhaps that was why—like any child who lives solely in the company of adults—she found solace in what became her lifelong passion for books. She graduated from Amherst at twenty-one, well-versed in music and literature in addition to a working knowledge of several foreign languages.

The Bakers encouraged her intellectual pursuits by including her when they entertained their brilliant circle of friends, all of whom provided further incentive for her admiration of learning. One of their closest friends, Alexander Hill Everett, a prominent diplomat, politician and former editor of *The North American Review*, became romantically interested in Louise. A writer himself, and more than twice her age, Everett earnestly courted her for some years, both in person and by letter. Dubbing himself her "father confessor," he early advised her in one of his letters, "If you were to add to the love of reading the habit of writing, you would find a new and inexhaustible source of comfort and satisfaction opening upon you." Louise gave him no encouragement as a suitor but kept him as a mentor. Before his death in 1847—the year Louise married—he wrote that he was pleased to see in print "a few of the products of her attentive mind."

The record of Louise's twenties is hazy. But in 1847, at thirty, she wed Fayette Clapp, the son of a printer and her junior by five years. He had planned to follow the ministry, but changed his mind and studied medicine instead. Presumably his first name came equipped with its *e*, but Louise inevitably added an *e* to his last name to give it a bit of dash.

Her whereabouts and activities for the next few years are undocumented. She may well have taught children at the elementary level to send her new husband through medical school. For when he graduated from Brown University in 1848, and went on to take his doctor's degree at Castleton Medical College in Vermont, they were already married.

Both Louise and Fayette suffered delicate health; Fayette from various undisclosed ailments, Louise with dreadful migraines. They may or may not have known about the gold rush, but in search of a kinder climate, in 1849 they sailed around the Horn on the good ship *Manilla*, her destination California. After putting up with a year of San Francisco's inclement winds, rains and fogs that tended to exacerbate their physical problems, they moved inland to Marysville, a northern California town at the confluence of the two forks of the Feather River. Equally unhappy there, they settled briefly in the soon-to-be extinct, neighboring village of Plumas City.

By June of 1851, when none of these places proved beneficial, a desperate Fayette left Louise to take the trail for the Upper Feather River to test life in the mines. Warned against the rigorous climate, he trusted the cleaner air in the mountains would effect a magic cure. He also intended to set up a medical practice somewhere, for he had heard that accident-prone miners could always use a good doctor.

Once arrived in the region, he wrote Louise his surprise at finding "a rash of doctors had broken out in the diggings." He chose to settle in Rich Bar, a camp in a narrow valley high in the mountains. A small bustling place at the base of a canyon, it was only eight hundred yards long by thirty yards wide. Later, in detailing her first impressions, Louise would romanticize over "the panoramic picture gallery" of miners bound for further diggings who formed a constant procession past her door. It should be remembered that these were the earliest years in the gold fields when a brand new kind of society was quickly born and just as quickly died.

Almost immediately Fayette reported a renewed sense of

vigor. He took rooms at the Empire Hotel, its name emblazoned in paint on its canvas side. Within a week he had opened an office with a dirt floor whose walls were also of canvas, its only furniture a few stout wooden crates. This period must have been a bonanza for the manufacturers of canvas, for that sturdy fabric was as popular as calico and used for almost everything. Soon established, Fayette sent for Louise who joined him there in late summer.

In the journal she kept, from which she extracted her tidbits to sister Molly, Louise grew lyrical over her first trip upcountry. "The meadows and oak and sycamore-studded prairies . . ." she wrote, "were carpeted with flowers and the air was full of birds." Most intrigued by the Indian women they passed who stooped to harvest a crop of nuts, she reported how very attractive she found them with their pretty brown skin and finely-shaped arms and legs.

She wrote of crossing broad stretches of plains she termed "chappard," fantasizing that the low antler-resembling skeletal shrubs looked "like a herd of crouching deer."

"It was worth the whole wearisome journey," she related to Molly, "the danger from Indians, grizzly bears, sleeping under the stars and all, to behold this beautiful vision."

Gaining the summit of the final hill, Louise thrilled to the sight below. "Deep in the shadowy nooks of the far down valleys, like wasted jewels dropped from the radiant sky above, lay half a dozen blue-bosomed lagoons, glittering and gleaming and sparkling in the sunlight." Commended for her endurance during the hard journey, she replied that her courage was merely a result of "the intensity of my fear, that kept me so still."

Like most writers of the day, Louise tended to use extra verbiage and over-flowery descriptions. "Too many flowers and too little fruit," as Sir Walter Scott remarked in damning a piece of writing he had been asked to critique. Inspired by the simple beauty of the natural setting, however, her prose soon moved beyond artificiality to a colorful but faithful recording of the daily realities she observed.

On one occasion, she and Fayette lost their way as they returned from Indian Bar. They had followed wrong trails all day and were finally forced to bed down in the woods for the night. The next day was no better, for though they could have stopped the next night at a so-called inn, Louise firmly opted for camping out on her saddle—"an excellent pillow"—rather than staying in that "hovel that called itself a hotel. Imagine the horror, the *creme de la creme* of Borosity," she went on, inventing her own word, "of remaining for twelve mortal hours of wakefulness in a filthy, uncomfortable, flea-bitten shanty, without books or papers, when Rich Bar, easily obtainable before night through the loveliest scenery shining in the yellow splendour of an autumnal morning, lay before us!"

Rich Bar sat—as she meticulously and humorously noted at the top of each letter—on the "East Branch of the North Fork of the Feather River." High in its canyon, it was inaccessible by any transport but a horse, a donkey, or one's own two feet.

Louise lavished a good many uncomplimentary words on the gold fields' poor excuses for hotels. All seemed to consist of ". . . a large apartment, level with the street, part of which is fitted up as a barroom, with that eternal crimson calico which flushes the whole social life of the Golden State with its everlasting red, in the center of a fluted mass of which gleams a really elegant mirror, set off by a background of decanters, cigar vases, and jars of brandied fruit, the whole forming a *tout ensemble* of dazzling splendor. A table covered with a green cloth upon which lies a pack of monte-cards, a backgammon board, and a sickening pile of 'yellow-kivered' literature, with several uncomfortable-looking benches, complete the furniture."

Hotel bedrooms were eight by ten foot spaces formed by fabric walls "curtained in red calico, but the color monotony is relieved by purple calico walls and a door of blue drill cloth hung on leather hinges." Her comment on the building was, "It is just such a piece of carpentering as a child two years old, gifted with the strength of a man, would produce if it wanted to play at making grown-up houses."

As Western writer Dee Brown conjectured in his book *The Gentle Tamers*:

> A sociologist probably could make a good case for the proposition that the germinating point of women's rebellion against masculine authority was in the American frontier hotel. Here, for the first time in our history, thousands of women came to close quarters with thousands of strange males; they saw the dominant sex as he really was, learned his empty secrets through thin canvas walls, and viewed the nakedness of his body and soul. In that locale may have been born the American woman's first doubts of the male's superiority, of his right to claim mastery over the female, doubts that soon would lead to demands for the right to vote, and for complete social and legal equality.

After a time of living in what she termed "this rag and cardboard house," enduring the noises of a bowling alley next door and the "moaning and shrieking suggestive of a suffering child from a nearby flume," Louise was happy to move a short distance away to the camp at Indian Bar.

Indian Bar was so small it had only twenty cabins and tents along with several ersatz dwellings created with pine boughs and calico shirts. But Fayette had new friends there. "Excepting the paths leading to these homes, the entire Bar is spotted with mining holes, next to which repose the immense piles of dirt and stones they removed." She reported that while the areas of level ground were bare, the mountains—that for three months of the year blocked the sun from reaching down into Indian Bar—still were haloed by sun and "beautifully verdant with pine trees."

By October, Louise and Fayette had built their own cabin. They didn't escape from the noise of a bowling alley, however, for they built on a piece of land behind the Humboldt Hotel which, Louise reported, "had a really excellent bowling alley attached to it." But at least it was a place of their own. The hotel, ". . . a larger shanty, was roofed . . . with a rude kind of shingles . . . and the barroom has a floor upon which the miners can dance, and above all a cook who can play the violin, it is very popular."

Of course, she went on, the only way to reach their cabin was through the hotel dining room and kitchen. Her detailed account of how it looked was prefaced by the engaging invitation, "Enter, my dear; you are perfectly welcome; besides, we could not keep you out if we would, as there is not even a latch on the canvas door, though we really intend in a day or two to have a hook put on to it."

Their cabin was one room, twenty by twenty, its ceiling a white cotton cloth sewn together in only a few places, leaving openings where the roof shingles showed through. The room's sides were hung in "gaudy chintz, a pattern of roses of every size, in every configuration imaginable, from garlands and bouquets to single flowers in brown, purple, green, black and blue." A curtain of the same patterned chintz shut off the bedroom area.

Their fireplace was made of stones mortared with mud, its chimney built of sticks and mud. Its mantel was a wooden beam covered with pieces of tin stripped from cans on which "piquant legends like 'Preserved Peaches,' 'Canned Cherries,' 'Pickled Oysters,' etc.," could still be discerned on their fire-blackened labels. Two smooth stones served as firedogs. "I suppose it would be no more than civil to call a hole two feet square in one side of the room a window, although it is as yet guiltless of glass," she wrote.

While waiting for the glass to be delivered from Marysville, by 1851 a city of 10,000 souls, they tacked a piece of cloth over the opening to combat cold weather, adding a blanket if there was wind.

Louise's toilet table was a trunk resting on two empty claret cases. On it sat her workbox of rosewood, a large cushion of crimson brocade, some Chinese ornaments of exquisitely carved ivory, and two or three Bohemian glass "cologne stands." Her looking glass sat in a paper case for a doll's house. Her washstand was a large vegetable dish next to a dining room pitcher, all sitting on another trunk covered by a towel. Nearby, a pail filled with river water stood on a small cask.

As for the rest, they brought from Marysville a carpet, a hair mattress, pillows, bed linens, quilts, blankets, towels, four chairs and a crude bench which Louise covered in a neat plaid to act as their sofa. An oilcloth-covered pine table held chess and cribbage boards, and a large raw pine table draped with old monte table covers was their dining table. Her bookcase was a converted candle-box for her library, as well as the mandatory Bible and prayer book. On their crude mantel two Brittania-ware candlesticks flanked Fayette's display of pipes and tobacco, "for you know the aforesaid individual is a perfect devotee of the Indian weed."

Louise ended her description of their new home by mentioning that their makeshift furniture all sat on "a floor so uneven that no article of furniture gifted with four legs pretends to stand upon but three at once, so that the chairs, tables, etc., remind you constantly of a dog with a sore foot."

She asks her sister, "dainty Lady Molly," how would she feel if she had to spend the winter in such an abode?

In a place where there are no newspapers, no churches, lectures, concerts or theater; no fresh books, no shopping, calling or gossiping little tea-drinkings; no parties, no

balls, no picnics, no tableaux, no charades, no latest fashions, no daily mail (we have an express once a month,
charging $2.50 a letter, $1.50 a newspaper and forty cents
per pound for all other freight), no promenades, no rides,
no drives; no vegetables but potatoes and onions, no milk,
no eggs, no nothing?

Yet in the next sentence she writes,

Now I expect to be very happy here. This strange odd life
fascinates me. . . . In good sooth I fancy that nature intended me for an Arab or some other Nomadic barbarian, and
by mistake my soul got packed up in a christianized set of
bones and muscles. How shall I ever be able to content
myself to live in a decent, proper, well-behaved house,
where toilet tables are toilet tables . . . where lanterns are
not broken bottles.

She adds that she trusts "when it is again my lot to live amid the
refinements and luxuries of civilization, that I shall endure them
with becoming philosophy and fortitude."

While there were no equivalent groups for the few women in
the camps, Louise makes note of the social clubs for men who —
"back in the States"— had belonged to the Odd Fellows, Masonry,
and other fraternal orders. One of the oldest and oddest of these
fraternal orders was known as The Honorable Order of E
Clampsus Vitus (Clampsus said without the middle *s*). Though its
origins are unknown, Carl Wheat and Ezra Dane, self-proclaimed
official historians of the organization, maintained:

The order dates back to 4004 B.C., the Garden of Eden,
and the first clampatriarch, Adam. The group counted in
its roster of members such luminaries as St. Vitus,

Solomon, the Caesars, the Louis', Henry VIII, Hee-Lai, Sir Francis Drake, and an assortment of Presidents and Senators.

The outlandish fraternal order spread like wildfire, and soon every town in the diggings had its own chapter. According to John W. Caughey, author of *The California Gold Rush*, its official purpose was the care of widows and orphans, especially widows. But in reality it mostly gave itself over to the playing of practical jokes and other mischiefs. Its rites were elaborate and impressive and the order still exists, its practices shrouded in secrecy. It is publicly known, however, that when the Royal Grand Musician sounds the "hewgag" to assemble the brethren to the Hall of Comparative Oblations, it is to initiate a new member into the order, who then is required to treat the rest. Caughey maintains that "the convivial, raucous, fun-loving 'Clampers' best exemplified the spirit of gold rush society."

After gambling, dancing was the favorite camp pastime. Because women were in such short supply — Louise was one of only three females at Indian Bar — the men worked out a partner-rationing system. If they lost patience while waiting for a turn about the floor with one of the ladies, they would dance with each other, the female partner of the pair indicated by a kerchief tied about his upper arm. In writing of the weekly balls held at the saloon, Louise saucily reported that, though clean and festive with the "ubiquitous red calico" at the start of the evening, the miners soon messed things up. They danced so vigorously that their boot heels sent splinters flying off the wood floor, and their nasty habit of chewing and spitting from cheeks full of tobacco created "some danger of being swept away in a flood of tobacco juice, but luckily the floor was uneven, and it lay around in puddles, which with care one could avoid, merely running a minor risk of falling prostrate upon the wet boards in the midst of a galopade."

Louise delighted in the fact that the lonesome and lovelorn miners often carried courtesy and respect for the female gender to lengths unknown since the days of chivalry. Touched by their small deceptions, she cited an occasion when some young miners, hoping to thrill lady visitors they'd invited to try their hands at panning for gold, "salted" their digs (buried small nuggets for them to find) to let "the dear creatures go home with their treasures, firmly believing that mining is the prettiest pastime in the world."

Fascinated by others' hunger for gold, she wrote Molly, "In a little more than a week after two men obtained two hundred and fifty-six dollars from a pan of dirt, two others got thirty-three pounds of gold in eight hours, the largest amount taken from a panful of dirt being fifteen hundred dollars."

Even conservative Fayette was seduced into investing in claims. Or, as Louise put it, "sinking his money into claims." Once he foolishly paid a thousand dollars for a claim that proved worthless. "He might better have thrown his money into the river than to have bought it," she complained.

Over the summer as word of success filtered back to San Francisco, five hundred men descended on the area. Smith Bar was a half mile from Indian Bar on the same side of their river; Missouri Bar sat on the other side. When the finding of gold came too slow or played out, the impatient miners would simply pack up their "goods and chattels, which generally consisted of a pair of blankets, a frying pan, some flour, salt pork, brandy, pick-axe and shovel," and move on to the newest Dorado.

Louise found camp law equally intriguing and appalling. She described Indian Bar's "His Honor" as a stout, balding man "with a meek, gentle air and a satanic goatee." He had gone to the county seat to get himself a paper that entitled him to call himself a Justice of the Peace and mete out the law in those parts. When his judgments ran contrary to what the miners thought right, they took matters into their own hands and practiced "Miner's Law," their name for the code of "Judge Lynch." At which point His Honor was summarily invited to "walk over the hill" or, in today's parlance, "get lost."

"How oddly do life and death jostle each other in this strange world of ours! How nearly allied are smiles and tears," Louise philosophized, as she tried to convey the darker side of their lives. In one instance where money was missing and presumed stolen, the trial of the accused man proceeded with exceptional speed. "At one o'clock," Louise reported, "so rapidly was the trial conducted, the judge charged the jury, and gently insinuated that they could do no less than to bring in with their verdict of guilty a sentence of death!" The foreman handed the judge a paper from which he read the will of the people, "condemning him to be hung in one hour."

Granted a respite of two more hours, the man (a Swede) used the time in consuming a great deal of liquor and writing his goodbyes to friends abroad. "The hanging was carried out on schedule by the same jury that convicted him." But even as they tied the cord about his neck and threw the other end over a tree limb next to the graveyard, ready to hoist him up, Louise noted that, like her, "most of those present expected his sentence to be commuted at the last minute."

When they actually went through with the hanging her bleak observation contained more than the usual three-dot punctuations she was so fond of:

> In truth, life was only crushed out of him by hauling the writhing body up and down several times in succession. . . . many of the drunkards, who form a large part of the community on these Bars, shouted and laughed, as if it were a spectacle got up for their particular amusement. . . . The whole affair, indeed, was a piece of cruel butchery, although that was not intentional but arose from the ignorance of those who made the preparations. . . . if he had

committed a murder, or had even attacked a man for his money . . . it would have been a different affair. But with the exception of the crime for which he perished . . . he was a harmless, quiet, inoffensive person. . . .

Louise's compassion for wrongdoers was even more remarkable given her stringent New England rearing and feminine nature. So alien, one would think, to that "coarse, barbarous life."

On the light side, she described a procession of miners from Chile, every man ". . . intensely drunk. I never saw anything more diverting than the whole affair. I ought to have been shocked and horrified, to have shed salt tears and have uttered melancholy Jeremiads over their degradation. But the world is so full of platitudes, my dear, that I think you will easily forgive me for not boring you with a temperance lecture, and will good naturedly let me have my laugh and not think me very wicked after all."

In that remote and rowdy setting, motivated by the books she'd brought along—Burns, Spenser, Shakespeare, Coleridge, Shelley, even a volume of Isaac Walton's Compleat Angler—the inquisitive and pretty New Englander began composing her wonderfully entertaining letters to sister Molly. She took great pains with them, polishing each episode until it adequately reflected her opinions and growing literary skills.

She was trying to accurately convey to Molly how it felt to live in a place where the mean age was twenty-four, and men and women alike carried guns, whips, and knives as a matter of course, and invariably got into serious fights after too much liquor.

Her twelfth letter, dated January 25, 1852, expressed her genuine need to write of all this. "I am bound, Molly, by my promise to give you a true picture (as much as in me lies) of mining life and its peculiar temptations. . . ." Yet it is equally evident that her lively stories of that life, even the disagreeable parts, were proof of her enjoyment of it.

In 1852 the Clappes were forced to return to San Francisco because the companies that built the dams and flumes, unable to meet their payroll, were forced to abandon the camp. On departing from the gold country, her last letter to Molly contained the following dolorous comment: "My heart is heavy at the thought of departing forever from this place. I like this wild and barbarous life. I leave it with regret."

It was in San Francisco a year later that Louise's friend, Ferdinand C. Ewer, asked to read the copies she'd kept of her "Dame Shirley" letters. Fascinated, he got her permission to publish them. From January of 1854 to December of 1855 they appeared serially in his new magazine *The Pioneer*. A rumor has persisted ever since that Bret Harte borrowed his best story ideas from Louise's letters.

The Clappe's marriage ended in San Francisco in the same year her letters saw publication. History does not record the cause of their breakup. Fayette left and Louise stayed in San Francisco despite the climate. She was granted a divorce in April of 1857. By then she had applied for, and been awarded a teaching post in the city's public school system. She was an inspired and inspiring teacher who took special delight in her brightest pupils, strongly encouraging them to pursue their talents and dreams.

A lover of outings, she often treated her favorite students to Saturday picnics at local beaches or parks. When asked, she enjoyed organizing theatrical or literary recitals for worthy causes.

Following her editor friend Ewer's ordainment as an Episcopal clergyman, Louise kept busy with an active role in the affairs of his parish. Childless, she legally adopted and raised a niece, Genevive Stebbins who, when grown, moved in 1878 to New York City. Louise soon followed. Her last nineteen years were lived on the kindness of friends.

In 1897, at the age of seventy-eight, Louise was moved to Overlook Farm, an institutional home near Morristown, New

Jersey. Ironically, it was managed by Bret Harte's nieces. And it was in that home at the venerable age of eighty-six that Louise Clappe ended her days. Her death certificate records that she died ignominiously of "chronic diarrhea and senility." She was buried in Morristown's Evergreen Cemetery.

A source for scholars, and known the world over today, *The Shirley Letters* have been published three times. The first was a small edition privately printed in 1922 by Thomas C. Russell. The second publication in 1933, edited by Carl I. Wheat, was a two-volume limited edition put out by Grabhorn Press. The third edition, also edited by Wheat, was a commercial one published in 1949 which contained his biographical Introduction. In it he truthfully characterized Louise Clappe's life in the gold country as "The one great, the one truly dramatic experience of her life."

Clappe, Louisa. *The Shirley Letters.* Edited by Carl I.Wheat. New York City: Alfred A Knopf, Inc., Borzoi Book, 1949.

Levy, Jo Ann. *They Saw the Elephant.* Hamden, Conn: Archon Books, Shoestring Press, 1990.

Brown, Dee. *The Gentle Tamers.* London: Barrie & Enkins, 1958.

Margo, Elizabeth. *Taming the Forty-Niner.* New York City: Rhinehart & Co., 1955.

Davis, Stephen Chapin. *California Gold Rush Merchant, the Journal of Stephen Chapin Davis.* Edited by Benjamin B. Richards. The Huntington Library, San Marino, Calif.: 1956.

Zauner, Phyllis. *Those Spirited Women of the Early West - A Mini-History.* Sonoma, Calif.: Zanel Publications, 1989.

Gray, Dorothy. *Women of the West.* Millbrae, Calif.: Les Femmes, 1976.

CHAPTER 3

Stargazer Maria Mitchell

In 1831, a distinguished looking bewhiskered gentleman peered through his low powered telescope at a lunar eclipse, tracking the exact path of the moon's motion as it traveled across the face of the sun. A white card, a pinpoint puncture at its center, covered the telescope lens to protect his eyes.

"Remember not to look at it directly, Maria," he cautioned his plain-faced twelve-year-old daughter. She darted a fond, amused glance at him. Of course she knew better than to look directly at the sun. He'd warned her enough times. Smiling to herself, she shifted her gaze back to the small notebook open in her hand, ready for his next entry. Her father was the cleverest and most intelligent man on Nantucket Island. She was proud that she was the one, of all his ten children, he chose to instruct in the mysteries of the skies, the one to record his nightly computations on the roof of their house where they did their stargazing.

"Next. . ." he cried to alert her, then reeled off a new series of entries. Balancing the notebook on the chimney ledge, she dipped the pen in the inkstand she had brought, and noted down his computations in the neat script she'd learned from him. To work with him — in a way that none of the other children could — was worth the taunting she got from her siblings, and the naggings both of them received from her overworked mother. It was worth having the shivers in winter and the sweats on their hot, humid summer nights.

A primary requirement of those who love learning is a healthily curious nature. Maria Mitchell—she insisted her name be pronounced Mah-rye-ah—was insatiably curious, even as a tiny child. She was also very attached to her father. William Mitchell was a man of many trades and interests, but his consuming passion was astronomy. He whetted her growing affinity for this study by keeping her on their roof at his side until all hours, even on the coldest winter nights, instilling in her his ardor for the mysteries of the heavens. Understandably, she adored him—later describing him as "mild and winning in his manners, firm and resolute in his purposes." Her mother Lydia, on the other hand, with no time for such indulgences, she characterized merely as "stern and hardworking."

From the age of twelve for nearly six decades, Maria's thoughts centered on the heavens. She was never far from a telescope. Her father's patronage undoubtedly spared her the kind of resistance nineteenth century women usually encountered if their ambitions outreached the conventions of the time, for Maria suffered only minor setbacks on her way to a career.

When she was growing up, there were no colleges that admitted women. They were either self-taught, therefore, or had to content themselves with learning the household arts from their mothers.

Maria maintained it was a fascination with mathmatics that propelled her into the serious practice of studying the heavens. However, being born a Massachusetts Nantucket Islander in 1819 also had a great deal to do with it.

In the opening years of the nineteenth century, Nantucket was the most important whaling port in the world. It was a given that the island's fathers, husbands, sons and brothers needed a working knowledge of skies and weather conditions. It enabled them to navigate distant seas in their constant pursuit of the sperm whale which they hunted for tallow and other commodities. And because their men were often gone for years at a stretch, Nantucket women were expected to keep the homefires burning and family business-es afloat. Island girls learned as a part of growing up how to iden-tify the constellations, read a sextant and check the barometer for weather changes.

Maria was third in a Quaker family of ten children. When her forebears—staunch members of England's Society of Friends—migrated to America, they brought their religion across the seas with them. A cooper by trade, in 1827 William Mitchell filled the post of master of the first free school on the island. In 1836 he was made cashier, or principal officer, of the Pacific Bank of Nantucket. The sciences were his avocation, a bent inherited by both Maria and a brother, Henry, who grew up to become a dis-tinguished hydrographer.

When William Mitchell took up astronomy as a serious pur-suit instead of the hobby it had been, one of his jobs was rating chronometers—the time-keeping instruments used by the fishing fleet—checking their accuracy by stellar observations. He had a small observatory built to his order on the roof of his bank, which allowed him to pursue stargazing unobstructed.

As a small child Maria had to attend the local dame schools; she was happy to transfer to the rather unorthodox school her father ran for a time on Harvard Street. His curriculum empha-sized the study of nature and punishments were a thing unknown. She graduated to Cyrus Pierce's school where life was sterner. Pierce was master of America's first normal school. During her time in that school Maria first began to apply herself and take her studies seriously. Later, in speaking of those years, she said, "I was born of only ordinary capacity, but of extraordinary persistency." It was her good fortune that the education she received there pro-moted so useful and necessary an attribute.

She was Pierce's assistant for a brief period, then opened an experimental girl's school of her own. She wanted to try out in practice her strong convictions regarding both education for females and education in general. But after one year she closed it down. Apparently she saw it as a failure, for when offered the post of librarian of Nantucket's newly opened Atheneum—a job that came with a salary—she was pleased to accept.

The library observed quite limited hours. Maria was only required to keep it open afternoons and a couple of evenings a week. The hours suited Maria. In prized solitude, she used the mornings to devour the resources the library could provide. They allowed her to work her way through technical tomes like Bowditch's *Practical Navigator*. She read works by Lagrange, Laplace and Legendre in French. She taught herself German, and pored over Gauss' *Theoria Motus Corporeum Coelestium* or *The Theory of the Motion of Heavenly Bodies* as a way to learn Latin. She attended lyceum lectures a few evenings throughout the winter to hear celebrated orators of the day like Ralph Waldo Emerson, William Ellery Channing, Theodore Parker, Horace Greeley and Lucy Stone. She remained the Atheneum's librarian for twenty years.

But most of her evenings were spent with her father up at his observatory. There the two recorded thousands of observations of meridian altitudes of stars to determine times and latitudes, plus equal thousands of observations of moon culminations and occultations for longitude. And this was accomplished with only an altitude and azimuth circle, a four-inch equatorial telescope and a two-inch Dolland telescope.

Word of their in-depth findings came to the notice of renowned experts William C. Bond, director of Harvard College Observatory, his son George Bond and Alexander Dallas Bache, superintendent of the United States Coast Survey. All of them were impressed by the breadth and accuracy of the Mitchells' stellar research. The Nantucket lookout was added to their list of Survey stations. Mitchell was overjoyed to be appointed to the visiting committee of the Harvard Observatory.

They were doing their usual research on the night of October 1, 1847, with twenty-eight-year-old Maria at the telescope, when she called out, "Father, Father!" in a voice quavery with excitement.

"What is it, Maria?" He rushed to her side, worried that she was ill. "What's wrong?" His daughter turned to glance at him for an instant, then glued her eye to their telescope again.

"Look there, Father. Just above Polaris," she exclaimed. "It's a. . . I do believe it's a new comet! I've never seen it before!"

"Let me look," he said, now as excited as his daughter.

On that night, William entered an important notation in his journal. "This evening at half past ten Maria discovered a telescopic comet five degrees above Polaris. Persuaded that no nebula could occupy that position unnoticed, it scarcely needed the evidence of motion to give it the character of a comet." Her discovery brought Maria immediate international friendship and acclaim. As soon as it was established that she was the first person to discover it, the comet was officially named after her.

Because the great sixteenth century astronomer Tyco Brahe had been one of its revered citizens, Denmark held stargazers in high esteem. In recognition of her achievement, King Frederick sent Maria a specially minted gold medal, an award he established in her honor. It was the first such prize ever given to an American, and the first given to a woman anywhere. That same year the noted writer, Elias Loomis, included a chapter in his book *The Recent Progress of Astronomy* entitled, "Miss Mitchell's Comet."

In 1848 Maria was elected to membership in the Academy of Arts and Sciences, the first and only woman to be so honored until 1943. The next year she was one of the original "computers" selected to compile data for the new *American Ephemeris and Nautical Almanac*, a recognition which brought with it a welcome honorarium to augment her small librarian's salary. In 1850 the renowned scientist Louis Agassiz nominated her to membership in the

American Association for the Advancement of Science. She was elected by a unanimous vote. She received honorary degrees from Hanover, Columbia and Rutgers Universities. Remarkably, in a day when females with talent and creativity were frequently intimidated, repressed, and ridiculed or otherwise dissuaded from pursuing their gifts, Maria stood out as a frank and passionate believer in the potential of her sex.

"Until women throw off their reverence for authority," she stated unequivocally, "they will not develop."

Despite all the accrued honors, Maria retained her job at the library and continued to do her own housework. She also kept up with her nightly observations, urged on by her feeling that, ". . . the world of learning is so broad and the human soul is so limited in power. We reach forward and strain every nerve, but we seize hold only of a bit of the curtain that hides the infinite from us."

By 1857 she was able to afford a trip to Europe, a long-desired prize. There Maria met famous scientists like Mary Somerville, Alexander von Humboldt and Sir John Herschel. On her return, she was touched to tears when a woman's group gifted her with a fine new five-inch Alvan Clark telescope, the most powerful one she had ever used. Humble in the face of so many accolades, Maria sincerely saw herself as undeserving.

An unsettling matter at this time was her "disownment"—at her request—by a local Quaker meeting. She did not hold their beliefs, so it seemed to her the only right thing to have happen. There was a great deal of dissension at the time over Darwin's *The Origin of Species*. In Maria's view, it was so clear. God and His Realm—as portrayed in the Bible—were not in conflict with Darwin's theories. "If they seem to be," she observed, "it is because you do not understand one or the other." Plagued by religious doubts, for a time she attended services at the Unitarian church, but never joined it. Her personal creed remained simply, there is a God—and He is good.

When her mother Lydia died in 1861, Maria and her father moved to Lynn, Massachusetts, to be closer to a married sister. In Poughkeepsie, not far from Lynn, lived a wealthy and visionary brewer named Matthew Vassar who had just endowed, and was in the process of building, a new college for women. He intended for it to rival the finest of American men's colleges. Learning of Maria, he contacted her with an exceptional offer.

"I will build you an observatory on the new campus," he proposed, "with a twelve-inch telescope (it would be the third largest in the country) if you will come to Vassar Female College as mentor and professor of Astronomy."

In that era the notion of educating women troubled both sexes. The new college had many detractors and provoked much negative comment. Some called it Vassar's Folly. "Open the doors of your college to women," they predicted, "and you will accomplish the ruin of the commonwealth." It was the prevailing point of view.

Maria hesitated, not because she disagreed with the idea of educating women but, lacking a college education herself, she feared she was poorly qualified to teach girls who were trying to acquire one. Matthew Vassar had faith in her, however, and kept pressing her for an affirmative answer. Finally she agreed to try.

She moved with her father into Vassar's completed observatory in September of 1865, just in time for the official opening of the school. They used the clock room as their sitting room, surrounded by a brass chronograph, a marble sidereal clock and a bookcase full of volumes on astronomy.

Maria hoped to find there the calibre of ". . . students who would tax my utmost powers, and the assurance that some shall go far beyond me." Over time this prophecy was fulfilled.

With neither husband nor child to say her nay, forthright and wonderfully homely Maria was ever an independent thinker. Her scientific studies had given her a mistrust of what she termed "mindless authority." Honest and ethical to a fault, tactless and often undiplomatic in the way she expressed her thoughts, she warned her students, "We cannot accept anything as granted beyond the first mathematical formulae. Question everything else. Nature made woman an observer. The schools and schoolbooks have spoiled her. . . . So many of the natural sciences are well fitted for woman's power of minute observation that it seems strange that the hammer of the geologist is not seen in her hand, or the tin box of the botanist."

One day hearing a lady remark, "I am but a woman," Maria indignantly retorted, "No woman should say, 'I am but a woman.' But a woman! What more could you ask to be?"

Initially, Maria absolutely refused to attend compulsory chapel services. She finally condescended to go when it was pointed out to her that her absence would reflect on the school and be a bad influence on her students. She came, but chose to sit well in the back of their chapel in order to be able, as she put it, "to think of something pleasant." When her own religious convictions were called into question, she replied with certain melodrama, ". . . the prison and the stake have passed away, but the scientist who ventured to push his thoughts beyond received tradition must even yet expect to hear himself branded with the name infidel."

It was immediately obvious Maria was a brilliant choice for the post as well as a rebel against her culture. An exceptional grasp of her subject and a true empathy and understanding of her students made her a superb and exacting teacher. Her gift was that of stimulus, not of drill. She wasn't demanding in the expected ways. She merely insisted her students give their best and strive for complete accuracy, thus hoping to infuse in them her own appreciation for the beauty and order of the universe. She differed from most teachers in refusing to grade her pupils' papers. "You cannot mark a human mind," she said, "because there is no intellectual unit."

She also refused to report absences. "Given a small class and a teacher of any magnetism," she contended, "there need be no required attendance. To some the precision of military drill is the poetry of motion. I mourn over any loss of individuality." Restrictions such as dress codes struck her as absurd. She considered them part of the artificial manners and prissy disciplines required of proper nineteenth century young ladies. For herself, she wore what was handy, sometimes provoking her students to whisper to each other of the paucity and poor quality of her wardrobe. Her avant-garde ideas shocked her peers and were considered extreme if not downright radical. Her rebuttal to any who criticized her was, "We must have a different kind of teaching. It must not be textbook teaching. . . . It is a feeble kind of science which can be put on a blackboard, placed in array upon a table, or arranged upon shelves. If the spirit of science can be developed at all in school rooms, it must be by free debate; free thought and free inquiry are the very first steps in the path of science."

Her outspokenness and divisive opinions on proper conduct and school matters often exacerbated her colleagues' sensibilities. Once or twice her own career was in jeopardy. It was Maria's contention that questions were an incentive to pupils' imaginations, but her fellow professors mistrusted a teacher who not only allowed, but welcomed questions from her students. It was her habit to share her findings with her students, some of whom would stay night after night to work with her at the observatory. Six of them even brought their own telescopes to school. Twice she chaperoned groups of girls on trips to the West. The first occasion was in 1869 when they traveled west to Burlington, Iowa, to observe a solar eclipse. The second trip in 1878 took them to Denver for the same purpose.

Maria realized that few of her students would follow in her footsteps and choose astronomy as their life's work. But she hoped to instill in them the kind of good mental discipline that would serve them well no matter what direction their lives took.

Once asked about her childhood, Maria replied, "Our want of opportunity was our opportunity, our privations were our privileges, our needs were our stimulants. We are what we are because we had little and wanted much."

During her teaching years at Vassar, Maria kept up her own research. She pioneered the process of the daily photography of sunspots and faculae, the bright spots and streaks observable on the sun. She noted the hitherto unknown fact that faculae were not clouds above the sun's surface, as so many astronomers believed, but whirling vertical cavities. In published reports she always included her notes on solar eclipses and any changes she observed on planetary surfaces, with particular reference to Jupiter and Saturn and their satellites.

A second trip abroad renewed her European contacts and allowed her a much anticipated entree into the great Russian observatory at Pulkova, which she found fascinating.

As she grew older Maria devoted more of her time to the fight for women's rights in the field of education, striving to achieve for them the goal of equality with men. "I wish," she said, "something of the physicist's readiness to try experiments would come into our moral reform work. We are all afraid of new experiments, as if the law of growth through failure were not similar in moral, mental and material work."

She also worked unceasingly to advance women's presence in the fields of science, as an ardent advocate of suffrage, as a renowned Vassar College professor, and finally, as president of the Association for the Advancement of Women—an organization she helped found in 1873. In this regard, year after year Maria took time from her busy schedule to appear at scientific meetings and A.A.W. congresses.

Her lectures stressed the urgent need for recognition of women's scientific abilities. She was desperate to bring the adventurous spirit of the true scientist to the process of social development, and to generate a search for solutions to perplexing social problems. "I wish we could give to every woman who has a novel theory dear to her soul for the improvement of the world a chance to work out her theory in real life."

In truth, she was an inspiration to those young women who followed her lead, both in the sciences and many other fields. Twenty-five of her students are listed in *Who's Who in America*, including Miss Mitchell's own assistant and successor at Vassar, a bright young woman named Mary W. Whitney.

Maria retired from teaching in 1888 at the age of seventy when her health declined and she found herself increasingly ill. She intended to continue her research in the small observatory at Lynn. However, she grew worse, too sick to work. In a matter of months, on her death bed, Maria was heard to deliver herself of what was possibly her most unique and pithy remark.

"Well," she said, "if this is dying, there is nothing very unpleasant about it."

The year was 1889. Maria Mitchell passed away peacefully, from "brain disease," or at least that is what her doctor wrote on her death certificate. She was buried with the rest of the Mitchell clan in the family plot on Nantucket Island.

Almost immediately, Vassar alumnae undertook to fund an endowment in her memory. By 1890, the next year, they had raised the munificent sum of $50,000.

In 1922 the Hall of Fame at New York University received the gift of a bust of Maria Mitchell. It was placed in an honored spot where it can be viewed to this day.

Maria's home on Nantucket Island has been preserved and is open to the public. Visitors will see her comfortable old rocker, notebooks open on her desk, full of her careful calculations. There are even two of her dresses with matching bonnets on the hooks where she hung them. Next door to her home is a museum with her books and telescopes and other artifacts used throughout her career. She remains Nantucket's most distinguished citizen.

But down-to-earth Maria would find such adulation laughable. Her well developed honesty and humility, her innate sweetness, and her outlook on life itself is best expressed in her own assessment of what her life's work was all about:

> The greatest benefit derived from the study of science, is that it lifts you out of and above the littleness of daily trials. We learn to live in the universe as a part of it. We cannot separate ourselves from it. Our every act connects us with it. Our every act affects the whole.
>
> Standing under the canopy of the stars, and remembering their presence, you could scarcely do a petty deed or think a wicked thought.

Ketchum, Richard. "Maria Mitchell," *Faces From The Past*. New York City: American Heritage Press, 1970.

Stephens, Autumn. *Wild Women*. Berkeley, Calif.: Conari Press, 1992.

Wright, Helen."Maria Mitchell," *Notable American Women*,Vol. 2. Edited by Edward T. James & Janet W. James. Cambridge, Mass.: Harvard University Press, Bellknap Press, 1971.

Video created for Maria Mitchell Museum, Nantucket, Mass., 1995.

CHAPTER 4

Sojourner Truth: God Talker

For more than thirty years the tall distinguished African American woman wearing Quaker's garb — white turban, white shawl, apron and long black dress — captivated audiences gathered to hear her declare, "Chillin, I speaks to God and God speaks back to me."

A slave born of slaves in upper New York state in 1797, her given name was Isabella. When she finally won her freedom, she took the name of Sojourner Truth: Sojourner, for the journey of faith she traveled, and Truth, for the truths she would impart.

Throughout her long life she had a knack for making news. Though she was illiterate we know quite a lot about the first half of her life because of a book she later dictated to a white friend named Olive Gilbert.

Her mother had taught her about God. "God will see that you're treated right," she told her. "Just obey." Nine-year-old Isabella prayed mightily, trying to obey. But having to do what she was told regardless of her own feelings went against her grain. Many years after her own children were grown, when she had met many famous people including President Lincoln and President Grant, she still recalled with a chill the day she was sold on the block.

"She's only about nine, folks!" the auctioneer had said. "When she's full grown she'll do a man's work. This is a strong little girl." He grabbed Belle and whirled her around. "Come on, now. What am I bid?" When no one bid, he sent for a half-dozen sheep. Belle stood in their midst in the paddock as he coaxed, "Now, what am I bid for both this strong girl and this fine lot of sheep?" Belle tried not to show fear or weep as the brisk bidding began. Before the auction her mother had told her not to lie, or steal, or be scared of her new owners. But she was scared.

The man who bought her spoke English, but Belle spoke only Dutch. They couldn't communicate. He bought Belle only because he wanted the sheep. Inexperienced in owning another person, her new masters assumed that training a slave was like breaking a horse. They gave Belle only enough food to enable her to work, and enough whippings to keep her in line. She worked outside in winter in bare feet, often nearly frostbitten. Horses got to wear shoes, but slaves didn't.

She begged God for another master. Soon after, a tavern owner bought Belle and treated her well. Already six feet tall at thirteen, Belle was slim and comely, and carried herself with a certain grace. A Mr. Dumont from New Palz, following her every move as he drank his ale at the tavern, offered her master seventy pounds for her. Since that was three times her purchase price, her second master readily agreed.

Dumont owned Belle until she gained her freedom. Over those years she learned to speak English. Dumont took over his daughter's bedroom when she married and left home. Belle, meanwhile, was ordered to spend her nights under Mrs. Dumont's bed. She enjoyed that, because the rug she laid on was softer than barn straw. Being wakened to perform some whim of her mistress was preferable to fending off the kisses of a new slave who always wanted to have sex with her.

On the first night his wife slept away at their daughter's, Dumont woke Belle from a sound sleep and ordered her into his bed. Belle complied. It was understood that if the master wanted her, that was just one more task to perform. But she disliked it.

The narrative she would later dictate to Olive Gilbert, skipped over this part; her reluctance to divulge that relationship was due to her innate delicacy. At this point, undoubtedly to cover himself, her master decided to breed her, and arranged a mock marriage with a slave named Tom. Before the year's end, Belle had a baby girl that was probably Dumont's.

On July 4, 1817, New York State abolished involuntary servitude for those forty or older. Younger slaves like Belle, condemned to wait another decade, wondered what they would do with their freedom when it came. Belle bore four more children over those ten years. Three lived: a boy named Peter, after a brother she'd never seen, a girl named Elizabeth, after her dead mother, and the youngest girl, Sophia, for Belle's sister, who was reputed to be living free somewhere in New York State. When Peter was five, Dumont sold him to a friend who, planning a trip abroad, thought it would be amusing to have the little blackamoor in his party. Ashamed to face Belle, Dumont promised her freedom a year sooner. But an injury to her hand and the birth of Sophia cut back on her work.

When she asked for her "free papers," Dumont refused, claiming her poor work had cost him and she must put in another year. A hundred pounds of wool sat in the barn, waiting to be spun. Belle decided if she stayed long enough to spin it, that would compensate him for his losses. She finished spinning the wool, then stayed on to help with the heavy fall work. Now, she felt entitled to leave. But how? And where to go?

"God," she prayed, "I'm afraid to go in the night, and in daylight everybody'll see me. What can I do?"

"Go at dawn," the answer came to her.

"Thank you, God. That's a good idea."

She started out at dawn, her girl baby under one arm and food and all the clothes she wasn't wearing tied in a cotton kerchief in her other hand. She walked quickly without looking back, only stopping to feed the baby. "Well, God," she declared, "you've started me out; now please show me where to go."

She stopped to knock at the door of a house in a small village, and told her story to the Van Wageners, a kindly Quaker couple who lived there. In them she found friends. The wife led her to a clean bedroom with a big beautiful bed and bade her goodnight. Belle couldn't bring herself to use it. She crawled under the bed and slept there with her baby until sunrise.

Dumont came for her in the morning as she had known he would. She stood on her new friends' porch; he sat his horse. "Well, Belle," he said, "so you have run away from me." She shook her head.

"I did not run away. I walked away by daylight, and all because you promised me a year of my time." He said she would have to come back with him. Belle refused.

"Well, I'll take the child then," he said, dismounting. Belle cried out in terror that he could not. Van Wagener came outside carrying his purse.

"Friend," he said. "I have never been in the practice of buying and selling slaves — I do not believe in slavery — but rather than have this woman taken back by force, I'll buy her services for the remainder of the year. I'll pay twenty dollars, and five more for the child."

Dumont looked long at Belle, nodded, took the money and rode away. Belle was choked with gratitude over this kindness.

"Master. . ." she began. He shook his head. "Your Master is mine." She was now a Van Wagener and free, he said, adding, "Before God, all of us are equal." Then he read to her from his Bible, "I am the Way, the Truth, and the Life." Elated, Belle clapped her hands.

"Is that in there? I knew that! God told me."

They took her to their white church. She stayed outside thrilling to the choir, and the hymns they sang, remembering them all her life. She loved especially the one that went:

It was early in the morning,
Just at the break of day,
When He rose — when He rose
— when He rose
And went to heaven on a cloud.

It remained her favorite for the rest of her life.

For the first time in her life Isabella felt like a person. She was happy, though she longed for the children she'd left behind, especially for sold-away little Peter. One day after church, a lady who had visited at the Dumont home brought Isabella news of Peter. Concluding the child was really too small to take along, his new owner sent him to a brother who sold the child to a relative in Alabama named Fowler. Belle went pale. She remembered having seen that cruel-appearing man at a house where she still worked.

The law, Van Wagener declared, forbade the selling of slaves out of state. "The law is bigger than people!"

"It is?" Isabella asked. The man repeated that it was. "I'll go and get my child," she declared.

Belle managed to find supporters in a nearby community of Quakers. Then followed a series of events unprecedented in the dealings between whites and slaves She not only found a lawyer to represent her, but he won the suit against Fowler for her.

When her boy was turned over to her, she carried him home to change his stiff, uncomfortable clothes and found his poor little body covered with sores and scars. He said that Fowler had whipped and kicked him. Her fingers shook as they traced the scars. How had he borne it?

"That's nothing, Mammy. If you'd see Phyllis, I guess you'd scare. She had a little baby and Fowler cut her till the blood and milk both was running down her. You'd scare to see Phyllis, Mammy." Isabella froze. "God," she whispered, "render unto them double!"

It wasn't long after that the daughter of this new house where Belle worked came one day in a hysterical state, bearing a letter with tragic word of her sister's death. Before running upstairs she told Belle the Alabama man who beat her boy had now actually killed someone.

"No wonder," Isabella retorted, "he like to have killed my child. Nothing saved him but God." An inner voice commanded her, "Go up and hear." She went upstairs to the bedroom and, entering unseen, shut the bedroom door behind her. She listened as the husband read from the letter. It was a horrible tale about the murder of her employer's daughter.

> He knocked her down with his fist, jumped on her with his knees, he broke her collarbone, and tore out her windpipe. He then attempted his escape, but was pursued and arrested and put in an iron bank for safekeeping. . . .

"My child," sobbed the old lady. "My Eliza!"

Isabella felt as if she'd been poleaxed. No one noticed her leave to return to her work. Was this what she was supposed to hear? This horror? Had God made her dreadful prayer come true? "Oh, God," she groaned, "that's too much! I didn't mean that much, God!"

One morning, while working at another house, she remarked that her former master would be coming that day to take her home. Surprised, the woman asked, "Who told you?" No one, Isabella replied, she just knew. Sure enough, before nightfall Dumont's open wagon stopped by the entrance. He brought news. The mother of the murdered woman had lost her wits over her daughter's tragic death, and her grandchildren were back from Alabama and living in New York State.

Suddenly he changed topics. It was almost Whitsuntide, why didn't Belle come back and spend it with him and her daughters?

Remembering happy times in the past, Belle donned her bonnet and shawl, gathered up baby Sophia, and went out to his carriage. She froze in the act of climbing in, as if physically prevented from moving. She stared into space standing there, the child pressed to her bosom. Getting no answers to his questions, Dumont finally drove away.

The family found her still frozen in place when they returned, unable to respond to their questions, either. They brought her inside with difficulty, and the wife put the baby back in her cradle.

"What happened?" they asked again. Isabella shivered.

"God. . . God gave me a look," she said through stiff lips.

"You saw God?"

"He gave me a look," she said again, trembling all over. The wife led her into her bedroom and lit her candle. Isabella whispered, "I didn't know God was so big. He's all over!"

Alone, Isabella was overcome by fear. Another look like that, she told herself, and I will be gone forever, just like a blown-out lamp. She pictured a shadow advancing on her; it suddenly became rays of light. They made her feel warm all over, melting her hate and bitterness. She shut her eyes.

The light became music. When she opened them, she felt a great joy. God had forgiven her. She could pray again, she could sleep. She would later say, "That was when I found Jesus."

She marveled, discovering others also knew of Jesus. She learned that the hymn she loved, "When he rose," referred to Him and his resurrection. Sometimes, listening to people argue whether Jesus was the Son of God, or God himself, or the Christ, or a mere mortal, she would shake her head and say, "I didn't see him to be God, or else how could he stand between me and God? I saw him as a friend."

In 1829, deciding Belle needed a change of scene, her white lady friend took her and son Peter to New York by Hudson River boat. Eyes ashine, Peter boasted he would one day go to sea. Belle carried a letter from the Kingston Methodists to a church on John Street, and was welcomed by its black preacher.

She now prayed alongside black brothers and sisters, but did not try to make friends with any of them. Several women at church took her along on their soul-saving mission. On the way back, Isabella asked a young prostitute they had persuaded to accompany them what it meant to "live in sin?"

The girl said, "It means letting a man bed you for money." Isabella pondered this as they moved on. The slave she'd been was required to agree if her master felt like sleeping with her. Had she lived in sin all those years?

Isabella was talked into working for a cult whose leader called himself "the Messiah." It was a troubling period that ended in 1835 when the self-styled Messiah and some of his followers were jailed, accused of many allegations of wrongdoing, including holding orgies, and keeping concubines.

Now thirty-eight, Isabella was one of those supoenaed to testify in court to what she knew of the cult and its doings. She said while he might have been a false prophet, he was not really a bad man. Despite all the shouting and muttering and backing and filing, the judge found for acquittal, saying none of the allegations had been proved. Isabella was shocked. Without leaving the room, the jurors nodded in agreement with the judge. Confused, Isabella lost her faith, both in the Law and in the Spirit of Truth.

The death of an important cult member under odd circumstances caused a cult couple to accuse Isabella of poisoning him. The press got wind of this, and although his autopsy proved otherwise, they continued to incriminate her in their newspapers. Upset, Isabella engaged Mr. Western, a young white lawyer, who advised her to sue for slander to clear her name. As a further protection, Isabella got glowing character references from four former employers.

Western sent for her when her suit was coming to trial. Because the papers mentioned it, the courtroom was jam-packed. Both lawyers and citizens stared at her. What was the world coming to when a former slave could sue a white businessman and his erring wife for damages to her reputation?

A man named Vale, editor of a publication called *Citizen of the World*, asked to meet with her. He described her as having totally African features and no apparent mixture of blood:

> She is not exactly bad-looking, but there is nothing prepossessing or very observant or intelligent in her looks; yet throughout we find her reflecting . . .

After interrogating Isabella about "the Messiah and his kingdom," Vale concluded:

> This colored female is . . . not exactly what she seems. She has shrewd common sense, energetic manners, and apparently despises artifice. If circumstances did not prompt her to tell all she knows, it would be difficult to get at it.

The courtroom gasped when the jury found for Isabella, awarding her the sum of one hundred and twenty-five dollars. Her name was now worth more than the price she had once brought at auction. "I felt so tall within," she was quoted as saying, "as if the power of a nation was in me."

Vale wrote two books about her, baring every detail Isabella had related about the cults' love life. But interest in her faded when it was determined that, contrary to being a witch from the West Indies, she was only a plain servant from upstate New York.

The money awarded her allowed her to pay her lawyer. Added to her savings, she repaid debts her wayward son had contracted. During this period, Peter was constantly in trouble. Dropped from school for non-attendance, he soon landed in jail for selling the livery from the coachman's job Belle got him.

Twice she bailed him out for various offenses, and twice he resumed his thieving ways while Belle worked overtime polishing door knobs and shoveling snow to earn the extra needed money. She urged Peter to go to sea but he dallied, overfond of the wastrel's life. His next arrest for pandering did not bring his mother running.

He was jailed as Peter Williams, and by a freakish stroke of luck a man with the same name bailed him out, asking that Peter and his mother call on him. An elderly light-skinned African American man, he represented himself as a barber who liked to help delinquents in his spare time, putting them out of harm's way by shipping them out on whaling vessels. He knew of a ship, the *Zone* out of Nantucket, bound for a trip around the Horn. The very thing for Peter.

Isabella mixed her prayers of thanks with worry until she heard that her boy had actually sailed. Peter Williams returned to his place of business and, removing the muffler concealing his clergyman's collar, entered his church happy to have saved another lost soul.

In the spring of 1841 she received Peter's letter, written the previous fall. "I have seen more of the world than ever I expected," it said, "and if I ever should return home safe, I will tell you all my troubles and hardships." He ended hoping she would not forget him, and would forgive him for all he'd done wrong.

Isabella felt lost. Her children no longer needed her, not even rebellious Peter. She had forsaken her old faith to follow a false Messiah and, with him discredited, she had nothing to take its place. Peter's next two letters complained at receiving none from her. Unable to write back, she waited for his return "in fifteen months." The *Zone* put in to Nantucket following a very successful voyage. It offloaded three thousand tons of sperm oil, and sailed again. No one Belle queried could recall a black crewman named Peter.

Heartsick with guilt, praying for guidance, one night she again heard a voice. At daylight on the first of June, 1843, she packed a change of clothes in her pillowcase, some food and a bit of money, and told her employer she was leaving that day. The puzzled woman questioned "Where will you go?"

She replied that the Lord had given her the name Sojourner and told her to leave the city and go east. "I'll find friends there."

"What friends?" her mistress wanted to know.

"How should I know till I get there?" she replied.

Refusing even to eat breakfast, and guided by the rising sun, she left the home that had sheltered her so long, walked to where the street ended at the East River, bought a boat ride to Brooklyn, then started walking east on Long Island. Never looking back, she thanked God for saving her from Sodom. At midday she was given a drink by a Quaker woman at her well.

"What is thy name," she asked.

"Sojourner," she answered.

"Where dost thee get such a name as that?" the woman wondered.

"The Lord gave it to me, 'cause I'm to travel up and down the land." What had her name been before?

"Belle."

"Belle what?"

"Well, whatever my master's name was."

"And now thee says thy name is Sojourner. Sojourner what?" The former slave looked baffled. It had not occurred to her to think of a last name. So happy at first in setting out on her new life, now she was saddened, feeling somehow diminished and dispossessed.

"God," she prayed, "give me a name with a handle to it."
"Sojourner Truth," came the answer. She clapped her hands
and cried aloud, "Thank you, God—that's a good name!"
For most of her life from then on Sojourner lived hand to
mouth, eating if offered food, walking until she tired, resting
wherever she found to lay her head as she traveled in search of her
destiny. She worked, if work was offered, accepting only the smallest change in payment.

She looked for meetings, unconcerned with the sect they professed to be, only wanting to be allowed to speak. Listeners gave
her letters of introduction to friends in other places. She carried
them in her hand, so that those she met along the way could read
her destination. She carried one letter for thirty years. Sister Dean,
it began:

> I send you this living messenger as I believe her to be one
> that God loves. . . . Let her tell her story without interrup-
> tion . . . and you will see that God helps her to see where
> but few can. She cannot read or write, but God is in her
> heart.

By now a thin, somewhat angular woman, a sunbonnet on her
graying hair, Sojourner traveled constantly, talking about God to
all she met. She didn't tell her children what she had set out to do,
but had someone write them about it for her. When she heard she
would soon be a grandmother, she vowed never to be out of touch
with her children again.

Wary of false prophets, she went from one camp meeting to
another, her speeches moving the crowds who flocked to her. She
stayed for a short time in a religious community, one of those with
names like "Hopedale" and "Fruitlands," names promising the
sweet rest Sojourner was beginning to long for. Arriving at one
meeting near sundown, Sojourner tested her spellbinding talents

in quelling an unruly mob of young town hoodlums by singing and preaching to them.

The community was deeply concerned with matters like the Underground Railroad and Abolition. Sojourner had been much too involved with her own and Peter's slavery and her search for God to pay attention. But she started to listen when someone hurled a rock that only missed the head of the young Frederick Douglass by a few inches. Himself a self-taught ex-slave, on that evening he declared, "Once you know how to read the Bible, you will be forever unfit to remain a slave."

Sojourner's voice rang loud and clear. "You read," said she, "but God himself talks to me."

The era of great religious revivals had waned. More and more, people were turning away from conversion and concentrating on worldly things. Sojourner didn't know quite what to tell them anymore. "Wait," her inner voice advised, "Watch and pray." She waited, frustrated, and stayed on with a family as part guest, part servant.

It was there she was met by Olive Gilbert, a white Northerner who had recently returned from a visit to Southern relatives. At supper, having just bragged that Southerners never mistreated their slaves, Olive's cousin had then related a shocking tale. That morning a young local matron, furious at her black girl, hit her so hard on the head that she broke the girl's skull. Next she had her tied to a bedpost and whipped to death. Agonized, Olive was convinced something must be done to stop such ignorance and cruelty. She decided she would write a book on slavery and kept Sojourner talking while she took notes. How, she asked, had Sojourner begun to talk to God?

Sojourner told her story. When she had to face powerful enemies or the law, she said she always begged God, "Show them that you're my helper!"

"Oh, I felt so little," she recalled, "If you could have seen me in

my ignorance, trotting about the streets, bareheaded and barefoot-
ed. . . ." Only God was capable of making people hear her, she said.
Olive, studying her, was awed by the subtle transformation in the
ailing, old black woman. At first seeming broken, now she was a
veritable Joan of Arc.

Olive used Sojourner's words for the book she called *The
Narrative of Sojourner Truth*. Published in 1850, financed by a doc-
tor of her acquaintance, in addition to containing the letters
Sojourner carried it also related other accounts of slavery.

Although the troubled Union stayed intact another eleven
years, the new Fugitive Slave Law threatened every man and
woman of color; they could be arrested without warrant, or trial by
jury, not even allowed to testify on their own behalf. Whole communities of Blacks—both escapees and freed—fled to Canada
and England. Harriet Tubman, herself an escaped slave, led three
hundred slaves out of the South in nineteen perilous trips, defying
the forty-thousand dollar price on her head. Furious abolitionists
literally pulled recaptured slaves from the grip of the police.
Sentiment in the North was shifting in favor of Abolition.

When her physician benefactor went bankrupt, a still-solvent
friend gave Sojourner a cottage. She could pay for it gradually with
money from her book sales. The county record book has an entry
of a mortgage in her name, stating that one Isabella Van Wagener
gave her note for three hundred dollars, payable with interest one
year after the date.

Sojourner could hardly believe her good fortune. . . her own
house! But she had barely claimed it when she was back trudging
country roads, a bonnet shading her hair from the sun as she
lugged her bundle of earthly possessions, "a-testifyin' of the hope
that's in me."

Sojourner peddled her thin autobiography at the first woman's
rights convention held in Worcester, Massachusetts. Olive kept
copies for herself and friends, and gave the rest to Sojourner to

deal with the best way she could. It was a difficult transition for Sojourner, learning to shake hands with strangers, remember new names and the stories behind them.

One eager participant in the fray for America's white women was the Negro orator, Frederick Douglass. Some scoffed, but Douglass saw the suffrage movement as allied to the battle to free slaves. Women of the day were newly aware that they were governed without consent, stripped by marriage of property rights, claim to their children, or the fruits of their own labors — no matter what they earned.

She heard lectures by literary light Wendell Phillips, and women leaders like Lucretia Mott. At one meeting, the chairwoman pointed to Sojourner and mentioned her book. Some called for her to speak. She stood and said, "Sisters, I aren't clear what ye'd be after. If women want any rights more than they got, why don't they just take 'em and not be talking about it?"

All her books sold after that meeting. Many meetings threatened to erupt in riots, but Sojourner's dignified manner and opportune remarks always calmed and restored order.

After two months in Rochester, Sojourner set off for Pennsylvania and beyond. At a May woman's rights convention in Akron, Ohio, heavy rains attracted a mostly unsympathetic crowd which stirred uneasily at the sight of the tall black woman in a rain-soaked dress and dripping sunbonnet huddled in the aisle at the side of the pulpit.

Several women pleaded with the president, "Don't let her speak! It will ruin us! Every paper in the land will have our cause mixed up with abolition and niggers."

The next day's session consisted of arguments from delegates of the Presbyterian clergy. One warned they were "selling their birthright of consideration for a mess of equality pottage," another, the old argument, "If God had desired the equality of women, he would have given some token of His Will. . . ." Men and boys jeered and made rude noises. Unasked, Sojourner slowly got to her feet. "No," many cried, "Don't let her speak!"

Sojourner moved to the front, took off her old bonnet and looked to the president. There was some hissing, but the church quieted when they were commanded. All eyes upon her, her deep voice easily hearable, she made some preliminary remarks on the trouble between North and South, then delivered one of her most famous speeches.

> But what's all this here talking about? That man over there says that women needs to be helped into carriages, and lifted over ditches, and to have the best place everywhere. Nobody ever helps me into carriages, or over mud puddles, or gives me any best place. . . and ain't I a woman? Look at me! Look at my arm! I've plowed and planted and gathered into barns, and no man could head me — and ain't I a woman? I could work as much as a man, and eat as much, when I could get it, and bear the lash as well. And ain't I a woman? They talks about this thing in the head. . . what they call it?

Intellect, someone said.

> That's it, honey. What's that got to do with women's rights or niggers' rights? If my cup won't hold but a pint and your'n holds a quart, wouldn't ye be mean not to let me have my little half-measure full?

While some cheered and guffawed, she pointed to one of the ministers.

> Then that little man in black there, he says women can't have as much rights as men 'cause Christ warn't a woman. Where did your Christ come from?"

No one spoke. She repeated the question. Then with a ringing voice she answered herself.

From God and a woman. Man had nothin' to do with it!

Deafening cheers.

Her new Ohio friends, most of them women, lived for "the cause" and there was work for her there, lecturing and selling subscriptions to the *Anti-Slavery Bugle*. A couple loaned her a horse and buggy for traveling about the pioneer land with its skimpy, cold and dirty log cabins, since she was no longer strong enough to walk from town to town. Unfamiliar with the terrain, unable to read the signs, at a crossroads she'd simply drop the horse's reins and say "God, you drive." He always landed her someplace where her horse got cared for, and she had a good meeting.

She wore glasses now and carried a cane, joking it was "mighty fine for crackin' skulls." She said she was "gone sixty," but she was actually fifty-five. She soon became a legend with stories told about her life experiences.

Instead of losing her accent, she used it. On the outskirts of civilization, plain speaking was an asset. But she didn't try to correct any of the many speculations she heard about herself, figuring these, like everything else she received along the way — her voice, her appearance, her songs, what she was was moved to say — all were God-given and not to be changed.

When a speaker dwelt on the sanctity of the Constitution, she had more to say. Weevils had destroyed thousands of acres of wheat that year.

Chillun, I talks to God, and God talks to me, I goes out and talks to God in the fields and in the woods. This morning I was walking out, and I got over the fence. I saw the wheat a-holding up its head, looking very big. I goes up and takes a-hold of it. You believe it, there was no wheat there? I says, "God, what is the matter with this wheat?" and he says to me, "Sojourner, there is a little weasel in it." Now I hears talking about the Constitution and the rights of man. I comes up and I takes hold of this Constitution. It looks mighty big, and I feels for my rights, but there aren't any there. Then I says, "God, what ails this Constitution?" He says to me, "Sojourner, there is a weasel in it."

She made her point.

Several events made her happy that autumn. She was able to pay off her mortgage and own her house. The doctor printed another edition of her book after she sold out the first. And she decided to go north to meet the famous author of *Uncle Tom's Cabin*, Harriet Beecher Stowe. Mrs. Stowe knew of the black woman who spoke at anti-slavery meetings, and intended that their interview be a brief one.

In her usual gray dress, Sojourner was dusty from her trip. On her head a bright madras kerchief was wound into a turban. Self-assured and relaxed, she towered over the small New Englander. "So this is you," Sojourner began. Mrs. Stowe agreed. "Well, honey, the Lord bless ye. I just thought I'd like to come and have a look at ye. You've heard of me, I reckon?"

"Yes, I think I have. You go about lecturing, do you not?"

"Yes, honey, that's what I do. The Lord has made me a sign unto this nation and I go round a-testifyin' and showin' them their sins against my people." She sat down where indicated.

Intrigued by Sojourner, Mrs. Stowe first called in Dr. Beecher, her father, to meet Sojourner, then the rest of her family. The black woman received them all with poise. When she met Dr. Beecher, Sojourner remarked, "I love preachers. I'm a kind of preacher myself."

"You are?" he asked. "Do you preach from the Bible?"

"No, honey, can't preach from the Bible. . . can't read a letter."

"Why, Sojourner, what then do you preach from?"

"When I preaches," she replied solemnly, "I has just one text to preach from, and I always preaches from this one. My text is, WHEN I FOUND JESUS! "

He said she couldn't have a better one. Mrs. Stowe, fascinated, felt this unique woman did have a message to impart, and readily gave it whenever and wherever she found an audience. Unable to part with her, they kept her for days.

The slavery issue was clear by this time — the battleground Ohio to Kansas, where audiences might grow violent. One evening a noted speaker, badgered by a local lawyer, was at his wit's end. Were they men or mice to let a nigger-lover tell them slaves were human beings? The lawyer went on, "Why, everyone knew niggers were low, lecherous, no better than monkeys, a tribe of utter baboons!" The audience shouted its assent.

"Don't dirty your hands with that critter," Sojourner whispered to the speaker, "Let me tend to him." She waited until the diatribe ended then stood to face the audience.

"Chillun," she began as always, "I'm one of them monkey tribes. I was born a slave. I had the dirty work to do. The scullion work." She added that talking to the man who had said those things was the dirtiest work she'd ever had to do. She got applause. But after the meeting, the lawyer she had denounced came to her.

"You think your talk does any good, old woman? Why, I don't care any more for it than a fleabite."

"Maybe not," she said, "But the Lord willing, I'll keep you scratchin."

Sojourner went back to Northhampton only long enough to sign her 'X' between the words Isabella and Van Wagener on a document deeding her house to a Daniel Ives for seven hundred and forty dollars. It was the last time she used that name from a human master.

By year's end she had her new house in Harmonia, six miles west of Battle Creek, Michigan, bought in the name of Sojourner Truth. In the 1860 census it was listed also as the home of her daughter Elizabeth Banks and two grandsons. She had a new stock of books to pay her way, a new frontispiece showing her older face, and a brand new preface by the famous Harriet Beecher Stowe. One by one the rest of her family drifted west to join her but she spent little time there.

In criss-crossing northern Indiana in the fall of 1858, she heard rumors that she was a pretender. At a meeting packed with pro-slavery Democrats led by a Dr. Strain, they let her speak. As she finished and was about to step down, he said there was a question of her sex; it seemed that some of the audience believed they had been listening to a man speak.

"It is for the benefit of the speaker," the doctor said with a broad smile, "that I ask for the speaker's breast to be submitted to inspection by some of the ladies present, so the doubt may be removed."

Sojourner pounded her cane and the noises subsided. Why did they think her a man? she demanded. Their answer was because her voice was so low. Strain wanted a vote of agreement. Sojourner did not wait for their vote, or the inspection of the ladies. She opened her dress.

"It's to your shame I'm doing this, not to mine." She bared her breasts, saying they had suckled many a white baby. When two men stepped up to hide her nudity, she pushed them away. Holding her flaccid breasts in both hands, she said scornfully to Dr. Strain, "Maybe you'd like to suck." This defiance of propriety, strangely enough, empowered both her and her embarrassed white sisters.

In all those years, she only crossed paths with Frederick Douglass once more. All were aware of the cerebral lion-headed speaker, while few knew of Sojourner or her role in the good fight.

On this evening, Sojourner sat in the front below the speaker's platform, one of the very few blacks in a predominantly white audience.

"They have no hope of justice from the whites," Douglass declared, "no possible hope except in their own right arms. . ."

A deathly hush swept the hall as Sojourner rose to face Douglass.

"Frederick," she asked, "is God dead?" She was outraged at his lack of faith.

The break between between the North and South was imminent. During another meeting pro-slavers yelled at Sojourner.

"Down with you! We think the niggers have done enough! We won't have you speak! Shut your mouth!"

Not the least intimidated, Sojourner yelled back, "The Union people will make you shut your mouths." She was staying at the time with a family who lived five miles from Angola, Indiana. On the evening of her next meeting two women came to report that her host had been arrested for housing her. The family wanted to hide her but she refused. "I'd sooner go to jail." A constable turned up with a warrant for her arrest. Soon after, as if by divine intervention, he was joined by a Captain of the Union Home Guard.

"She is my prisoner," the Captain announced, producing his orders.

Disgusted, the constable retorted, "I ain't going to bother my head with niggers; I'll resign my office first." The captain said it was unlikely there'd be a meeting, for the Copperheads (Northerners who sympathized with the South) had sworn to burn their town hall if she tried to speak.

"Then I'll speak on the ashes," she replied.

The women decided she should wear a sort of uniform, and outfitted her in a red, white and blue shawl, with a matching apron, a cap with a star on it for her head and a star on each shoulder. She glanced in a mirror, "I could scare myself," was her only comment. She refused the sword or pistol they offered her. "The Lord will preserve me without weapons. The truth is powerful and will prevail."

"What business are you now in?" asked a man who had known her in New York.

"In New York my business was scouring brass door knobs; now, I go about scouring Copperheads." She kept on until winter, when she fell ill.

"Help me live a little longer to praise God and speak to the people in this glorious day of 'mancipation," she prayed. She wanted very much to see Mr. Lincoln and hoped to do so before his term ended.

The *Anti-Slavery Standard* carried a piece by Harriet Beecher Stowe titled "Sojourner Truth, the Libyan Sibyl," that filled the whole back page. Though ten years had passed, Mrs. Stowe fondly recalled all of their conversations. When it was read to her, a bedridden Sojourner mistook the word for "symbol." When someone started to read it again, she interrupted, "Oh, I don't want to hear about that old symbol. Read me somethin' that's going on now, somethin' about this great war!"

Word of her illness traveled far. Letters and gifts came to her from all over, from as far away as Dublin, Ireland. She was dumbfounded. How could they know her so far away? She asked a friend to reply that she was better than ever. "I've budded out with the trees," was her expression.

Almost sold out of books, she let a photographer take her picture to use in the next printing. "Sell the shadow to support the substance," she joked. She sent the first batch of books to *The Anti-Slavery Standard* in New York, which quickly announced "a card photograph of that noble woman, Sojourner Truth," was for sale to the public.

Her first grandson and fellow traveler, James, was off fighting for the Union; she traveled now with thirteen-year-old Sammy

Banks, a grandson who could both read and write. She said he almost made her feel young again.

James was reported missing but Sojourner insisted God told her he was alive and would return. One June day, finishing up the washing, she told her current employer she must leave and go to Washington. When asked why, she said she had to see the president before his four years were up.

From friend to friend and meeting to meeting, the trip was long and full of memories. They traversed on foot the states she had walked years before—Ohio, Pennsylvania, and Upper New York State—carrying a "Book of Life" whose empty pages she filled with names of friends. Finally arriving in New York, the city she left to go journeying so long before, she made sure to call on editors of newspapers to show she was not dead as reported.

She and Sammy reached Washington at summer's end. The capitol had not been free soil all that long and a host of her people were adrift in the city, hungry, thirsty, ragged and currently homeless. Mere children prowled the streets picking pockets, robbing to live; hundreds of black families were crowded together in filth and squalor. But they were free. A few caring souls had set up camps and put men to work on the land. Sojourner stopped to visit one called Freedman's Village. She promptly organized a meeting and reminded them that "cleanliness was next to Godliness." They asked her to stay, and she did for a while.

It was harder to call on the President than she'd thought. She needed an appointment. She was one of the speakers at a celebration of the end of slavery in Maryland where Lincoln made an appearance and was soundly cheered.

Finally a friend got Sojourner and herself an appointment for eight on a Saturday morning on October 29, 1864. The President's door was open and she could hear what he said to others before them. At last their turn came.

The friend introduced Sojourner, saying she'd come all the way from Michigan to meet him. Lincoln rose and bowed, giving the black woman his hand. "I am pleased to see you," he said simply.

"Mr. Lincoln," Sojourner replied, "I'd never heard tell of you before they put you up for president."

He smiled. "But I had heard of you." She went on to liken him to Daniel in the lion's den, being saved by God. As God had spared her, here she was seeing him for herself. He congratulated her on being spared. She told him he was "the best president who's ever taken the seat." He said there were others before him who were just as good, and would have done the same as he, if the time had been right for them.

"And if the people over there," he pointed across the Potomac, "had behaved themselves, I couldn't have done what I have; but they didn't, which gave me the opportunity to do these things." She thanked God that he was the instrument chosen by Him and the people to do it. He showed her a beautiful Bible the Blacks of Baltimore had presented to him, and read her its touching inscription. Reaching for her Book of Life, he spoke the words he wrote in it: "For Aunty Sojourner Truth, October 29, 1864. A. Lincoln." He would be pleased to have her call again, he said. The interview was over. Before she could call on him again, so was Mr. Lincoln's life.

The law against slavery was still being fought in the courts. The war ended when she'd been five months at Arlington Heights, but Lincoln lay in his coffin in the East Room of the White House. Two columns of hushed people, many of them black, filed by for a last tender look. Sojourner's cheeks were wet as she passed the bier.

The parade celebrating the end of war took two days to finish. Among the marching black soldiers, she was thrilled to see her grandson James, many months a prisoner.

A one-armed officer who rode with Sherman's army sought Sojourner out. He had just been appointed head of the new

Freedman's Bureau. He spoke to her, then listened to what she had to say. Subsequently a report was issued from the War Department in charge of Abandoned Lands, Refugees and Freedmen. It was dated Washington, September 13, 1865, and read:

> Sojourner Truth had good ideas about the industry and virtue of the colored people. I commend her energetic and faithful efforts to Surgeon Gluman, in charge of Freedman's Hospital, and shall be happy to have him give her all facilities and authority so far as she can aid him in promoting order, cleanliness, industry, and virtue among the patients.

Her hospital work did not occupy all her time. She still spoke at meetings in churches, and made new friends, one of them Elizabeth Cady Stanton. As Mrs. Stanton's guest at an equal rights convention in New York, Sojourner said:

> I want women to have their rights, and while the water is stirring I'll step into the pool. Now that there's a stir about colored mens' rights is the time for women to get theirs. I'm sometimes told, "Women ain't fit to vote; don't you know a woman had seven devils in her?" Seven devils ain't no account. A man had a legion in him.

The house broke up in laughter. She explained to Mrs. Stanton. "You never lose anything by asking everything."

One day she quit her jobs and left for Battle Creek with Sammy. Now that she had all her family around for the first time, she bought a barn on College Street on credit as a place for them to live. But she stayed less than six months, and set out West again, telling her ideas to those she met. They were subsequently transposed into a petition which asked for land in the West for former slaves, plus care for the aged and infirm Blacks.

When she arrived back in Washington in mid-March, she managed to get a letter from the Commissioner of the Freedman's Bureau requesting an interview for her with President Grant. Seated in the next room waiting for her interview, a gentleman also waiting spoke to her.

"I recollect having seen you at Arlington Heights. How old do you call yourself now?"

"I get five dollars for telling my age." The man smiled and asked her to stop in and see him at City Hall. She'd been talking to Washington's Mayor Bowen.

She met Ulysses Grant, who shook her hand and replied he too was happy her people had won the right to vote. Her visit to the Capitol caused a stir among wide-eyed clerks and pages as she passed on her way to the Chamber, marveling at the changed way people reacted to "coloreds." A Washington newspaper reported her visit as:

> An hour not to be forgotten, for it is not often even in this magnanimous age of progress that we see revered senators — even him that holds the second chair in the gift of the Republic — vacate their seats in the hall of State to extend the hand of welcome, the meed of praise, and substantial blessings, to a poor negro woman. . . . It was as refreshing as it was strange to see her who had served in the shackles of slavery . . . for a quarter of a century before a majority of the senators were born now holding a levee with them in the marble room. . . . Truly the spirit of progress is abroad in the land. . . .

But every trip Sojourner made to the capitol had its share of fights with streetcar drivers and conductors, as well as angry passengers. She would sneak on, resisting every attempt to throw her off, yelling "I want to ride!" as loud as she could. Walking with a white woman one afternoon, she kept moving as her friend stopped a streetcar with a signal. Her friend climbed on board in a leisurely fashion. Sojourner reversed course and jumped aboard as well.

A man asked indignantly, "Conductor! Do niggers ride these cars?"

The conductor pulled at Sojourner to get her off, and dislocated her shoulder as he shouted to her friend, "Does she belong to you, lady?"

"No," she answered. "She belongs to humanity."

"I hope he's just been anticipatin'." Sojourner responded to a letter from a man who had heard a rumor of her death. It took years instead of weeks to fill the petitions she'd had printed at her own expense. They asked for land for former slaves. She spoke in twenty-one states over four years, until they were filled with names and could be presented to Congress. She was told they needed one more push and some luck.

Her grandson Sammy fell ill. Sojourner took him to Battle Creek, where he died in 1875. Her own health declined until she, too, was expected to die. But a young Dr. Kellogg who would make a fortune in health foods and corn flakes undertook her treatment. Soon Sojourner walked more youthfully than before; she even gave up the eyeglasses she had worn for years.

She would joke about herself, "I have a white skin underneath. Just scratch deep enough." She continued to lecture for woman's rights, temperance and penal reform, talking as often as three times a week. In 1878 she gave speeches in thirty-six Michigan towns as well as a woman's rights convention in Rochester.

She was now reputed to be over one hundred, a fiction she encouraged. Figuring from her slave days, she was probably eighty-six. In days to come, when she felt herself weakening, she began to speak of how she perceived dying would be.

"Stepping out into the light. Won't that be glorious!" she cried.

Her three daughters began to keep watch by her side each night. Just before dawn on November 26, 1883, she died just as she said she would. . . "going out like a shooting star."

They buried her the day before Thanksgiving. The minister finished the Lord's Prayer as her casket was lowered into her grave. Spontaneously many voices broke into her favorite hymn.

It was early in the morning,
Just at the break of day,
When he rose—when he rose. . . .

The original stone marker her friends set on her grave was a simple one. The black painted letters on it read:

In Memoriam
SOJOURNER TRUTH
Born a slave in Ulster County, New York, in the 18th century.
Died in Battle Creek, Nov. 26, 1883, aged about 105 years.
"IS GOD DEAD?"

Frederick Douglass, hearing the news of her death, wrote, "We were all for the moment brought to a standstill, just as if someone had thrown a brick through the window."

Truth, Sojourner. *Narrative of Sojourner Truth*. As told to Olive Gilbert 1850. New York City: Random House, Vintage Books, 1993.

Pauli, Hertha. *Her Name Was Sojourner Truth*. New York City: Appleton-Century-Crofts, 1962.

Redding, Saunders. "Sojourner Truth," *Notable American Women*, Vol.3. Edited by Edward T. & Janet W. James. Cambridge, Mass.: Harvard University Press, Bellknap Press,1971.

Painter, Nell Irvin. *Sojourner Truth: A Life, A Symbol*.W. W. Norton & Company New York City, 1996.

CHAPTER 5

The Three Charleys

We tend to think of 19th Century women as virtually entrapped in high-necked, long-sleeved, ankle-length dresses that barely revealed the toes of their shoes. Their dresses covered a myriad of petticoats and other unmentionables, and were meant to conceal . . . not reveal. But at least three unconventional women of that century spent all or a part of their lives as men, enjoying the liberty men's clothes permitted, employing that disguise for their own purposes.

It would take courage, determination and stamina in any age for a woman to live as a man, but this was especially true in the inhibiting 1800s. To hide her gender would have necessitated being a "loner," trusting no one of either sex, guarding her identity as closely as if the law were after her. An intriguing aspect of these three intrepid women was that they all came West within a couple of years of each other, and all used the name Charley — a fact which confused future legends. And they never met.

COCKEYED CHARLEY

The first of them, Charley Parkhurst, was known at different times as Charley Darkey Parkhurst, Charles Parkhurst, D. B. Ransom, "Six-Horse Charley," "One-eyed Charley," "Cockeyed Charley," and plain "Old Charley."

But her given name was Charlotte Darkey Parkhurst, and she was born in Lebanon, New Hampshire in 1812, although others have set her place of birth the same year in Providence, Rhode Island. Regardless of which was her true birthplace, all agree she was abandoned by her parents and raised in an orphanage. Wiry and strong, in her early teens she stole a boy's clothes and walked away from her grim beginnings never to return. From then on, she spent her life as a male. To avoid confusion, from here on we will refer to Charlotte Parkhurst as "he."

While hunting a job in Worcester, Massachusetts, he met a livery stable owner named Ebenezer Balch. Balch took Charley into his home and started the kid out washing carriages, cleaning stables and currying horses. Finding him an apt pupil, Balch next taught Charley how to drive a horse team. By the time he was in his late teens, he could handle a six-horse coach.

When Balch moved to Providence, Rhode Island, he took Charley with him. He bought a house and the What Cheer Stables, from which Charley was hired out as a driver. Within months, Charley had acquired a name as a fast and safe "whip," and was often requested for outings by rich families.

Charley next spent time driving in Georgia. He grew bored traveling the same routes so when two friends, John Birch and Frank Stevens—owners of a stage line in California during the Gold Rush—wrote they needed able drivers, Charley moved West. In 1851 he commenced his long career by driving stages between Stockton and Mariposa.

This was only the first of the many routes and many companies he drove for, both in Mother Lode country and up and down the coast. Yet no one seemed to suspect Charley was a woman. Full grown, he stood five-foot-seven, with broad shoulders, muscular long arms and a sunburnt face the color of saddle leather. His voice was soft except in anger, when he could cuss with the best of them. Asked about the patch over his eye, he replied truthfully, "When I first was drivin' in Californy, I was involved in an incident outside Redwood City. I was kicked in the face by my lead horse while attempting to calm her down after a rattler jumped out on the trail. From that time on I been called Cockeyed Charley by my friends and acquaintances and I placed a black patch over my blinded left eye."

He did all the manly things like throwing dice, playing poker, drinking his whiskey straight, and arguing politics. Charley disguised his gender with embroidered gloves, blue jeans, a double-breasted coat, and a wide leather belt about his midriff. And he always wore a hat. People remarked on the fact that Charley never allowed a woman to ride the top seat by his side, nor did he seek female companionship. Once he even left a good Sierra run he'd held for three years because some of his female riders bothered him by speaking of marriage.

Even as a youngster in his first job, Charley exhibited real talent for working with animals. If he chose to live in stables with them rather than in houses, it was either a ploy to help conceal his true identity or because his claim that he got along much better with horses than with his own kind was true.

Men in Charley's profession were well respected. In the words of writer Georgina Kingsley Rose, "The western stage driver, on his box, with the 'lines' in his hand, is inferior to no one in the Republic. Even the President, were he on board, must submit to his higher authority."

Ben Truman, writing in the *Overland Monthly* of March 1898 said of them:

> The old stage drivers of the Pacific Slope during the fifties and sixties — nearly all of whom have themselves been driven over the "Great Divide"— were the last of their race. Time was, however, when the man who held the ribbons over a six-horse team on the summits of the Sierra and in

the canyons of the coast was more highly esteemed than the millionaire or the statesman who rode behind him. He was, moreover, the best liked and the most honored personage in the country through which he took his right of way. . . . He was the autocrat of the road at all times.

According to Craig MacDonald in *Cockeyed Charley Parkhurst, The West's Most Unusual Stagewhip*, it was bad form to tip a stagedriver with money. Appreciation for his expertise was better expressed with a nice slouch hat, a pair of fine boots, nice new gloves, silk handkerchiefs or a gift of good cigars.

Charley became an inveterate tobacco chewer. The more deadly the trail on which he was guiding the team pulling a Concord coach, and the more risk, the more tobacco Charley packed into his cheek. It was probably this habit that led to his death, which was ascribed to cancer of the tongue.

Charley's sex remained a secret until he died on December 28, 1879, at the age of sixty-seven. In *Anybody's Gold* noted Western writer Joseph Henry Jackson said, "Charley was as skillful, as resourceful and as hard-boiled as any driver in the Sierras."

In his book, *Westward*, historian W. H. Hutchinson noted:

Charley Parkhurst was not only the most skillful reinswoman the world has ever known, but typified the devotion to calling, the pride in accomplishment, and the determination of all drivers who made it possible for stagecoaching to play the glorious role it did in the opening and development of the American West.

In *They Saw the Elephant*, Jo Ann Levy cites the following accounts of Parkhurst which appeared shortly after his death. A brief obituary in San Francisco's *Morning Call* informed its readers:

He was in his day one of the most dextrous and celebrated of the famous California drivers, ranking with Foss, Hank Monk, and George Gordon, and it was an honor to occupy the spare end of the driver's seat when the fearless Charley Parkhurst held the reins of a four or six-in-hand.

The *Providence Journal* had this to say:

> Now that it is known that Charley was a woman there are plenty of people to say they always thought he was. . . . His hands were small and smooth, and so far from being proud of the fact, it disgusted him and he wore gloves Summer and Winter. He was thought to be putting on style, but as he always dressed well, the gloves were looked upon only as a part of his high-toned ideas. He was beardless, and his voice was a little thin . . . but Charley weighed a hundred and seventy-five pounds, and could handle almost everyone that ever took hold of him, smoked with the placidity of an Oriental, and would take one or two glasses of whiskey punch without winking.

Another man named George F. Harmon who, as a young boy, knew Charley in retirement, was quoted in *The Pajaronian* about the legendary stagedriver:

> What caused Parkhurst to adopt male attire and follow a man's work will never be known, as the secret died with her. My father and mother were her most intimate friends. . . . A short time before her death she said that she had something to tell him, but there was no hurry about it. She kept postponing telling him, and he was not present when the end came. I have no doubt that she intended to tell him the secret of her life, what caused her to dress and live the way she did.

After his death, when it became known that Charley had been a woman, gossip abounded on why she had chosen to hide her identity behind a man's facade. People conjectured she had loved not wisely, but too well or had borne a child out of wedlock and vanished from the East to appear in the West as a man. It was even suggested she might have been a "hermaphrodite," a rumor the coroner's inquest dispelled.

Not long after her death the town of Soquel, California, which is near Santa Cruz and Watsonville, honored her with a brass plaque — not for her achievements as a man and career stagedriver, which would have pleased her — but for being the first woman to vote in the Presidential election of 1868, which definitely would not. She had registered to vote as Charley Parkhurst, male.

MOUNTAIN CHARLEY

Though Charley Parkhurst apparently felt no regret at spending her life as a man, the next Charley's feelings about her thirteen years in men's guise, five spent in the West, were quite different. We know this because in 1859, when her identity was disclosed, she wrote and published an explanatory autobiography she called *Mountain Charley* in which she described those years as, "deeply disturbing."

Her given name was Elsa Jane. She was the illegitimate child of a union between a wealthy young Louisiana plantation owner and an even younger woman he adored and planned to marry. He left on a business trip, telling her the wedding day would take place on his return. Elsa discovered she was pregnant — a fix precipitous lovers have gotten themselves into since time began.

When he failed to return on schedule, in her desperation she wed the first available man, her lover's overseer. He proved a cruel, surly brute of a husband.

Shortly after their unacknowledged daughter, Elsa Jane, was born, the baby's bachelor father took the child to live in his mansion as his niece. In her early years she was visited from time to time by a woman she was told to call "Aunt Anna," a woman who frantically "embraced her, covered her with kisses" and called her "dear child."

In her autobiography *Mountain Charley* she states, "My remembrances of the place and its people are all misty. All about it seems more like something I once saw in a dream." Many years later Elsa learned that the kindly older man she'd been taught to address as "Uncle" was her real father, and "Aunt Anna" her natural mother, their love denied them by convention.

From the age of five until she was twelve, Elsa Jane was educated in a select New Orleans boarding school. There she received fond notes from her Aunt Anna, and sporadic communiques from her Uncle, usually with spending money enclosed. Occasionally he would arrive in person and take her on a day's outing to, as she put it, "observe my progress. My life there passed without much variation." But something happened when she reached the age of twelve that, in her own words, "gave it a direction never before traveled by any other woman." She claimed she was physically matured, "with a rapidity marvelous even in that hot-bed, the South." She considered herself, "as womanly in form, stature, and appearance as most women at sixteen. My mind was, perhaps, not so much in advance of my years, yet it was not of a character to do discredit to my appearance of maturity."

The event she referred to was her elopement. At the precocious age of twelve, Elsa ran off with the first young man who courted her to become Mrs. Forest, wife of a Mississippi riverboat pilot, "a fact of which I had never thought to inquire prior to our marriage." The newlyweds rented a modest cottage in St. Louis, the point of departure of all her husband's trips.

Apprising both Uncle and Aunt of her new status, she wrote

how supremely happy she was, and that her husband was "a noble fellow" who "well repaid the sacrifice I made for him." Within three years their union was blessed by two children, a boy and a girl. However, her baby daughter was just three months old when a man brought her heartbreaking news. Elsa's beloved young husband was dead as the result of an altercation with one of his crew. A certain Jamieson had fatally shot him in the heat of an argument. Arrested, Jamieson was duly tried, convicted, and then set free on a technicality.

For devastated fifteen-year-old Elsa the next few days passed in a kind of nightmare. She saw "a hearse—funeral trappings—was aware of the rigid body of my husband," was subjected to "meaningless words of comfort—whispered directions, until finally I was left alone with my children. It was terrible, so much so that I wonder it did not drive me to insanity."

Before she had time to recover from her first shock, a letter came to inform her that Aunt Anna had died. Enclosed was Aunt Anna's final letter. In it she revealed to her daughter the true details of her birth, and why she and Elsa's father could never marry or acknowledge her as their child. And now a new burden was laid on her young shoulders when she was told that her dear improvident husband had spent his money as he earned it, and had left her nothing—not even enough to pay for his funeral. This fearful news would have destroyed the average fifteen-year-old, but it only served to strengthen Elsa's resolve. She hated the villain who had made her a widow and burned with a desire for revenge. She swore somehow to punish him and find a way to support her babies.

Her husband's brother Masons came to her aid; they advanced her the sum of seventy dollars and paid for his burial. Solvent for the moment, she settled her bills and fed her children while racking her brain for a solution. She refused to appeal to her father who hadn't cared to contact her since hearing of her marriage. But, with no skill or trade in a world prejudiced against the idea of a gentlewoman with children working, what could she do?

Casting about for the answer, she came upon the idea of changing gender, knowing if she could bring it off it would give her a chance at a better living. Her "soul filled with poignant grief," she bid her children goodbye and left them in the paid care of the Sisters of Charity. She next persuaded a friend of her late husband's to buy her a good boy's suit; she cut her luxuriant long hair, and — donning the new outfit — practiced acting the part of a young male until it felt natural. Not tall, Elsa easily passed for a teenager. Reminding herself constantly to use rough language and speak in a lower, gravelly voice, within three weeks she felt able to go anywhere without fearing detection.

Her early efforts to get work brought rude treatment and countless rebuffs. But she finally got a job that paid a handsome thirty-five dollars per month as a cabin boy on the *Alec Scott*, a steamer plying the Mississippi River between St. Louis and New Orleans. Successful in her charade, she wrote of it, "I found myself able to banish almost wholly the woman from my countenance. I buried my sex in my heart and roughened the surface so that the grave would not be discovered." Between trips, she donned her woman's clothes to visit her children. Each time was a joy, she wrote, and each parting a wrenching sadness at day's end when she had to leave them and resume her disguise.

She served under the captain of the *Alec Scott* for almost a year. If he suspected her deception, he was chivalrous enough not to indicate it in any way. Learning of a better paying job on the *Bay State*, she left to become its second waiter. She quit after six months when the chance came to resume working for her "kindly captain" of the *Alex Scott*. In 1854, after she'd spent four years on the river, her captain suddenly sickened and died. Grieving, Elsa quit the river for a land job. Incredibly, she found one as a brakeman on the Illinois Central Railroad.

In her autobiography she recorded her innermost emotions: "It is needless for me to deny that during this time I heard and saw much entirely unfit for the eyes and ears of a woman, yet when tempted to resume my sex, I was invariably met with the thought—what then?" The money she earned covered her children's education and support as well as her own frugal living expenses. No job she might get as a woman would equal the thousand dollars she'd been able to save doing a man's work. And being able to go wherever she pleased without being saddled by cumbersome female clothes made her present lifestyle most appealing.

A few months into her railroad job, the conductor, who was also her boss, became overly friendly, asking for details of her life, inviting her to evening entertainments and dinners she found hard to refuse without seeming ungrateful. One evening in Chicago, in a private dining room, her boss excused himself to go and meet a friend he'd asked to join them. Elsa also left the room momentarily to hunt down a discarded newspaper with which to occupy herself until their return. Spying one through an open door of an empty room, she went to pick it up and heard a man say, "I tell you I haven't a doubt as to his being a woman—I'll bet my life on it!" Dismayed, she recognized her conductor's voice.

"Well, suppose he is," a second male voice responded, "what are you going to do about it?" Elsa stood, overhearing their exchange, her mood one of mixed rage and and humiliation. Their simple-minded plan was to ply her with enough liquor to disrobe her and have sex with her. And she discovered this friend of her boss was a police officer!

She forced herself to sit through the meal, laughing at their dirty jokes and suggestive banter as she feigned growing intoxication. Walking ahead of them as they left the restaurant, she quickened her steps, turned a corner out of their sight, climbed a low wall, and fled back to their lodgings. There she packed some money and a few necessities, then slipped into an empty room as she heard them approach, still discussing her. Stealing quietly down the stairs, she raced the few blocks to the river and booked passage on a boat about to up-anchor and sail. By morning she was well beyond their reach.

She returned some days later to St. Louis in leisurely fashion by way of Niagara Falls and other points of interest she'd always wanted to see. Again wearing dresses, she spent long hours with her children, "mingling in their frolics, learning their childish secrets, sympathizing with their young sorrows, admiring their development, and in short doing all such things and enjoying them, as would any mother who for nearly five years had been separated from her fatherless children. I found them all I could wish and progressing rapidly under the truly maternal care of the kind sisters."

Grateful for her perfect health, grateful to have risen by her own efforts from the severest poverty to comparative wealth, Elsa rejoiced daily and "thanked Fate" for her good fortune.

Strolling through the town one evening, garbed again as a man, she found herself face to face with the man her vengeful heart had been praying to find one day. There in the flesh stood her nemesis, Jamieson, with a group of his friends. To a description of him as "a medium-sized swarthy individual . . . haggard and careworn in appearance," she added that his pallor and unhealthy appearance was undoubtedly "the result of reflecting upon the friend he had slaughtered."

Her fingers itched and tightened on the grip of the concealed revolver she always carried. Then, her heart racing, she thought of a more sensible plan. She would simply follow him until he was alone.

Jamieson and his friends went to a gambling hall. While they gambled at cards, Elsa sat close, her eyes fixed on his face, savoring the justice she meant to mete out to him before the night ended. The game finally broke up in the early morning hours with

Jamieson somewhat drunk, but the big winner of the evening. Each man eventually took a different direction home so that soon Jamieson was ambling along by himself. Elsa, unseen, followed as close as she dared. Within a few blocks she accosted him, her revolver aimed at his heart. Caught off-guard, he didn't know her. Instead of sensibly shooting him with dispatch, she gave in to the need to berate him, and remind him of their interwoven past history. When she finally shot, he was faster at pulling his trigger. His shot entered her thigh, while hers merely grazed his shoulder as he staggered away. Elsa had the presence of mind to creep into a near-by alley, where she fainted.

She woke to find herself in a comfortable but unfamiliar bed, with a strange man she presumed to be a doctor taking her pulse. A matronly lady by his side smiled down at her encouragingly. Elsa protested weakly when the doctor wanted to view her wound. She whispered a few secret words to the lady of the house, who banished him from the room so she could dress Elsa in clothes suitable to her sex before summoning him back.

Her thigh bone, fractured by the bullet, needed six months to heal. But she passed those months pleasantly enough in the company of the gentle woman who had befriended her. Her convalescence was spiced with frequents visits from her children. By the time she was able to walk again without limping, she wrote, "a considerable hole had been made in my finances. I began to look around for something to do."

Back in men's clothing and admittedly sick of life on the river, in 1855 Elsa decided to try her luck in California. St. Louis was one of the main jumping-off places for the beckoning West. Full of soon-to-be pioneers buying up supplies, forming up wagon trains and setting forth on their great adventure, the city literally churned with activity. Elsa wrote that she "steeled herself against all pleading by my maternal nature not to go," her rationale being that if she met with success she could then retire, stay in woman's dress, and enjoy the rest of her life with her children.

Elsa invested what was left of her savings in an outfit, joined a west-bound party and left St. Louis on the overland route. By the spring of 1855, so many wagons had passed that way that "the trail was a hundred feet wide." Their wagons kicked up so much dust that they literally could not see ten feet ahead. The dry sections of the trail were dreaded, Elsa recorded, for the alkaline dust blistered and blotched women's tender skins. The alkaline water in rivers and streams weakened and killed trail animals by the thousands. Elsa, on someone's good advice, had brought an ample supply of glycerine to counteract the effects of alkali, which she secretly rubbed into her skin before rejoining the men each night to bed down.

They had begun the trek in the spring of 1855; she wrote that their party "was composed of sixty men, one six-mule team, fifty oxen, ten cows, fifteen saddle horses and mules. There were among us a doctor, a carpenter, blacksmith, and the balance were miners and armourers, exclusive of three passengers accompanied by their negro servants." The only female in the party, Elsa somehow succeeded in passing as a man.

If her story seems the product of an overactive imagination, reading the detailed journal entries she made on the way makes it credible. She wrote well, and kept to the facts. After a fairly easy and uneventful overland trip, their wagon train reached the Sacramento Valley in October, a matter of five month's travel. Elsa noted in her journal the exhorbitant cost of all the provisions she had to buy to go to the mines, not really mines at all but "johnny jump up" settlements that sprang up overnight like mushrooms by icy mountain streams where gold waited to be pried from its bedrocks.

"Flour," she complained, "is fifty cents a pound, Beef, twenty-five, Bacon, fifty cents, Pickles twenty-five cents each and everything in proportion. Board, the poorest and cheapest, is three dollars a day." It didn't take her long to discover she hadn't the physical strength to endure the hard toil of panning or digging for gold up to her hips in freezing water.

Elsa returned to Sacramento to look for a job. She found one in a saloon at a surprisingly generous salary of one hundred dollars a month. Ever thrifty, in six months she had saved enough to pay five hundred dollars to the owner, with another five hundred owed, for a partnership in what was demonstrably a good money-making occupation.

Ever alert to a better proposition, eight months later she sold her half interest and went into the pack mule business. Instantly successful at this new enterprise, she sold it in turn when offered the princely sum of twenty-five hundred dollars. A rare woman with a real head for business and its opportunities, she next purchased her own mule train and "packed goods and provisions" to the mines, doing well in this undertaking also. By then, longing to see her children, she left her business in the hands of a trusted employee and made the trip back to St. Louis by way of the Isthmus of Panama and New Orleans, whether as a man or a woman, her autobiography doesn't say.

Restless again after being at home only a few months, she decided to return to California. "Not wanting to go empty-handed," she bought some cattle and began the long trek west almost two years to the day from her original trip. This time she made up her own party, taking fifteen men, twenty mules and horses, and the cattle. But disaster befell them en route; one hundred and ten head of cattle died from drinking alkaline waters and their party was suddenly set upon by a small band of Blackfeet Indians.

During the ensuing fracas, one of her men was killed and Elsa was wounded in the arm. Her journal notation told triumphantly that she had shot and killed one of the Indians and severely wounded another by stabbing him, an act which finally sent the marauders packing.

Her party arrived in Shasta Valley without further incident.

There she purchased a small ranch on which to leave her cattle until they could be sold. She then traveled to Sacramento to meet with the man she had left in charge of her pack mule business. Finding it in order and still successful, she resumed the running of it. But as usual, she soon tired of the routine. Deciding she had money enough, she sold out again and was able to send thirty thousand dollars to her savings account in a St. Louis bank.

Unable to bear inactivity, adventurous Elsa joined a unit of the American Fur Trading Company and spent most of that next summer trading in furs with the Indians on the North and South Platte Rivers. By now addicted, both to her wanderlust and her money-making ventures, she moved on to Colorado, arriving just ahead of the gold strike of 1858. "Pike's Peak or bust" became the slogan of the miners who rushed into the state and swelled its population to 100,000 by the height of the strike. "Finding nothing better to do," Elsa reported, "I opened a Bakery and Saloon forty-two miles from Denver. I was making money rapidly," she continued, "when in the Fall I was taken sick with the mountain fever, and was most unwillingly obliged to give up my business and go back to Denver."

However, constitutionally strong, she soon recovered her health. Again looking for "something to do," she came across a bar for rent by the name of "Mountain Boy's Saloon." She took it on and ran it during the next winter. She also worked several claims which proved worthless. She acquired some others a hundred miles from Denver. In the spring she hired six men to go and work them, still hoping for gold. She spent the summer on them, plus another claim she had staked at the mouth of the Platte. When she found she cleared only two hundred dollars over expenses, she gave up hunting for gold.

Returning to Denver, she bought her old saloon and managed it through the winter. Elsa's ongoing journal records that throughout her time in Colorado she was accepted just as if she were a man, and everyone addressed her as "Mountain Charley."

In the spring of 1860 when she was twenty-eight, she had the luck to fulfill her dearest wish. While jogging along on her mule on the way to visit a sick miner friend, to her amazement and delight who should she see approaching her on his mule from the opposite direction but Jamieson! We can assume her heart beat with savage joy knowing revenge was to be hers after all. He saw her in the same moment when they both drew their weapons. This time Elsa was a second quicker. Her first shot tumbled Jamieson to the ground while his whistled harmlessly past her head.

"I emptied my revolver upon him as he lay," she wrote, explaining she had intended to do the same with her other revolver but was prevented by the arrival on the scene of two hunters who stopped her. Creating a tree branch litter, they carted the injured man back to town.

Though the wounds she'd inflicted were severe, in time Jamieson healed and left Denver. Prior to departing, however, he gave his story to the local newspapers, revealing Elsa's masquerade, but exonerating her of all blame.

"The story soon got out and I found myself famous — so much so that [Horace] Greeley, in letters from Pike's Peak to the New York Tribune, makes some allusion to my story and personal appearance." Pleased by that, Elsa was also quietly gratified when word came back from New Orleans that, as soon as he arrived there, Jamieson had contracted yellow fever and died.

> I continued in my male attire, notwithstanding the knowledge of my sex, and kept my saloon during the winter of 1859-60. I had a barkeeper named H. L. Guerin, whom I married, and in the spring we sold out the saloon and went into the mountains where we opened a boarding house and commenced mining. We left in the fall with a view of returning to the States. We did so, and reached St. Joseph in safety where my husband now resides. My children are

at school in Georgia. My father still lives on his plantation near Baton Rouge, and has written me to come home and live with him, but I shall not as I wish to devote myself to selling this work.

This is all the ambitious, industrious and driven lady named Elsa Jane Forrest Guerin, alias "Mountain Charley," left us about the rest of her life.

COLORADO'S MOUNTAIN CHARLEY

The third woman who posed as a man and also called herself "Mountain Charley" often made no attempt to conceal her feminine gender. Her tale comes to us through articles by a Colorado newspaperman named George West who, using the initials G.W., wrote for the *Golden Transcript*. It was to him alone that she confided her history, making him swear to honor her confidences and keep them secret for at least twenty-five years.

"Mountain Charley," he wrote, came riding into the town of Golden on her hand-picked little mule in the summer of 1859. He described her as "merely an overgrown, pretty boy, but for a woman she was rather above the average size, fresh looking, and without the slightest indication of dissipation, but always with a watchful look in her eyes, especially when approaching a strange crowd. Her age was given to me as twenty-two, and she looked no older."

He tells how she never went out without a revolver or two in her belt as well as a long sheath knife in her boot leg, ready to defend herself against men who might think it an easy matter to "get away" with her. To their chagrin, she told him, they found her not "that kind of hairpin." It was a phrase she was fond of using to describe herself.

"From frequent meetings upon the road and long rides together both in the valleys and mountains," G.W. continued, "I had become interested in her strange conduct and on several occasions had attempted an interview, but totally without success until circumstances threw her under my protection."

On Christmas day, a crowd of young fellows got drunk celebrating the holiday. Learning Charley was in town, they took it into their heads to come after her as an added fillip to the evening. Both G.W. and Charley were stopping overnight at Golden's Johnson House. She had mentioned that she would be rising earlier than usual the next day to hunt down the mule she had turned out overnight, and then be leaving immediately for the mountains. But instead of turning in when G.W. did, Charley went into town. A tired G.W. was jolted awake by a barrage of pistol shots, followed by a woman's scream.

Recognizing Charley's voice, he jumped up and hurriedly threw on some clothes with the noise of a squabble as a backdrop. Next he heard a shot discharged in the street, sounding as though it had happened right in front of the lodge. Then he heard Charley's shrill voice.

"How do you like that, you d___d drunken cowards? You'd better get back across the bridge or you'll get another one!"

Before G.W. could get to the door, Charley threw it open and rushed into the downstairs store where he stood. Bareheaded and flushed of face, she held a pistol in each hand. She dropped into a chair. He wrote that "her eyes gleamed like a tiger at bay." Her motionless body simply masked her extreme agitation.

"What's the row, Charley?" he asked, moving to where she sat.

"Oh, three or four of those cowardly cusses thought they were going to get away with me, I reckon!" she replied with emotion. "I winged one of them though, the sneak! And maybe he won't want to try it again in a hurry."

The gang of drunken brawlers were still in front of the Johnson House, bragging to each other about who was going to assault Charley next. Able to hear their boasts, the woman's poise began to slip. Her face went white at their taunts and her hands, still gripping the two pistols, began to shake. Telling her to stay put, and that he would take care of the ruffians, G.W. relieved her of one pistol and went outside. As he closed the front door, Elsa slipped from her chair to the floor in a faint. While the others who had gotten up to see what the row was all about rubbed her wrists to revive her, G. W. managed to persuade the clutch of drunken youths to disperse.

He came back in to find her conscious, but weak. He and other men made a comfortable "shakedown" bed for her on the floor, and as soon as she was sound asleep they returned to their own beds. Rising early the next morning, G. W. found her already gone. But in her note of thanks she asked that he find her mule and meet her with it on the following Saturday at a deserted location known to them both. On Friday morning a boy rode in with a second communique from her. In it she asked that he ride out part way with her while she told him about herself, if he could spare the time.

In her words, "I must tell my story to someone, for it is burning my heart out. You have been my friend and must hear it, or it shall die with me." She also requested that he not let anyone know where he was going. G. W. promised and told everyone he would be away most of that next day.

Setting out well before sunrise with her saddled mule tied and trotting next to his, he tried to imagine what sort of secrets a young girl like Elsa would have to reveal. Had she suffered a star-crossed love? Perhaps run away from her parents and home? He couldn't imagine it being anything more serious than that.

He arrived at their rendezvous as the first shafts of sunlight highlighted the peak of nearby Table Mountain. He circled the projecting lime-ledge that gave shape to the southern extremity of the "hog-back" at a sharp gallop. There she stood, calmly leaning against the rock wall, waiting for him.

"Before I had time to check the headlong speed of my animals, she jumped out alongside the mule, threw her heavy poncho over its neck, seized the pommel and cantle of the saddle with either hand and, after running a few steps in this position threw herself lightly into the saddle from the ground." G. W. wrote that as he started to hand her the reins for her mule, Charley reached over and clasped his one hand in both of hers, exclaiming, "God bless you, my good friend! I knew you would not fail me."

With no need to slow their pace, they continued on at a gallop. By mid-morning they came upon a deserted claim cabin where they halted to let the mules rest and feed. G.W. had brought along the makings of a late breakfast. Removing them from his saddlebag and readying their meal, he couldn't help comparing the way Charley looked this morning with the "buxom, full-cheeked healthy girl" she had been when he met her. Today she was a "pale, hollow-eyed, cadaverous woman, full of anxiety" who kept glancing back over her shoulder with a "saddened, shuddering glance." He wondered why.

"Seated here, in this lonely cabin, miles from my habitation, Mountain Charley confided her story, after personally exacting my solemn promise that none of it be revealed to the public before the lapse of twenty-five years, unless I was certain that she had 'passed over the range' before the limit expired. It was a thrilling, saddening narrative of young and trusting love ... desertion and revenge."

She told him Charlotte was her given name and that even in her Iowa school days, her friends had always called her Charley. Her mother had died when she was eighteen, leaving her in the care of a harsh, overbearing stepfather whose main interest in her was keeping her a drudge. He drove away every young man who expressed interest in her. He had no intention of losing her unpaid housekeeping services. She recounted:

> I grew tired of this, and in an evil hour ran away with a
> dandified looking young man who was almost a total

stranger to the neighborhood. Like all girls of my age who are passably pretty they always told me I was pretty, and I believed it. I was ambitious to marry above my station. We were legally married in Des Moines when I was nineteen, over three years ago. He professed to love me, and O, my God! I loved him with all my heart, even after I found out that he was nothing but a gambler and a villain of the deepest cast. His "profession" as he called it, kept him much from me, but I clung to him like a true and loving wife. We remained in Des Moines for more than a year, and there my baby was laid in my arms — dead!

She sobbed recalling how she had wept and mourned for her poor dead child, and how she was "cruelly chided" by her "unfeeling husband" who struck her and left her destitute.

They told me he had gone away with another woman. One he had been seeing throughout our married life. All my great love for him turned to hate. . . .This feeling of hatred for my husband and the low-down wench for whom he had left me, buoyed me up to strive for a livelihood and the means to follow them to secure my revenge.

She found a job in St. Joseph that allowed her to save over six hundred dollars, the first money she had ever earned. For a lark she had put on male attire the preceding spring, and discovered she was able to get away with passing as a boy. Certain that her erstwhile husband and his doxy would head for Colorado and its gold, Charley bought her mule and joined a party of emigrants. She said she soon found the going aggravatingly slow, and got into the habit of riding alone ahead of her party.

"I saw you many times while we were crossing the plains," she told G.W., "and was one of the big crowd that arrived at Cherry

Creek with you when our journey was ended, but you did not know it." At several stops along the way she got word of her husband and his paramour. "I knew I would find them, and I did! It took me all summer . . . and until yesterday. I found them!" Nearly screaming this last remark, she jumped to her feet and ran madly into the open air.

To G.W.'s astonishment, she jumped astride her mule and galloped off at a fearful pace, bridle dangling loose from the horn of her saddle and lariat dragging on the ground, and disappeared back of a jutting mesa. He was slowly readying his mount to depart when she returned, this time at a calm hand-gallop, having recovered her composure. Leaning from her saddle she placed both her hands on his shoulders and gasped, "Oh! I wish I could cry!" then jumped to the ground.

As she fixed her bridle and lariat, he tried to say something soothing. Charley stopped him with a sudden, "Hush! You know it all now, as I told you you should. I am so glad you come [sic] out with me, for if you had not I should have been plumb crazy by this time. I don't want to take you any further away, for it will take you 'til midnight to get home as it is. You will hear from me bye and bye, if anybody does." They said their goodbyes and parted, he going west, she going east. And the years went by.

In finally publishing her story, G.W. wrote, "I have kept my promise to her of secrecy for twenty-five years, as that promise was given to her on one of the last days of December, in the year of our Lord 1859."

To his surprise, he did hear from her again after the story was published. In addition to a letter, she sent him a package containing her diary, saying she was giving it to him to allow him to complete that part of her story. He published it under the title "Mountain Charley: A Sequel." In her diary she recorded further incidents of her amazing life; in particular, her stint as a soldier during the Civil War. Again G.W.'s article, drawn from her diary, told how Charley went south to New Mexico in the spring of '62, and did some prospecting near Albuquerque, spending time in the mountains west of Maxwell's Ranch, at the headwaters of Ute Creek.

At Fort Union she signed on with a government train headed for "the states" as a "mule-whacker," its destination Leavenworth, Kansas. Soon after they were underway she was promoted to assistant wagon master in place of a man dismissed for drunkenness. G.W. notes, "Not even her most intimate acquaintants in the train suspected her sex." Arrived at Leavenworth, at the request of the quartermaster she stayed to oversee the loading of the train, then left for Iowa. When she arrived in Keokuk in September, the war had begun and she enlisted in the Iowa Cavalry under General Curtis, using the name of Charles Hatfield. Recruits were so badly needed that she was accepted without the usual physical examination. She served first as a clerk at headquarters, then as an orderly to Major Charlot, Curtis' adjutant general.

Throughout the campaign, the fighting at the front in Missouri in the fall of 1864, Charley rode "here and there over the field carrying orders and messages between different parts of the command." One evening, while the company was camped in the suburbs of Kansas City for the night, she overheard General Curtis wishing he could know the intentions of his enemy, General Price.

A plan in mind, Charley rigged herself out in an old dress and a regulation Missouri butternut sunbonnet borrowed from a local house servant, and rapped on Charlot's tentpole.

"Come in." Major Charlot was busy writing.

"Please sir," Charley said in a girlish tone, "my pau wants to know if you'uns wouldn't like to buy some eggs for your supper."

Barely looking up, Charlot responded, "Why no, my girl; you will have to see our mess cook about that."

"Be you the general?"

Considerably amused, Charlot said he wasn't, but the general entered the tent at that moment, so he introduced them. "General, here is a young lady enquiring for you." Curtis kindly asked what he could do for her.

"Oh, nothing much. Only I told my pau I was bound to get a good look at you'uns down here and now I'm ready to "lite out." Saying this, Charley pulled off her sunbonnet and standing rigid, saluted. For a moment, totally astonished, the officers could only laugh.

"Well, well, Hatfield," Curtis asked, "what does this mean?"

Charley explained this was a test to see if she could be recognized in her disguise, then asked permission to try to get behind their enemy's lines. Curtis said yes and instructed her just what to ask. A few evenings later, on a clear star-lit night, as the pickets of the opposing armies ranged on both shores of the Big Blue heckled each other, Charley slipped across.

Confederate General Joseph Orville Shelby's Field-Officer-of-the-Day, Major Arthur McCoy, followed by his orderly, was riding back through a stand of woods from visiting his outposts when he heard a suppressed sob. He turned in his saddle to see a female sobbing as she leaned against a tree trunk.

"What's the matter, my girl?" he asked. After more convincing weeping, she calmed enough to answer in broken sentences.

"Why, mister, I've been so scared all the afternoon that I'm e'n amost crazy. My man wanted me to go to Kansas City with some eggs. I hadn't got down to the branch here before them Yankees began to pile down the road." Some more frightened words, explaining how she'd hidden, then she wailed, "When I seen you'uns had druv them over the branch I was jest as 'fraid and didn't know what to do."

The officer sympathized, asked how far she was from home, and wanted to know if her people were Union or Confederate. "We all have to be Union while the Yanks are here," Charley answered with a little laugh, "but now you all are here I reckon we'll have to be rebs."

McCoy took her to General Shelby's headquarters where she would be furnished an escort to her home. Though that was what she'd hoped for, she pretended to be afraid to enter Shelby's camp. Directing his orderly to dismount, McCoy lifted Charley and her basket of eggs onto the horse's saddle and led her into their camp. Here she found some soldiers and their general hunkered down around a fire, roasting chunks of meat on sticks for their supper. Once she had repeated her tale, General Shelby pumped her for word of the Union forces in the area. Charley played her part well, except when he directed a question at a nearby officer, and Charley recognized the man from her days in Golden, Colorado. Trying to keep her face blank, she discovered three more familiar faces. She was greatly relieved that none of them saw through her disguise. As a distraction, she gave the men her basket of eggs, a welcome addition to their scant supper, and gratefully received. They talked casually of their intended maneuvers in front of Charley. General Shelby was just assigning an officer as her escort home when a messenger rode in with an urgent communique. Charley faded into the shadows and watched as the general first scribbled a note for the messenger, then dispersed his men on various assignments before riding off with his orderly, forgetting Charley.

She dashed out to retrieve a paper he had dropped and made for the river. She slipped in, then realized she wouldn't be able to swim in her cumbersome dress. She clenched the precious paper between her teeth, hitched her skirt up around her hips and laying on her back, floated noiselessly down river in the dark past the armed pickets. By using her feet, she made the other shore about a half mile downriver. Chilled to the bone, she was challenged by a Union lookout as she climbed from the icy water. He marched her to his commanding officer who, upon hearing her story, furnished her with a horse and escort to General Curtis' headquar-

ters, where she arrived at one in the morning. Major Charlot was
still up, and wakened the general. The paper she retrieved turned
out to be crucial, disclosing all of Shelby's orders for the day which
became the first battle of Westport.

Charley had another adventure while carrying orders from
General Curtis to one of the generals under his command.
Stopped on the way and held at gunpoint by two lost reb soldiers
hiding in a thicket, she convinced them she was one of them in a
stolen Union uniform. She promised to lead them safely to their
lines. Instead she turned them over as prisoners to a company of
Illinois Cavalry they encountered.

After a skirmish between the two sides, Shelby's men found
Charley on the ground by her dead horse, and took her by ambu-
lance to their Headquarters surgeon. She fainted from loss of
blood from a shot that entered her leg above one knee and a serious sabre-cut in one shoulder. The doctor treating her was surprised at her gender but kept her identity their secret and sent her
to Newtonia where he was able to remove the ball from her leg.
Soon after, the fighting ended and she and other wounded soldiers
were returned to Fort Leavenworth.

Recovered and reporting to her new post, Charley had a happy
surprise. Because of her courage and the success of the hazardous
spying sortie she made behind enemy lines into General Shelby's
camp, Curtis wrote to Iowa's governor, recommending her promo-
tion.

An elated Charley found herself granted a full commission.
Hereafter she would be addressed as First Lieutenant Charles
Hatfield, assigned to General Curtis' staff as an aide-de-camp,
again reporting to Major Charlot. Lieutenant Hatfield was further
edified at receiving "an shiny officer's sword and equipments complete," an order that included a complimentary new uniform suitable to her rank. The latter was a gift from the general and the
gentlemen of his staff as a testimony to her courage.

In a final letter to G.W., dated February 8, 1885, she wrote:

My old friend G.W.:
You may well realize my surprise when yesterday I was shown a copy of your paper by a friend. . . .This lady was much interested in your sketch of Mountain Charley, as she said her husband well remembered her when he was a resident of Golden twenty-five years ago. Her surprise and interest was nothing, you may imagine, to what it would have been had she known that the staid matron to whom she was showing the paper was the veritable heroine of that tale of the wild early days in your beautiful valley and mountains. My surprise and interest were also great as was my gratification to find that you had kept your promise made to me so many years ago. And now, in part payment for the kindly manner in which you have treated my wild escapade, fully assured that my secret, so far as it relates to my present whereabouts will be safe with you, I resolved to at once write you of it. I have been married to one of God's noblemen now for more than eighteen years. . . . you will not look upon it as egotism when I tell you I am beloved by him and my four children as few women are loved. God knows I would not for the whole world that he should know of my former life, and that is the only secret I ever had from him. If you use my diary to complete my wild, strange masquerade as Mountain Charley, it may prove of interest to many of the old timers—"Barnacles" I see you call them now, and I shall be satisfied as long as they have no means of penetrating our secret. Goodby and God bless you.

This is where G.W. ended his friend's history. Both he and the lady in question refer to those times as "wild," but wildness isn't apparent in his account to the reader. He termed her story "A thrilling, saddening narrative of young and trusting love, desertion and revenge." We can't help but wonder whether he deliberately omitted the most salient facts.

Having finally located her husband and his paramour, what did she do about them? She was certainly highly emotional when she met him at the "hog-back" rendezvous, declaring that at last she had found the husband who betrayed her trust. And despite her extreme excitement, he inferred a sense of triumph in what she said to him. Had she just come from their killing ground?

Undoubtedly she told G.W. the whole story, but we shall never know the truth. For he withheld the key information from his account, no doubt to continue protecting the lady of whom he had grown so fond—his grateful friend, the third Mountain Charley.

MacDonald, Craig. *Cockeyed Charley Parkhurst: The West's Most Unusual Whip.* Palmer Lake, Colo: Filter Press, 1973.

Guerin, Elsa Jane. *Mountain Charley or The Adventures of Mrs. E. J. Guerin Who Was Thirteen Years in Male Attire*: Dubuque, Iowa: 1861. Tulsa: University of Oklahoma Press, 1968 and 1985.

Curtis, Mabel R. *The Coachman Was A Lady.* Watsonville, Calif.: Pajaro Valley Historical Society, 1959.

Stephens, Autumn. *Wild Women.* Berkeley, Calif. Conari Press, 1992.

Brown, Dee. *The Gentle Tamers*, London: Barrie & Enkins, 1958.

Levy, JoAnn. *They Saw The Elephant.* Hamden, Conn.: Archon Books, Shoestring Press, 1990.

Reiter, Joan Swallow. *The Old West*, Volume 23: "The Women." Alexandria, Va.: Time/Life Books, 1978.

Seagraves, Anne. *Women of the Sierra.* Hayden, Idaho: Wesanne Publications, 1990.

West, George. "Mountain Charley, A Colorado Story of Love, Lunacy and
Revenge," *Golden Transcript.* Golden, Colo.: January 14, 1885, Vol. XIX, No.8.
Following letter: February 4, 1885. No. 11.
Sequel: February 25, 1885. No. 14.
Continuation: March 4, 1885. No. 15.
Conclusion: March 11, 1885. No. 16.

Margo, Elizabeth. *Taming the Forty-Niner.* New York City: Rhinehart & Co.,
1955.

Steamboats on the Mississippi. New York City: American Heritage Publishing Co.,
Inc. NYC: 1962

Shirley, Glenn. Law West Of Fort Smith. New York City: Henry Holt & Co.,
1957.

Wellman, Paul I. *Glory, God & Gold.* Garden City, N.Y.: Doubleday & Company,
1954.

CHAPTER 6

Nellie Cashman: Miners' Angel

The tough men who prospected the newly opened gold fields of the Cassiar District in upper British Columbia gave no quarter and gave in to no man. They froze by day in the precarious and difficult search for gold. They spent their evenings and sometimes their nights in the local saloons, getting warm, getting drunk, getting overheated, overexcited and going broke over life-or-death card games and wagers.

One particular night, one of the men saw a figure in skirts push through the swinging doors. Usually there were at least three "parlor girls" hanging about the tables or sitting on laps, mostly to earn small change. Females who made it this far north were generally homely and no longer young; even so, the men appreciated them.

But the woman entering was both young and beautiful. The man at the bar whistled, a secret signal. At the sound, every man in the dingy room turned; the card players put down their cards and stood, and all of them snatched off their ever present hats as she passed by.

The word was whispered for the newcomers, "Get yer hat off, man. That's Miss Nellie, Nellie Cashman." Those slow to perform were dragged to their feet, and had their hats slapped off. Their eyes followed her dainty figure as she paused at the center of the bar and turned to face them. Only an inch or two over five feet, twenty-year-old Nellie was a dream, slender and delicately featured, with copper-colored hair and dark eyes.

"Why, thank you kindly, boys. Good evening to you all," she said in her Irish brogue, her pretty brown eyes sparkling in secret delight. Her glance traveled the room. "I'm after tryin' to locate the Swede. I hear he's broke his back. Any of you know where he's been put?"

"Sure, Nellie," several men answered together, still standing and hiding their grubby hands behind their hats.

"He's been settled in at Purvey's boarding house. He's in terrible pain," a large bear of a man said. "But doctor's down in Victoria, and they sure as h___, 'scuse me, Miss Nellie. I mean they sure as heck don't know what to do fer him."

"That's all right, fellas. I know what to do. Thanks again. You all be good now. Not too much drinkin'! Good night to you." They parted as she went back to the swinging doors and exited.

Only then did the clamor and normal business of the room resume. One of the newcomers nudged the big bear of a man as they resumed their places at the monte table.

"What was that all about? Is the Swede her boyfriend?"

"Hell, no. Miss Nellie doesn't take boyfriends, though some has tried. Like as not, she's going to see if the Swede needs money. Then she'll probably fix a brace to his broken back, make him some chicken soup and nurse him till he gets back on his feet. It's almost worth being sick."

"But why this standin' up, and doffin' yer hats? It's not like she's a royalty or somethin'."

"Better not show your ignorance. There ain't a man jack here she ain't been good to, some time or other. She goes wherever there's gold or silver to be dug. Miners call her special names like 'Miners' Angel,' 'Saint of the Sourdoughs,' and 'The Frontier Angel'. Miss Nellie's got a heart as big as a mountain. She'll stake a man who's lost his gear, or feed him when he's hungry. That's why every man pays his respects, even if she ain't done nothin' fer him personally. It's fer what she does fer everybody else."

It was true. During the fifty years Nellie was to travel from Alaska to Mexico in search of pay dirt, she became one of the best known and most revered women of her time. She won the undying devotion of those men whose lives she touched, and never neglected anyone in need.

Coupled with her strong sense of compassion was a large thirst for adventure. Nellie was lucky in that she was good at something she loved to do: namely, making money. She struck it rich several times in her life. In addition to maintaining her always successful mining camp businesses, Nellie earned at least half a dozen fortunes. But she gave them away to those less fortunate, and donated large sums to frontier hospitals and church missions.

She took under her wing and personally fed, housed, nursed back to health and grubstaked an indeterminate number of miners down on their luck. Her friends were fond of saying Nellie only made money to underwrite her true vocation, doing good.

"The best woman I ever knew," was the accolade paid her by one of her many ardent admirers.

In Nellie's trips far afield, she frequently risked her life in daring and strenuous exploits. For those who had never seen her, the image her deeds evoked was of a grim-faced, muscular Amazon-like figure. Her nephew, Michael Cunningham, a prominent banker of Bisbee, Arizona, bragged, "if she were in my office, and you walked in and met and talked with her, not knowing who she was, you would never think that she was Nellie Cashman."

Nellie broke with convention while still in her teens when she persuaded her sister Frances to run away from Ireland to America. Their boat docked in Boston in the mid 1860s, so that is where they settled. One account of Nellie's jobs had her working for a time in a local hotel as a bellhop and messenger, because most of the men were away fighting the Civil War.

As soon as the transcontinental railway was completed in 1869, Nellie's inherent wanderlust took over: she convinced her sister they should leave the East and entrain for the West. Newly arrived in San Francisco, sister Fannie met a man named Cunningham, lost her heart, married, and started her large family. Despite many proposals received by Nellie, she wasn't anywhere near ready to settle down.

Ever restive, she moved in 1872 to the burgeoning silver mining town of Virginia City, Nevada. There she earned a living while indulging her penchant for feeding hungry men by opening a short-order restaurant. She ran it at a profit for two years, then shut it down in 1874 to join the "rush" to newly opened gold fields in the Cassiar district of upper British Columbia. In a remote area Nellie described in a letter to Fannie as "practically unknown," the gold fields lay east of Alaska's Panhandle at the end of a tough grind of a journey.

The strike there proved a bonanza. Always ambitiously industrious, Nellie prospected claims with one hand while running a boardinghouse for miners with the other. In autumn she moved on to settle in Victoria, a respectable and civilized city in British Columbia just a boat ride from Seattle.

But when she heard that the men she had fed so well were now falling ill with scurvy, Nellie — barely twenty years old — felt it incumbent upon her to go save them. She bought fifteen hundred pounds of provisions, including plenty of lime juice to fight scurvy; she hired six men to carry the loads and started the trek north to the diggings in the midst of winter. The local army commander, presuming her ignorant of the truly hazardous weather, sent a party of soldiers after her, hoping to reach and rescue her in time.

Victoria's newspaper, *The Daily British Colonist*, reported the scene when the soldiers caught up with Nellie's party at the Stickeen River.

"Why hello there." Nellie broke off the lively air she'd been humming. She gave a delicious-smelling pot of stew hanging above a wood fire a final stir as the little group of six soldiers came toward them across the frozen river. Far from being in trouble, she and her men were comfortably camped right on the ice.

"How nice of you boys to drop in," she cooed, knowing full well why they had been sent after her. "A nice cup of hot tea to warm you?" They were very cold. The men gratefully drank the tea she poured them. "And are ye hungry, lads? There's plenty of rabbit stew." After they more than eagerly gulped down helpings of stew, the embarrassed soldiers sheepishly retreated to Victoria. The next dawn Nellie, traveling on snowshoes and pulling her own sled, continued on north with her six carriers through high drifts, foul weather and sub-zero temperatures.

"One night," she recalled with a smile, "the men put my tent up on the side of a steep hill where the snow was ten feet deep. The next morning one of my men came to where my tent had been to bring me coffee. It had snowed heavily in the night and, to his surprise, he couldn't find the tent. Finally they discovered me a quarter of a mile down the hill, where my tent, my bed and myself and all the rest of my belongings had been carried by a snowslide." The intrepid Nellie had already dug herself out by the time they came to rescue her.

When they finally arrived at the diggings by Dease Lake, Nellie found seventy-five of the original two hundred men half-dead from scurvy. She was able to slowly and successfully nurse them back to health.

The year 1880 found Nellie in the new boomtown of Tombstone, Arizona, where a huge silver lode had been discovered. This time, instead of prospecting, Nellie bought a hotel named The Russ House and became noted for serving the best meals in town. In her spare time she took up collections and put on benefits for every good cause, more often than not on behalf of men in need—like one unlucky prospector who broke both his legs when he fell down his mine shaft. Nellie pried the money for his hospital and doctor bills from the town's most disreputable citizens.

One oldtimer remembered, "Nellie Cashman always called for help from 'Black Jack,' the queen of Tombstone's red light district, and Nellie said her greatest help came from the back street which had no name on the map."

Nellie showed no fear. Indeed, she seemed especially fearless where her own principles of right and wrong were concerned. She held extremely strong views, and was just as strong in acting upon them. Once, five convicted murderers were sentenced to hang in the courtyard of Tombstone's jail. Incensed when she saw a carpenter busily constructing a grandstand in the yard next door so he could charge spectators to watch the hangings, Nellie rounded up some miner friends. Waiting until the middle of the night, with their help she dismantled the grandstand ahead of the event. Even convicted men, she felt, should be allowed to die in dignity and not be gaped and jeered at by insensitive townspeople. She went further and led a boycott against hiring that carpenter. Now unemployable, he soon got the message and moved to another town.

If she felt they were wrong, Nellie was just as unforgiving where her beloved miners were concerned. During a strike against the Grand Central Mining Company, someone alerted her to the fact that the strikers were plotting to kidnap and lynch a Mr. Gage, one of the mine's owners.

On the night the lynching was supposed to occur, Nellie drove her buggy to Gage's home and, without mentioning the plot, invited him out for a late evening drive. Any man there would have been thrilled at the chance to be alone with Nellie Cashman; Gage was no different. He was surprised, however, when she chose to travel right through Tombstone's back streets, then proceed beyond to the town of Benson, a railroad spur for the Santa Fe.

There, parked at the deserted station in her buggy, she set the reins and turned to him. "I expect you're wondering why I asked you out, Mr. Gage."

"Why. . . why, yes, Miss Nellie, I am," the important executive stuttered, imagining a tender scene developing in the next few minutes when he might take her in his arms and kiss her.

"I confess I did not tell you the truth before, because I was afraid you might do something foolish and be more at risk than you are now."

At risk? he asked himself, confused. There was nothing dangerous about a midnight drive with a beautiful young woman — or was there? "I don't understand," he said.

"Of course you don't. You see, Mr. Gage, don't ask me how I got to know — that's a secret — it's that some of your disloyal men hatched a plot to kidnap and, I fear, kill you."

"My God! Are you serious, Miss Nellie? You're not just joking with me?"

"No, Mr. Gage. It's no joke. I got to you just in time."

"Then, if it's true, you've saved my life, Miss Nellie. How can I ever thank you?"

"No thanks needed, Mr. Gage. We'll stay here until the wee hours when the train is due. You'll take it to Tucson where you will stay until I can send word that the culprits have been taken into custody and it is safe for you to return."

"Thank you. Thank you, Miss Nellie Cashman. You have my eternal devotion. Remember to ask me if you ever need anything."

"Don't worry, Mr. Gage. I will. Indeed I will."

An adventuress in the best sense of the word, Nellie's gallantry, big brown eyes, comely face and figure, along with her appealing Irish accent, certainly turned the heads and enchanted the hearts of most of the men she encountered along the way. And one thing is certain. Nellie's zest for life never flagged, and each new promise of adventure beckoned her more seductively than the one before.

Gage was one of many influential men over time to whom Nellie endeared herself with her beauty and generous heart. Another was a future U. S. senator she met as a prospector; a third was one of British Columbia's chief justices she'd known at Dease

Lake as a young lawyer; and a fourth was Edward Doheny, multi-millionaire-to-be, who had done time as a "pearl diver" (dishwasher) in one of Nellie's Alaska hotels. Nellie had only to ask, and they would have granted her every wish. But independent Nellie chose to get by on her own efforts, and never asked for anyone's help.

One day in Arizona a desperately ill Mexican collapsed before the entrance to her hotel. Nellie had him carried inside to begin ministering to him. However, he was in very bad shape. All he seemed to be able to say was, "Mulege. . . Go to Mulege." He died in her arms still muttering that word which she knew was the name of a town on California's Baja peninsula. When she turned out his pockets looking for some identification, she found, to her surprise, that they were filled with gold nuggets.

Soon after, despite three successful years as a hotelier, Nellie — again bitten by the prospecting bug — sold the hotel to go after gold. She left Tombstone headed for Guaymas with twenty male prospectors in late May of 1883, clad in the obligatory miner's costume: overalls and red flannel shirt, with a miner's pick slung over her shoulder.

At Guaymas they were ferried across the Sea of Cortez and landed at Mulege on the east coast of the Baja peninsula. From there they set off on foot across the barren terrain, unaware that they took less water than the trip required.

In mid-June, the *Phoenix Herald* reported that the failed Cashman party was making its way back to Arizona, but that Nellie and two others, having died of thirst, would not be with them. This was just hearsay.

What had happened was, when they stopped at intervals to test the gravel and sand for signs of gold, her party found themselves out of water; at the same time they made the unpleasant discovery that they had wandered off-course into unknown territory and were hopelessly lost.

Apparently in better physical shape than the men, Nellie volunteered and was allowed to set off alone across the hot sands to seek water. Ready to give up, and parched for water herself, Nellie stumbled upon an isolated Catholic mission. Its priests tried to prevail on her to rest. But explaining her fellow prospector's need, Nellie quickly organized a rescue party among the Mexicans who worked at the mission. Leading a borrowed burro train, each animal loaded with heavy goatskins full of lifesaving water, Nellie was able to retrace her steps and reach the stranded men in time to save them. As soon as they could travel, the party of would-be prospectors abandoned all thought of their expedition and returned to Tombstone.

But even this close call didn't dampen Nellie's love of the game of prospecting. In her fifty years of hunting for pay dirt of one kind or another, her search took her from camp to camp all over the West and from Mexico to Alaska. It is even reported that in the late 1880s she tried her luck for a time in South Africa's diamond fields, but quit because she preferred gold.

Always a prime subject for interviews when she appeared in any town, newspapermen usually tried to pry information out of Nellie about her private life. Was she in love? Did she currently have a lover? A fiance? A husband somewhere? They hounded her until even Nellie lost patience. To each of their questions Nellie shook her pretty head and answered with a resounding, "None of yer business!" When asked if, living among all-male mining camps as she did, she'd ever had cause to fear for her virtue, she countered, "Bless your soul, no! I never have had a word said to me out of the way. The 'boys' would sure see to it that anyone who ever offered to insult me could never be able to repeat the offense."

Nor could the reporters who dogged her steps ever learn whether Nellie had a love life. She always refused to answer such personal questions. The curious finally had to conclude that being loved, admired and praised by so many must satisfy her need for a lover.

In any case, her legend grew with each passing year. Reporting in October of 1895, *The Arizona Star* carried this item, "Yesterday Tucson was visited by one of the most extraordinary women in America, Nellie Cashman, whose name and face have been familiar in every important mining camp or district on the coast for more than twenty years. She rode into town from Casa Grande on horseback, a jaunt that would have nearly prostrated the average man with fatigue. She showed no sign of weariness, and went about town in that calm businesslike manner that belongs particularly to her." Nellie was in her forties at that time.

Soon lured by the 1898 strike in the Klondike, Nellie struggled over the murderous Chilkoot Pass with the rest of the male goldseekers, camping with them all winter on Canada's Lake Laberge, waiting for the ice to break on the Yukon River. When it did, she and her companions were ready with boats they'd built, and they shot the wild rapids down to Dawson City.

There, repeating past successes, she opened a short-order restaurant in a hotel with a grocery store in its basement. As always, Nellie undertook to help everyone crossing her path who was broke or hungry or needed a grubstake. They dubbed her basement store, "The Prospector's Haven of Rest." There she gave away cigars, and set a space aside so they could read and write letters home.

Dawson proved lucky for Nellie. One claim she staked brought her more than $100,000. When asked, "What did I do with it?" she laughed. "I spent every red cent of it buying other claims and prospecting the country. I went out with my dog team or on snowshoes all over that district looking for rich claims."

Nellie chose to make the North her permanent home, leaving only infrequently on stateside visits. Seven years after moving to Dawson, she went farther inland to Alaska's desolate interior. There she operated a grocery business in the settlement of Fairbanks during that town's first heyday. Three years later she moved on to the Koyukuk, making her home in a district literally on the rim of the Arctic Circle, five hundred miles from any town. She was probably the only white woman who ever dared venture into that vast wilderness all by herself.

In July of 1908, a Fairbanks newspaperman meant flattery when he described Nellie as "hard as flint, with endurance on the trail equal to that of any man, but with an inexhaustible fund of good humor and a cheery word and a helping hand for anyone in need. She frankly states her age to be sixty, but she doesn't look it by any means." A couple of summers after that interview in 1910, Nellie decided to make a trip down the Koyukuk River. Lacking either boat or canoe, she talked a fellow miner into building a raft and making the trip with her. They finished the raft and started down the swift-running river. While navigating its rapids they hit a rock. The raft broke up and was destroyed.

"We almost went under that time," she said of the incident, "but managed to make it to shore. It just goes to show that you can never tell in this business when you will be called to cash in your chips."

Undaunted, Nellie continued to mine her claim on Nolan Creek year after year. Over time Nellie acquired and operated eleven mines in the area. None, however, proved as fruitful as her Dawson claim. In 1922, at seventy-one, Nellie mushed a dog team on a trek across Alaska's trackless frozen wastes for 750 miles, and did it alone. In 1923, discovering she lacked machines to probe deeper, she headed for New York and raised the needed capital. Always making news wherever she went, her age was variously reported as being in her sixties, seventies, even her early eighties.

That was her last trip. In 1924 she fell ill with double pneumonia. She managed to survive the trek from her cabin at Coldfoot to the hospital at Fairbanks where she stayed until recovered, and left in fine spirits. But the many years of physical hardship when she pushed her body to extremes had undermined her health.

"You're not a youngster any longer," her nephew had cautioned when she stopped over in Bisbee, "and that's a hard country up there."

"Pooh," countered Nellie. "Why, there's nothing to it these days. I'll take the boat to Seward and the train from there to Fairbanks. Then I can get an airplane to set me down within a hundred yards of my camp. Why, I'll hardly have to walk a step."

Instead of an airplane, Nellie took the little launch. Stricken with pnemonia a few days later, she was again hospitalized in Fairbanks. Certain she was well enough, she started off once more via steamer. It sailed on her birthday, a fact known because the ship's cook recorded that he had baked her a cake with her name on it.

Within eighty miles of her camp she had a relapse and was brought into a Catholic mission. The nuns nursed her until she could be returned to the Fairbanks hospital. A month later, she was so much better that they allowed her to move into a local hotel to complete her convalescence.

This pleased her because there were "more people to talk to." Within a couple of weeks Nellie was on her way again, traveling south by train, headed for the healing warmth of Bisbee.

"Don't worry," she told friends, "I'll be back when the water starts to run, ready for some more mining. See you in the Spring."

But she got only as far as Victoria and the hospital she had helped to finance. "Just until I catch my breath," she assured the nurses. Yet, lying in her bed she confessed to being tired. "Sometimes I can hardly wait until I can get together up there with all the fellers I used to know. Say, won't we do some mining, though? And yarns? Why, I bet there's never been yarns like the ones we'll spin when I get there."

It was only a matter of days before Nellie had her grand reunion. She died peacefully on January 4, 1925 at the recorded age of seventy-four. Two days later she was laid to rest next to the

Catholic Nuns Plot in Ross Bay Cemetery in Victoria, British Columbia. The restless spirit of the Miners' Angel had found a final resting place.

Ledbetter, Susan. *Nellie Cashman, Prospector & Trailblazer.* El Paso, Texas: University of Texas at El Paso, Western Press, 1993.

Reiter, Joan Swallow. *The Old West,* Volume 23: "The Women." Alexandria, Va.: Time/Life Books, 1978.

Seagraves, Anne. *High-Spirited Women of the West.* Hayden, Idaho: Wesanne Publishing, 1992.

Clum, John P. *Nellie Cashman.* Tombstone, Ariz.: Privately Printed,1931.

CHAPTER 7

Mystery Poet Ina Coolbrith

The shabbily dressed kid stopped before the doors of Oakland's two-story public library late one November evening. Although he appeared to be shivering from the cold, his trembling was caused by excitement. He knew about the library, that the street floor was given over to a reading room for magazines and newspapers. But the second floor. . . ah! the second floor was just for books! He need only climb those few steps and push open the swinging double doors and mount to the second floor to enter that dreamed-of magical world. He'd do it! Screwing up his courage, the kid darted inside.

Librarian Ina Coolbrith's desk faced the stairs. She glanced up to see the small figure approach along the windowless west wall whose shelves reached higher than he could see. She'd already snuffed out the kerosene table lamps, creating a shadow world out of the thirty-five-foot-square room. But the boy kept coming, oblivious of everything but the books, caressing their spines with his fingers as he passed, awe in his wide gray eyes. Ina's voice startled him.

"Sorry, young man, the library is closed."

Did she mean he was too late? After he'd braved his way in, too! His eyes glinted with sudden tears. She relented.

"Oh, all right. Come here, into the light." He came warily, expecting a rebuke as he twisted the worn cap in his small hands. Ina's desk lamp highlighted the face of an Irish street urchin badly in need of a good scrubbing and a trim for his unruly reddish-blond hair.

"You haven't been here before," she said. "What's your name?" The boy could only stare, speechless, at the loveliest creature he'd ever seen. Ina was tall and slender, with tendrils of light brown hair curling becomingly about her face. Pinned back, it bared her ears and her dangling earrings, and cascaded in waves below her shoulders onto the dark lace shawl worn over a lacy white high-necked blouse. Her eyes, as gray as his, were wide set and dreamy, her lips full and sensuous. She was unlike any other woman the boy had ever seen. How to speak to such a vision?

"I'm sure you didn't come at this hour to gawk. Did you hope to take out a book? Ah, but I fear you're too young for a library card. How old are you?" She paused between each sentence to let him reply, but he just kept swallowing. Take out a book? Was that allowed? He supposed they had to be read on the premises. Certain he would be denied, he gazed longingly at the full shelves before uttering a lie.

"I'm already ten." His birthday was still two months away, in January.

"Ten. . ." she echoed reflectively, aware of the yearning in his eyes. She recalled herself at ten, without schooling, trying to puzzle through the pages in her stepfather's books as their family's covered wagon jolted over the wide prairies en route to California. She supposed that was the beginning of her love of words and their sounds, and a sensitivity to the same love in others.

"Well, I might make a library card in your mother's name. . . What sort of books do you like?"

"Travel." He barely got out the word.

"We have many fine travel books. What country do you. . .?" But he was already gone, scurrying to the section he'd passed before and bringing back a thick tome. She checked its title, then regarded him with renewed curiosity. "*Pizarro in Peru*! You sure you can read this?" He nodded vigorously.

"All right. I'll make an exception this once if you promise to take the best possible care of any books I let you borrow, beginning with this one. Have your mother sign this card and return it with the book on or before this date," she pointed it out, "or you will be charged a penny for each day it's late. You understand?" Again the boy could only nod.

"Now I need your name to open a borrower's account." She poised her pen over the inkwell.

Shyly he said, "It's Johnny. . . no. . . I mean Jack. . . Jack London."

Ina smiled as he disappeared down the stairs lugging the big book. That encounter began many years of friendship between one of America's celebrated authors-to-be and California's poet laureate-to-be. Jack London once said of her, "I loved Ina Coolbrith above all womankind, and what I am and what I have done that is good I owe to her."

Ina cared deeply for her young readers. She set aside a corner of the library for them called The Children's Room. Because public education was a random thing then, libraries and librarians exerted a great influence on the communities they served. Oakland had one of the earliest free public libraries in California, and Ina was its first official librarian.

From 1874 to 1895, during her twenty years of service as its literary mentor, Ina Coolbrith would befriend and inspire many young talents like world-renowned dancer Isadora Duncan and Mary Austin, the writer who limned the Southwest with her lyrical prose. Jack London took the trouble to acknowledge the debt he felt he owed Ina in a loving letter of tribute written in December of 1906.

The old Oakland library days! Do you know you were the first one who ever complimented me on my choice of reading matter? Nobody at home bothered their heads over what I read. I was an eager, thirsty, hungry little kid and one day at the library I drew out a volume on Pizarro in Peru (I was ten years old). You . . . stamped it for me; and as you handed it to me you praised me for reading books of that nature. Proud! If you only knew how proud your words made me! For I thought a great deal of you. You were a goddess to me. I didn't know that you were a poet, or that you had ever done such a wonderful thing as write a line.

However, there was no praise — and Ina would garner much in her long life — that could heal the bitterness she harbored in her soul over the disruption of her career as a poet. For at age twenty-eight she had to get a full-time position in order to bring home a regular salary.

Ina was an exceptionally warm, open, gregarious woman, except in revealing anything of her past. That, she kept from friends all her life. Her random remarks let them surmise her childhood had been less than perfect but she would neither confirm nor deny such ideas. However they were all too evident in her poetry, which revealed her sense of sadness, frustration and unfulfilled dreams.

They did learn she'd lost an older sister at five to scarlet fever, that her father had died an untimely death at age twenty-five when she was an infant, and that William Pickett of St. Louis had married her mother when Ina was five years old. Pickett moved his new family to St. Louis where he worked as foreman of the printing office for the *Missouri Republican*, later called the *St. Louis Republican*. In their first year of marriage, Agnes gave birth to twin boys who were much loved and coddled by their doting older sisters.

With sad eyes Ina related the two tragedies that befell St.

Louis while it was their home, events that laid low many of their friends. The first was a fearful epidemic of dreaded cholera. As it swept the city it took the lives of over four thousand citizens in a matter of weeks. And while the fever still raged, *The White Cloud*, a fine sailing ship anchored at the city wharf, inexplicably caught fire and burst into flames. Though swiftly cut adrift, it did not float far enough away. Before its fire burned out, it had ignited and destroyed many other ships. Much of the waterfront section was also razed in what became an inferno; fifteen square city blocks went up in flames before the fire was under control. Fortunately, the Pickett family was spared harm from both cataclysmic incidents. But they left their mark on sensitive young Ina, and probably precipitated the family's departure.

In response to these disasters, or because this was the era of Manifest Destiny, Pickett was infected with gold fever. He sold all but their most precious possessions to buy the needed equipment for the long journey, getting his information — like so many others — from a popular pamphlet of the day written by a man who had never been west of New York City. The Picketts left for California in 1851 as part of a wagon train. They may have hoped that going West would leave behind not only the recent tragic episodes, but also their dark secret.

Ina loved to reminisce about having been the first white child to travel the just-opened Beckwourth Pass, riding with James Beckwourth himself. A well-known mulatto scout, Beckwourth had explored the new route through the Sierra Madre mountains, and financed its clearing with his own money. It leads from Reno, Nevada, to the town of Marysville in the Mother Lode country. The memory of that day as a little girl, perched in front of Beckwourth on his saddle to lead her parents' wagon train through the pass, still thrilled Ina in her old age.

Eventually his pass would carry the tracks of the Western Pacific Railroad. On today's maps, the nearby automobile road runs halfway through as Interstate Highway 80, goes on to finish as State Road 20.

Staying only briefly in Marysville, the Picketts detoured south to try San Francisco, but soon moved farther south to Los Angeles, then a village of two thousand souls referred to as a cowtown. Its population was half Mexican and half Indian, with but a sprinkling of Easterners. Due to its arid desert climate and position near the foothills, the town had few trees and hardly any gardens. General purpose water had to be hand carried from a *zanja* or ditch in the vicinity. Cooking and drinking water was dipped from the river at the exhorbitant charge of fifty cents a bucket.

The town's houses were all alike, with flat roofs, common walls, and tamped earth floors. Each had the same wood-barred windows and crude adjoining arcade to shade its interior from hot southern sun. But the Picketts had nothing but praise for the lively and welcoming small American colony; after enduring six grueling months on the trail with no creature comforts, the continued lack of many of them in the jump-up city of Los Angeles was a shortcoming they could easily forgive.

Pickett soon had his law practice underway. Agnes kept the home while her daughters attended the brand new two-room school, one side for girls and the other for boys. Ina studied there from ages fourteen to seventeen. It was her first and only brush with any sort of formal education.

From the first, the pretty Pickett girls were in demand for every party and dance. Ina also gained a certain celebrity at fifteen when a local newspaper published one of her poems. From then on she was so lost in poetic reverie while doing her chores that her amused stepfather would jolt her back to reality by teasing, "What is the matter with that girl?"

Her early poems were criticized as the "sentimental outpouring of a nineteenth century girl." But they grew remarkably more adult following an anonymous exchange of flirtatious verses with an unknown male admirer. Frequently their poems to each other ran simultaneously in both the Los Angeles and San Francisco papers.

When her sister Agnes Charlotte — eight years Ina's senior — became engaged at twenty-five, seventeen-year-old Ina decided she was also in love. The object of her affections was Robert B. Carsley, a handsome fellow in his late twenties who was a half-owner of a successful cast iron foundry. Following their marriage in 1857, Robert proved to be an insanely jealous and mentally unstable man who constantly accused Ina of adultery.

Fortunately, their doctor was a witness to his psychotic behavior the day Robert flew into such a towering rage that he threatened to kill both Ina and her mother. When he began wildly brandishing his pistol, the doctor drew his own weapon and shot Robert in the hand before he could fire. Besides the ugly three years Ina endured with him, the tragic death of their newborn baby and that terrifying incident wrote *finis* to their union. They were divorced with everyone's approval. Ina never referred to this segment of her life, nor to the years preceding it. No one but her mother knew that she had borne a child, or its sex. Covering up her past had become second nature to Ina, a way of life.

When twenty-year-old Ina and her parents moved to San Francisco to start a new life, her happily wed sister remained in Los Angeles. It was then that Ina took her mother's maiden name, thereafter being known as Ina Donna Coolbrith. Yet her poem of 1862 entitled "The Mother's Grief" reveals so clearly the emotions she was attempting to conceal:

> *So many woes my Heart hath known,*
> *So true a child, am I of suffering,*
> *That, judging time to be by time that's flown,*
> *I dare not dream what coming years may bring,*
> *Through all my life have pain and passion wove*

Their subtle network: by the grave of Love
I've knelt, and shed no tear! My soul hath borne,
Unmoved, the shafts of enmity and scorn
From an unpitying world! . . .
                    Ah, my God!
I'm weary, weary, would that I might sleep!

It wasn't only personal sorrows that kept Ina silent. In the Bay area's sophisticated environment—San Francisco was known as the city of poets—she was embarrassed to admit to having grown up in Los Angeles, a city right-minded San Franciscans looked down upon as provincial and lacking in culture. She feared if her origins were known it would be a black mark against her. Using the pen name of "Meg Merrilies" she saw some of her first poems in print in the *Golden Era* and *The Californian*, two of San Francisco's elite literary publications. Thereafter she simply signed her work "Ina."

It was also at this time that her stepfather William Pickett drifted out of their lives, leaving Ina with the full responsibility of her mother's as well as her own support. She found work as a teacher of English at private schools to augment the meager income she was able to realize from the sale of her poems. As a young woman in her early twenties, even though she dearly loved her mother, it was only natural for Ina to feel trapped and resentful. "Longing," which appeared in the first issue of *Overland Monthly*, was a forthright declaration of her secret rage at having to earn a living instead of being free to write and live as she wished.

O foolish wisdom sought in books!
O aimless fret of household tasks
O chains that bind the hand and mind —
A fuller life my spirit asks!

In the fall of 1864 an introduction to Bret Harte, the already famous publisher of the *Overland Monthly*, not only gave her life new meaning but began a friendship and collaboration that placed Ina at the center of the city's literary lights. Writers like Ambrose Bierce, Mark Twain, Bret Harte, Edwin Markham, and "Joaquin" Miller were her friends. (Vastly uncomfortable with his baptismal name of Cincinnatus Hiner Miller, he blessed Ina for having chosen his more poetic *nom de plume*.)

Whenever they were in town, these noted men were part of Ina's circle. If they were away, its hard core trio — dubbed "The Golden Gate Trinity" by some unknown and perhaps envious wag — remained a constant: Harte, poet Charles Stoddard, and Ina. The three friends were close as brothers and sister, and although they traded confidences, Ina always held back intimations of her past.

The three loved playing word games, and often made up limericks using exotic local place names. "There was a young girl from Yreka. . ." or "A solid young man from Vallejo. . ." One day when Ina found Harte out of sorts she sidled up to his desk, tipped her head and spouted extemporaneously:

There was a young writer named Francis
Who concocted such lurid romances
That his publishers said,
You will strike this firm dead
If you don't put a curb on your fancies.

Harte swiveled half around in his chair, his lips turned up in a half smile. Ina was always able to pull him out of the doldrums, not just because of her beauty, but because of her wit and intelligence. Without even looking at her, he countered:

There is a poetic divinity —
Number One of the "Overland Trinity" —

Who uses the Muses
Pretty much as she chooses —
This dark-eyed, young Sapphic divinity.

Ina's modest home on Russian Hill became their literary meeting place. Stoddard left an endearing word picture of her parlor as:

A cosy interior. . . . always a kind of twilight in that place,
. . . a faint odor of fresh violets, . . . an atmosphere of peace.
Here Bret Harte would discuss with his hostess his projected table of contents of the forthcoming *Overland Monthly*; here the genial "John Paul" (Charles H. Webb) talked over the prospects of his *Californian*, and here Joaquin Miller . . . met the gracious lady who was the pearl of her tribe.

Under Bret Harte's guidance, the *Overland Monthly* did wonderfully well from 1868 to 1871, publishing for the first time submissions from both Mark Twain and Ambrose Bierce; one of these was Twain's "The Luck of Roaring Camp," the story that made his literary reputation.

It was a glorious time full of promise for Ina, the woman Joaquin Miller called "A daughter of the gods! Divinely tall, And most divinely fair." Stoddard also wrote of Ina, "Her muse was speedily and cordially recognized in the best quarters. . . ."

However, several of her friends, the great naturalist John Muir in particular, grew anxious over Ina's unmarried state. Muir's one attempt at matchmaking caused Ina to "rhyme him," something she did to anyone who vexed her. Her rhyme about him began:

Up from her catalogues she sprung
And this the song she wildly sung:
Oh Johnny Muir! Oh Johnny Muir!

How could you leave your mountains pure,
Your meadow-breadths, and forest free,
A wily matchmaker to be?

and finished:

But O of this I pray there be
No more, John, an' thou lovest me!
Or if you smile, or if you frown
I DO NOT WANT YOUR MR. BROWN.

Under Harte's tutelage, these were Ina's three happiest and most productive years. During his tenure from 1868 to 1871 almost every issue of the *Overland Monthly* carried a poem by Ina. Sometime during these three years, Ina learned that her stepfather William Pickett had died. Now Ina was truly her mother's sole support.

By 1871, Charlie Stoddard was living in Tahiti, writing his *Idylls*. Harte, paying Ina a farewell call, left with his wife and children for Boston where he would write for *The Atlantic Monthly*, the country's leading journal. Although they would stay in touch for the remainder of his life, his leaving made a void in Ina's life that no one ever filled.

That same year she received a signal honor. She was asked to compose an ode for the young University of California's commencement exercises. The press faithfully carried the long ode *in toto*.

Ina found a new interest in 1872 with the founding of San Francisco's Bohemian Club, lauded as "an event of great importance in San Francisco's circle of arts and letters." Ina and her friend Mary Tingley sat for hours to hand sew the curtains for the large hall the club rented. Her close association with this "no females allowed" group led to her being admitted as its first honorary member. Her poem extolling the club's virtues ended:

The sparkling jest, the laughing lip,
The royal, genial fellowship —
Of these thy wealth, Bohemia.

With Harte gone, the *Overland Monthly* quickly lost its luster. To Ina's dismay, by 1875 the publisher decided to discontinue the magazine. Only one of her poems saw print in 1876, and that was in a newspaper.

Ina's sister Agnes Charlotte, herself not well, lost both her husband and her littlest son within a matter of days. Ina insisted she bring her other boy and girl for a visit. Depleted by grief, Agnes Charlotte's health declined even further and soon she too died. Ina made the grim trip to Los Angeles with the casket to let her sister lie beside her beloved husband. She returned, the only relative her orphaned niece and nephew had, and took on their raising with decent grace. As if that were not load enough, she learned Joaquin Miller's half-breed illegitimate child Callie was being turned out of her home and Miller, gallivanting about Europe, was unable to be reached. While Ina disapproved of the wayward poet's lack of concern for his child, her conscience wouldn't allow her to let the child be placed in an orphanage. Sending for her, Ina added Callie to her burgeoning family.

Now, with her elderly mother and three children to support, Ina looked for a job. The monies from teaching and the random sale of poems could not begin to cover their monthly expenses. Relinquishing all hopes and dreams of Europe and broader horizons, she took the the post of librarian at Oakland's new public library at a salary, an offer which came in the nick of time. She and her brood moved to Oakland in 1874.

Two years later, shortly after the demise of the *Overland Monthly*, Ina's mother died of a fatal illness in late December of 1876. Undone by so many losses in quick succession, Ina expressed her grief and loneliness in a verse that ended:

For I would leave the fairest clime
God ever decked for mortal eyes,
Shut from the lapse of earthly time,
Shut from the lapse of earthly skies;
Nor miss the dark, nor miss the day,
Nor flowering of the pleasant land —
Could I but hear her voice, and lay
My hand once more in her dear hand!

In later years an overenthusiastic fan would gush, "Oh, Miss Coolbrith, our whole family just lives on your poems!" Ina was heard to retort acidly, "How nice. That is more than I was ever able to do."

She held her post at the Oakland Library for twenty years, until her own ill health forced her resignation in 1894. Soon afterwards, a fever took her devoted Callie, dead at thirty-two after some years of marriage. By this time, however, Ina's other charges were grown and nearly on their own, but still living with her.

During her tenure at the library, several famous Westerners credited Ina with having given them special help and inspiration. World-renowned dancer Isadora Duncan, an Oakland native, wrote of Ina: "There was a public library in Oakland where we lived, but no matter how many miles we were from it, I ran or danced or skipped there and back. The librarian was a very wonderful and beautiful woman . . . Ina Coolbrith. She encouraged my reading. . . . She had very beautiful eyes that glowed with burning fire and passion." Isadora added that she always suspected her father, who often went with her to the library, of being secretly in love with Ina.

In the earlier years, beauteous Ina collected a number of would-be swains, all pressing for her hand, but refused every proposal. Only in old age would she express regret that she had not accepted one of them. "It would have been so nice," she told a friend, "to have a caring companion in my last years."

Along with her sweetness, Ina also had an acerbic side. A certain Henry Kirk, recalling his first visit to the library as a student, wrote of her: "She was a marvelously handsome woman. None of her pictures do her justice. . . . The first book I took out was a life of Mary Stuart. Ina opened it to the frontispiece, studied the portrait, and sniffed, "Humph! She was not so beautiful!"

Ina's outspokenness sometimes worked to her detriment. The most unfortunate example was the day when, as a career librarian, she was moved to write a high-handed letter to the library's brand new Board of Directors in which she detailed in vivid terms what she felt was wrong with the library—what it lacked and what it needed. To her shock, her candor brought her immediate dismissal. Her nephew Henry, who had worked as her assistant for some years, was appointed head librarian in her place. Ina found this a crushing insult.

Soon after being let go, she fell ill and was confined to her home. It was a few years before she was well enough to resume the duties of a librarian, this time for the San Franciscan Mercantile Library, a job she held for two years. Offered the librarian's post at her beloved Bohemian Club in 1899, she was proud to fulfill those duties until 1906. In her view, its distinguished writers, artists, and business tycoons were such interesting and stimulating company that she relished every day on the job.

In respect to her long career dispensing books, she said, "I am prouder of being the first public librarian in California than I am of being the first woman author, for I think the public libraries have been a greater help to the people."

While she continued to write poetry most of her life, Ina Coolbrith was not prolific. Her only two books were *A Perfect Day*, published in 1881 by subscription, and *Songs From the Golden Gate*, printed in 1895 by Houghton-Mifflin & Company, and republished several times. She always tried to buy the entire print run herself to augment her small income and realize a profit on the books' sales.

In her final decades Ina was revered as the focus of a San Francisco literary salon, as well as a symbol of an earlier golden time. By then Ina was always seen with a white mantilla on her silver hair. Having let herself grow quite stout, she suffered from intermittent bouts of rheumatism that often kept her housebound and even bedridden.

Following the devastating earthquake of April 1906, a worse tragedy befell Ina. Her home on Russian Hill—built by generous friends to her specifications—caught fire and burned to the ground. Her possessions and, most dear to her, all her books and papers went up in its smoke. Only because of the caring of the publisher of the *Overland Monthly*—who preserved the poems she had sent him—are Ina's original manuscripts still available to researchers in the Bankcroft Library archives at the University of California at Berkeley. Faced with the knowledge that the precious research she had so painstakingly gathered over many years was irretrievable, Ina lost heart. Gone were her notes, intended for the day when she would begin her history of frontier letters. Gone was the material for a personal project, her long-planned memoirs. Sadly she abandoned plans to write any of this.

When Ina judged her niece and nephew were of an age to understand and digest the information, she revealed her dark secret—confiding to them the tale of her birth and early youth—facts she had promised her mother never to disclose. She then exacted the same promise from them, a promise they honored until after her death. Today's world might not credit the seriousness of such a commitment, but in her day it damaged a person's reputation if an association with the controversial Mormon church was known.

She told them of their grandmother, whose maiden name was Agnes Coolbrith, and of her wedding in her mid-twenties to nineteen-year-old, six-foot-four Don Carlos Smith, the fourth and youngest brother of Joseph Smith, the founder of the Mormon faith. Although he died before she was old enough to know him, in speaking of him her eyes filled with tears.

"He was only a boy of twenty-five," she sighed. "His brother Joseph called him a 'lovely, a good-natured, a kind-hearted and . . . upright child.' Joseph loved him dearly," Ina added, "and said of him at his grave,'where his soul goes let mine go also.'"

She said both she and her sister—their mother—had been born in Nauvoo, herself on March 10, 1841. Her given name was Josephine Donna Smith but as a toddler they began calling her Ina, and the nickname stuck. She told them of the ugly years when masked citizens abused and killed Mormons—and boldly razed their properties as a result of Illinois Governor Hale Boggs' heinous order to "exterminate" all Mormons, which forced them from the state.

She described in all its horror the night their grandmother was turned out of her house as it was set afire and, eluding the manic mob, bravely carried her children through the dark to a safe house three miles away. She explained how the constant riots against their people ended in the second arrest and imprisonment of Joseph Smith and his brother Hyrum, leading to their lynching and cruel murder a few days later. And how their brother Samuel arrived too late to prevent their deaths and fell from his horse and died of shock and exhaustion outside the prison walls. So it was that the Mormons sustained their cruellest loss and all four Smith brothers, including her father, perished in the same year. Heartbroken, the Mormons prepared to move on.

Their grandmother, now totally dependent on the kindness of friends and family, sold Don Carlos' press and printing business for a pittance of seventy dollars. She had not finished grieving for him when her five-year-old, Sophronia, suddenly died of scarlet fever. Ina was but two and a half.

Ina let them see the grieving letter she had saved, the one their grandmother had written to her cousin George, sent on ahead to seek possible locations for settlement. She read aloud, "If there was a Carlos or Joseph or Hyrum, then how quickly I would be there." Devoted to the church and all its brethren, she wrote; "But, alas, there is an aching void I seem never able to fill." Ina explained that their grandmother and her sister-in-law Emma had chosen to stay behind in Nauvoo with Mother Smith. "Besides," her letter ended, "my beloved dead now rest under the sod of Emma's garden."

The forced exodus began under Brigham Young's leadership. All spring and summer, Ina recounted, they watched the wagonloads of their people be ferried across the river on flatboats, there to prepare for the long overland trek. They set off in 1846 in search of a new homeland. Brigham Young had promised them he would lead them so far west that they would never be persecuted again. Following many hard months of travel, they found their fertile Utah valley in the spring of 1847.

Back in Illinois, grandmother Agnes met and married William Pickett. On September 7 of the same year, the small band of Mormons still in Nauvoo were ordered to quit the city within sixty days. It didn't take much persuasion for Pickett to convince his new bride to move to St. Louis for a life in a "civilized society."

"They traveled the Mississippi to St. Louis by riverboat," Ina told her spellbound niece and nephew, "and as they stood at its bow holding hands and looking south toward their new home, Mr. Pickett exacted a promise from my mother never to tell anyone of her Mormon background, or that she had been first wed to a brother of the Prophet. Pickett did not ask this for his own sake, you understand, but to protect her from the cruelty of bigotry. And you, my dear niece and nephew, must make the same promise, must now give me your word that you will also guard this secret with your lives."

Years later, Ina would make poetic mention of "the blood-

stained couch of death." Yet her biographers Josephine De Witt
Rhodehamel and Raymund Wood in *Ina Coolbrith*, their definitive
delineation of her life, state that her only early exposure to death
would have been her sister Sophronia's funeral; although the
Saints' keening at her uncles' burial may also have left its mark.

In 1915 Ina was given the pleasant task of organizing and
heading a Congress of Authors for the Panama Pacific Exposition.
In 1919, in recognition of her accomplishments, the state legislature accorded her the honorary title of Loved Laurel-Crowned
Poet of California. Her acceptance speech, in addition to express-
ing her thanks and gratitude for the honor, was a candid acknow-
ledgment of her own shortcomings.

> By me poetry has been regarded not only as the supremest
> of arts, but as a divine gift, for the best use of which its
> recipient should be fitted by education, time, opportunity.
> None of these have been mine. The "higher education" was
> not open to my sex in my youth, although, singularly, I was
> the first woman to furnish a commencement poem to any
> university, which I did at the request of the faculty of the
> University of California; and in a life of unremitting labor,
> "time and opportunity" have been denied. So my meagre
> output of verse is the result of odd moments, and only
> done at all because so wholly a labor of love.

She was asked by a San Francisco newspaper reporter, "What
would you do with a million dollars, Miss Coolbrith?" Her answer
came from her own sense of need.

"Provide training schools in which girls and women wage-
earners might be educated and thoroughly fitted for some occupation that would ensure their freedom from slavery."

She reminded him of the many hundreds of women who had fought their way West over plain and desert with their frontier-minded men, hoping to hang onto the pitifully few books and melodeons they brought along to help preserve and recall something of the way of life they'd loved and left.

"And, as woman does not live by bread alone any more than man, I would have in connection therewith libraries and reading rooms, lectures and music, that the mind and heart might be fed as well as the body, and life be endowed with its greatest humanizing and moral influences, hope and happiness."

Ina Coolbrith died on Februrary 29, 1928 at her niece's home in Berkeley, ten days before her eighty-seventh birthday. Her casket was spread with a blanket of her favorite lilies-of-the-valley, a gift from the Bohemian Club to their most cherished female member. She was laid to rest by her mother's grave in Oakland's Mountain View Cemetery. Oddly, no tablet marks her resting place. If ever one is made, it should carry the passages from, "When The Grass Shall Cover Me," the most poignant of her poems, which begins:

When the grass shall cover me;
Head to foot where I am lying —
When not any wind that blows,
Summer blooms nor winter snows,
Shall awake me to your sighing:
Close above me as you pass,
You will say, "How kind she was,"
You will say, "How true she was,"
When the grass grows over me.

After her death, her collected works, *Wings of Sunset*, were published with a memoir written by a devoted young friend named Charles Phillips. A poetry prize is still given in her name. In

1932, members of the Ina Coolbrith Circle prevailed upon the California state legislature to name a mountain after her. Mount Ina Coolbrith is 8,059 feet high and can be seen from Beckwourth Pass.

Rhodehamel, Josephine De Witt & Wood, Raymund. *Ina Coolbrith*. Salt Lake City, Utah: Brigham Young University Press, 1992.

Reiter, Joan Swallow. *The Old West*, Volume 23: "The Women." Alexandria, Va.: Time/Life Books, 1978.

Bamford, Georgia L. *The Mystery of Jack London*. Privately printed. 1930.

Stone, Irving. *Sailor on Horseback*. New York City: Doubleday & Co. Inc., 1978.

Beckwourth, James P. *Life and Adventures of James P. Beckwourth*. New York City: MacMillan & Co., 1891.

After discovering an old cemetery record, the Pajaro Valley Historical Association placed this plaque in 1954, seventy-five years after Charley Parkhurst's death. *Courtesy of Wm. H. Volck Memorial Museum, Pajaro Valley Historical Association, Watsonville, California*

Nellie Cashman struck it rich in the gold fields, but she won love and respect from her fellow miners when she spent it helping those down on their luck. *Courtesy of the Traywick Collection, Tombstone, Arizona*

There is no known photograph of Louisa Clappe, who wrote under the *nom de plume* of Dame Shirley However, this daguerreotype taken in an Auburn, California ravine in 1852 is typical of the dress and gold field scenes she described. *Courtesy of the California History Room, California State Library, Sacramento, California*

▲ Spinster Maria Mitchell spent her nights watching the stars, her reward the discovery of a comet. For many years, she was the only female member of the American Academy of Arts and Sciences. *Courtesy of Special Collections, Vassar College Libraries*

Despite her difficult youth, Bethenia Owens-Adair determined that she would be a full-fledged doctor. She sacrificed to raise her son and gain her degree by middle age. After she retired, she was a force in Oregon politics and medical legislation. *Courtesy of Douglas County Museum, Oregon*

◄

This portrait was the frontispiece for the second edition of Sojourner Truth's autobiography, dictated to Olive Gilbert, for which Harriet Beecher Stowe wrote the introduction. *Courtesy of the Library of Congress*

During her tenure as California's first librarian, Poet Ina Coolbrith mentored Jack London and Isadora Duncan. Beloved by bay area intelligentsia, Ina guarded a deep secret from her past. *Courtesy of Oakland History Room, Oakland Public Library*, California

Pearl Hart was tough enough to hold up stage-coaches, stupid enough to get arrested, then wily enough to con herself out of Yuma Territorial Prison. *Photo at left Courtesy of Yuma Territorial Prison State Historic Park, Yuma, Arizona. Photo below Courtesy of Denver Public Library, Western/ Genealogy Department*

◄

When Ann Eliza W. Young divorced husband Brigham Young, then told the world of her unhappy life in the Mormon faith, she brought down the practice of polygamy almost singlehandedly. *Reproduced from the archives of the Church of Jesus Christ of Latter-Day Saints*

Mary Austin was a passionate writer, naturalist, feminist and mystic. Most men were intimidated by her intellect, but famed British writer H. G. Wells considered her "the most intelligent woman in America." *Courtesy of the California History Room, California State Library, Sacramento, California* ►

In 1895, at age twenty, Nellie Bly was a daring and resourceful reporter. When she undertook to beat the fictional Phileas Fogg's record of going around the world in eighty days, she had readers racing to read her latest byline. *Photo courtesy of UPI-Corbis Bettmann*

Carrie Chapman Catt upon her graduation from Iowa State
College in 1880. Inventor of brilliant campaigns, over time she
taught women how to confront men in politics, master-minding
the strategies that eventually won them the right to vote.
Schlesinger Library, Radcliffe College

CHAPTER 8

Pearl Hart, Highwayman

Late in the summer of 1899, two outlaws held up a stagecoach bound for Globe, Arizona. One was tall, the other small and slender with steady blue eyes. The hold-up netted them a man's watch, four hundred and thirty-one dollars and the dubious distinction of a tiny niche in history. They would become known as the last road agents. The shorter of the two was a woman, proud of her fame; she could boast she was one of the few female highwaymen in the West.

Her name was Pearl Hart. She was a small woman with a feminine figure which she disguised behind a large man's shirt, trousers, and boots. She kept her long dark hair tucked under the wide brim of a cowboy hat, letting only her eyes show above the kerchief that concealed most of her face.

Until caught and imprisoned, Pearl enjoyed a moderately successful career as a petty thief and road agent in association with her lover John Boot.

Their technique was simple but effective. On one occasion, a stage driver named Baker was concentrating on bringing his team of six horses and coach safely around a dangerous blind curve, when he suddenly saw a distraught Pearl at the side of the deserted road. Apparently near fainting as she leaned into the hillside, her long dark hair was wildly disheveled and her dress rumpled and torn, nearly revealing one tempting breast. In anyone's eyes she was the victim of foul play. Baker stomped down on his brakes, bringing the team of horses to an abrupt stop.

Before Baker could gather his wits, Pearl was aiming her twin six-shooters at his heart, her torn shoulder miraculously mended.

"Halt! Climb down out of there!" the little outlaw commanded in a gruffly disguised voice. Baker got down first and stood by the coach with his hands up. The passengers—one being her accomplice Boot—also jumped out. The real passengers obediently arranged themselves in a row beside Baker, their hands also in the air. Pearl, boss of the robber duo, relieved the passengers of their money and watches while Boot rifled the express and mail boxes for valuables.

Two of the men carried heavy revolvers but, having heard of Pearl's uncontrollable temper, neither of them risked drawing their guns. A drummer, O. J. Neal, had two hundred and ninety dollars on him, and the other two men each carried a hundred dollars. One passenger, a Chinese gentleman, his hands clamped over his head, chewed nervously on a colored string. Had Pearl checked, she would have found the string attached to a small pouch containing $200 in large bills which he'd popped into his mouth as soon as he saw they were being held up. Baker was not searched. Content with their haul, Pearl handed back two silver dollars to each of the victims "for grub 'n lodging" and waved the coach on its way.

A reporter for *The Phoenix Republican*, interviewing Baker later, asked the stagedriver why he had surrendered his six-shooter, and why none of the other men had even contested the holdup.

"I feel the same as Sheriff Bill Truman of Pinal County," Baker said. "He had a run-in with Pearl once. He said 'That crazy woman is a very tiger-cat for nerve and endurance. She'd kill you as soon as look at you.' She'd have shot me if I resisted." As word of their *modus operandi* spread, Pearl and Boot dropped the act and simply stepped out into roadways together to rob stagecoaches.

On the heels of their daring holdups, the way in which they were captured proved to be stupidly anticlimactic. After a poorly planned holdup, they backtracked only to discover they had traveled in a circle, and were barely a mile removed from the holdup encounter.

In the morning, while trying to ford a rushing stream, Boot fell from his shying horse and would have drowned if Pearl hadn't rescued him. The rest of this misspent day came to a soggy conclusion as a torrential downpour forced the two hapless road agents to take refuge in a cave already occupied by a wild pig. Boot managed to kill the animal and butcher it for their supper. Pearl's acerbic comments were later quoted as "I didn't know which was worse. The dead hog, the smell of gun smoke or Boot's snoring." Cold and soaking wet, they dined on half-cooked bacon and cold beans and slept uncomfortably on their saddles inside the cave entrance.

The following morning, Pearl and Boot awoke to find Sheriff Bill Truman and his posse standing over them, the posse's rifles pointed at their heads while their own weapons lay on the ground beside them within easy reach. Boot was taken into custody without a struggle but Pearl had to be overpowered.

They were first put behind bars in the prison at Florence, Arizona. Pearl was pleased by the size of the crowd waiting to see her incarcerated. People shouted and jeered at her.

"Would you do it again, Pearl?"

"Damn right, podner!" she snapped back.

While in Florence's prison, Pearl wallowed in her sudden notoriety. All the newspapers covered her sob story of having begun her outlaw career to raise money for a dying mother. Even *Cosmopolitan Magazine* sent someone to interview Pearl. Within a few days, however, when her name was no longer front page news, she swallowed a large dose of some unknown white substance. The doctor who was summoned told her dryly, "It doesn't matter how much talcum powder you swallow, Pearl. It'll never kill you." Next, influenced by woman suffrage articles, Pearl hit the headlines by declaring she would not let herself be tried "under a law which my sex had no voice in making."

Since Florence had no appropriate facilities for female prisoners, it was decided that Pearl should be sent on to Tucson while John Boot would stay where he was. That expectation was shattered the next morning when the turnkey bringing their morning meal found the fifteen-inch square Pearl had managed to cut in the thin outer wall of her cell. Both she and Boot were long gone. A week later, the venturesome but not terribly bright couple had the misfortune to run into a posse out hunting cattle rustlers near the town of Deming, New Mexico. They were brought back to Florence and sentenced the same day.

John was given thirty years, his time to be served in the territorial prison at Yuma, Arizona. Judge O'Connor hesitated over pronouncing sentence on the diminutive, ninety-five pound Pearl.

"What in hell are you waiting for, you silly old bastard?" she inquired in a sweet mocking tone.

"Five years in the same place," the judge pronounced, stiff-lipped, with a pound of his gavel.

Established in 1875 when Arizona was still a territory, Yuma's prison, like most Western prisons, was equally ill-equipped to house women. On the fateful day in 1899 when Yuma's warden, Captain Walter Ingalls, had to accept Pearl Hart as a ward of the state, he acquired a monumental headache.

Pearl's history is not reliable. It differs with each account. The little brunette of less than five feet confessed to being twenty-eight, but looked much younger except on those frequent occasions when she was acting tough. Then her face would freeze into hard and determined lines. She was supposedly born and raised in Lindsay, Ontario, Canada. At sixteen, it was reported, she gave birth to a child fathered by a small time gambler named Hart. They married, but Pearl quickly found marriage and motherhood irksome. According to one account, Hart got a job as a barker with the Chicago World's Fair of 1893. Pearl went along, leaving her old life and her baby in her mother's willing care, never looking back from the day she and Hart first crossed the border into the United States.

At the Fair, Pearl hung around the riders, ropers and sharp-shooters of a Wild West Show, learning those skills. An apt pupil, Pearl was so good that they let her perform in their show. She soon met a handsome fellow named Dan Bandman, the piano player for a theatrical company also performing at the Fair. Said to be a "tall, lean individual of Semitic origin," when he left town Pearl went with him. It was Bandman, she claimed, who taught her to smoke opium.

Later deserted by Bandman, Pearl drifted west from boom-town to boomtown, living off men she seduced. She sent all but pocket money back to support her mother and baby. She worked her way to Arizona, charging ever larger sums for her "favors." It was in a mining camp in New Mexico where she met a man she particularly liked. He told her his name was John Boot and he, like Pearl, also lived outside the law. Soon the two of them were part-nered in mugging both men and women at gunpoint for their money, gold dust or any other valuables.

Within a few months the effort of traveling from town to town to hold up unsuspecting victims began to wear on Pearl. Her mother's last letter said she was ill and that she needed to hire a girl to look after the baby while she recovered. Desperate for quick revenue, Pearl talked Boot into trying highway robbery. It should be easy. A lonely stretch of road and an unsuspecting stagecoach driver, and there the two of them would be, facing him with men-acing pistols. That was all the inventory their new business need-ed! Pearl said.

The pair of desperadoes did all right for a few months, always managing to disappear into the countryside with their loot, until the fateful day they let themselves be caught. Pearl and Boot were transported by train to the Yuma penitentiary in November. Facing Southern California across the dividing line of the Colorado River, the prison sat on a high bluff with a sheer drop to the water on three sides in a uniquely fortified position.

According to the *Coconio Sun*, Pearl entered the building with ". . . a big cigar in her mouth rivaling the efforts of the locomotive to charge the atmosphere with smoke." An inveterate smoker, Pearl stuffed a small plug of opium into her cigars and cigarettes whenever she could get it.

Warden Captain Ingalls had a son who served both as a guard and a sentry, in charge of the formidable Gatling gun mounted on a two-wheeled carriage at a corner tower which could be swung in any direction. Mrs. Ingalls was also trained to operate the Gatling, and was noted for having foiled at least one escape attempt.

The day Pearl and John were brought in, Pearl wore a pair of tight jeans and a man's shirt, and smoked and swore like an old sailor. "I shall make no defense," she was quoted as saying. "I don't care what the world does with me. Would do it all over again if I had the chance."

She had nothing but scorn for Boot. "Why, the fellow hadn't an ounce of sand. When I was 'going through' the passengers his hands were shaking like leaves. He was supposed to be holding the guns. Why, if I hadn't more nerve than that I'd jump off the earth." In contrast, John Boot was reserved in manner and soft-spoken, and actually seemed to sigh in relief at being separated from his mistress.

Pearl was carrying the money when they were arrested in the cave which was just twenty miles from the railway station at Benson. "Boot was to have helped me hit the train eastward," she sighed dramatically. "In a day more, I would have been home, my life here left behind forever."

"Truman (the sheriff) wonders why I fought him," she mused between drags on her ever-present cigarette. "How can anyone wonder why I fought who considers that the money I had would have taken me back to liberty and decency and happiness." Maybe, maybe not.

Captain Ingalls commissioned the town dressmaker to sew Pearl a proper jail uniform. Next, he had his carpenter rip the six-tiered bunks out of one cell, nailing boards over its door to give Pearl privacy. While a guard and Mrs. Ingalls escorted Pearl to her new home, the warden's very proper wife curtly explained the house rules. They had never had to house a woman prisoner before and she was wary of Pearl's loose talk and swaggering ways.

"We'd best keep that young woman away from the other inmates," she reported back to her husband. "She'll shock them with her language and corrupt their morals!"

Ingalls managed to distance Pearl from the rest of the prisoners, but he couldn't keep her quiet. Using foul language, she amused herself every night by calling out for a man to join her, an invitation that had the male population of the jail howling like coyotes through many sleepless nights.

Ingalls' final solution was to move the other prisoners out of the range of her voice, leaving Pearl in solitary possession of her cell block. He obviously didn't trust her either, for he also made a ruling that no one but him or his wife—always with a guard—would be allowed inside that cell block during her five-year term.

Finally permitted to see her, a reporter from *The Arizona Graphic* wrote in his interview:

> Pearl occupies a cell as large as an ordinary bedroom, which is excavated in the hillside, and she has a houseyard in which to take her constitutional whenever she is mind-ed. Several weeks of prison life had relieved her physical system of its load of opium, for Pearl was a "hop fiend" of insatiable appetite, but her wicked face is sallow for she has not been deprived of her cigarettes. She is talkative, and

delights to tell the story of her stage robbery. It is a long-spun tale, told in hobo slang and mixed with the philosophy of her kind. She holds her "pal" responsible for her capture, and knows that they never would have been captured if he had followed her advice. But he knew it all, so Pearl says, and had abiding faith in the protecting power of the Virgin Mary, to whom he continually prayed for guidance. "What do you think of a guy like dat?" she asked. "Praying to de Virgin Mary to take care of him! De Virgin Mary's all right, of course, but what can she do fer a man? I can see how God almighty can take care of a man if he wants to, but how can de Virgin Mary do anything? It's all rot!"

John Boot proved to be a model prisoner. His New England accent placed his origin as somewhere in the northeastern part of the United States, although other accounts claim he spoke with an English accent. The only information they managed to get out of him was that Boot wasn't his real name. He made himself so compliant and inconspicuous that before he had served out two years of his sentence, he vanished sometime between breakfast and the nightly bedcheck one day, never to be seen again.

Boot's disappearance brought about a remarkable change in Pearl. She became almost demure and soft-spoken. When she asked Mrs. Ingalls if she might have a dress and some toiletries, her reasonable requests were readily granted. Soon after, she asked to speak to a minister. Warden Ingalls sent for Yuma's leading cleric. He was closeted with Pearl for more than an hour. In reporting on his visit to Captain Ingalls, he said, "Pearl is most remorseful for her sins. I believe she was under the influence of Boot. Now he is gone, she can realize the error of her ways."

During the ensuing six months, the minister visited regularly, bringing Pearl a Bible and other uplifting books. She began to write poetry. Warden Ingalls gave permission for her to have visitors. They often brought gifts of money for the new life she would lead after her discharge from prison. The gratified minister suggested to Ingalls that since Pearl was now a changed soul and truly repentant, she should have the rest of her sentence reduced. He wanted to see her released into the custody of her parents who were, she had informed him, currently residing in Kansas City.

While Ingalls agreed in principle — anything to get her off his hands! — he explained that he had no authority to arrange such a move. The zealous clergyman took it upon himself to pen a letter to Arizona's Territorial Governor Alexander O. Brodie, and got several of his parishioners to write to him on her behalf as well.

Some months later in traveling the territory, Governor Brodie's route took him through Yuma. Recalling the minister's letter, he arranged to stop overnight and requested a visit with the prison's now-famous female inmate. Captain Ingalls was happy to oblige. First briefing Brodie, he waived his own rule and allowed the governor to talk with Pearl alone.

Brodie spent forty-five minutes with Pearl. In taking leave of Ingalls, he said he would seriously consider the matter of commuting Pearl's sentence with a pardon.

"I think this wretch Boot mesmerized her," he declared. "She will undoubtedly be much better off at home with her family." Ingalls agreed whole heartedly, feeling certain that his prison would be much better off without Pearl.

Both the warden and the clergyman eagerly awaited a communication from the governor, but the passage of three months failed to bring any word from Brodie. Warden Ingalls couldn't bring himself to overstep his authority and write a letter to jog the territorial governor's memory.

Matters remained at a standstill until the morning the guard brought Warden Ingalls word that Pearl was feeling so poorly she wanted to see a doctor.

"What's the matter with her?" Ingalls asked.

"She didn't say, sir," the guard replied with a shrug of his shoulders.

Instead of a doctor, Ingalls sent his wife. Mrs. Ingalls came back in minutes.

"The girl appears to be pregnant," she told him, her mouth tight with disapproval. "She has all the usual symptoms."

Ingalls was in shock. There were only two keys to Pearl's cell; one he carried and the other his wife had. Outside of their regular visits to check on her, only three other people had been near her; the seamstress, Yuma's leading clergyman, and Territorial Governor Brodie!

"How far along is she?" he asked, frowning deeply.

"She's missed three times," was the laconic reply.

Ingalls made a command decision. He sent his son to the train station with money to purchase Pearl a one-way ticket to Kansas City. Then, with his affronted wife and two sturdy guards, he entered Pearl's cell to break the good news to her.

"You'll be leaving on tomorrow's train," he informed her brusquely. "Your pardon's finally come through."

"Praise the Lord," Pearl responded devoutly.

Back in his office, Ingalls penned a hasty letter to the clergyman. Next he wrote a lengthy and confidential report on Pearl's condition to Governor Brodie in which he asked that she be pardoned, delicately suggesting that the governor back-date the official document by an appropriate period. This timely action might enable him, the clergyman, and the governor himself to sidestep what promised to be a most embarrassing predicament.

Clad in a new dress and hat, courtesy of the territory of Arizona, Pearl was escorted to the train station and put on the train. There she took up a celebrity position on the observation platform.

All of Yuma's townfolks turned out for Pearl's departure. Two elderly women pushed their way to the front of the crowd to see "the famous lady bandit," blatantly demanding her autograph for their little niece. Pearl found the idea engaging and leaned over the platform railing to comply. This started a rush of kids and grown-ups wanting Pearl's autograph. Pearl, like a queen, graciously obliged each one.

"What are you going to do now, Pearl?" asked an enterprising reporter.

"Vaudeville," she stated with aplomb. "I've already got a year's booking as a real life ex-con and stage robber."

"And I suppose you'll be meeting up with your friend John Boot?"

Pearl gazed at the reporter for a long moment, then her lips curled in a lazy scornful smile.

"Well, and aren't you the stupid bastard," she said as agreeably as if she were paying him a compliment. People laughed as he backed off in chagrin.

The train began to pull away. Pearl remained outside, waving to all who'd gathered to see her off, until the train disappeared into the distance.

Back at the prison, even before the train carrying Pearl had left the area, Ingalls had already restored Pearl's cell to its former crowded state of six-tier bunks peopled with inmates of the strict-ly male persuasion.

The sun was brightly shining on a pleasant afternoon
My partner speaking lightly said, "The stage will be here soon."
We saw it coming around the bend and called to them to halt,
And to their pockets we attended, if they got hurt it was their fault.

While the birds were sweetly singing, and the men stood up in line
And the silver softly ringing as it touched this palm of mine.

There we took away their money, but left them enough to eat
And the men looked so funny as they vaulted to their seats.
Then up the road we galloped, quickly through a canyon we did pass
Over the mountains we went swiftly, trying to find our horses grass,
Past the station we boldly went, now along the riverside,
And our horses being spent, of course we had to hide.

In the night we would travel in the daytime try and rest,
And throw ourselves on the gravel, to sleep we would try our best
Around us our horses were stamping looking for some hay or grain
On the road the Posse was tramping, looking for us all in vain.
One more day they would not have got us, but my horse got
*   sore and thin*
And my partner was a mean cuss, so Billy Truman roped us in.
Thirty years my partner got, I was given five,
He seemed contented with his lot, and I am still alive.

PEARL HART

Williams, Brad. *Legendary Women of the West.* New York City: David Mckay, Inc.
  1978

Reiter, Joan Swallow. *The Old West,* Volume 23: "The Women." Alexandria, Va.:
  Time/Life Books, Inc., 1978.

Williams, Brad & Pepper, Choral. *Lost Legends of the West.* New York City: Holt,
  Rinehart & Winston, 1970.

Stephens, Autumn. *Wild Women.* Berkeley, Calif.: Conari Press, 1992.

Archival Material furnished by Yuma Territorial Prison, Yuma, Ariz., 1996.

CHAPTER 9

Bethenia Owens-Adair: Pioneer M.D.

"It was father's custom to pat me on the head, and call me his boy," Bethenia noted in her autobiography, *Dr. Bethenia Owens-Adair: Some of Her Life Experiences*. Begun at the time she retired from medicine at age fifty-five, her material was culled from the daily journals she kept throughout her life.

Except that she was known in the neighborhood for being something of a tomboy, she gave no reason why he should have said that for she came from a family of nine children, several of them boys. "The regret of my life up to the age of thirty-five," the passage continued, "was that I had not been born a boy, for I realized very early in life that a girl was hampered and hemmed in on all sides simply by the accident of sex."

Born in Van Buren County, Missouri in 1840, she was the second child of Kentucky parents, Thomas and Sarah Owens. Bethenia also recalled being the family nurse. "It was seldom that I had not a child in my arms. When there is a baby every two years, there is no end of nursing to be done." In her day, boys and girls of fourteen and fifteen were considered grown, and expected to do a full day's work on the farm or in the house. Even younger ones were taught to be useful, and learned early to take responsibility.

Because of being labeled a boy while growing up, Bethenia constantly tested her strength against that of an older brother, trying to prove she was as strong as he. Once she even ". . . bet him I could carry four sacks of flour, or two hundred pounds." True, he helped load the sacks on her back and arms, but she carried them to win the bet.

In 1843 Tom Owens picked up his wife and three children and left Missouri. They were among the early overland travelers on the Oregon Trail; the family settled on the Clatsop Plains, an area southwest of Astoria on the Oregon coast.

Lacking formal schooling, at twelve Bethenia did her share of frontier farming chores and took care of the younger children. Not very prepossesing in looks, she developed a serious crush on a Mr. Beaumont, a young bachelor who boarded with them while conducting a three month school in their neighborhood. Certainly part of the emotional attraction was her admiration for his learning. Perhaps it was then she developed her passion for books and knowledge.

"School books were extremely scarce," she noted, "and sometimes whole families were taught out of one book. Every child over four years old attended school, and children did not remain babies long when other babies crowded them out of the cradle."

Heartsick when Beaumont's teaching stint finished and he was moving on, Bethenia hovered near him, barely managing not to cry, as the family said their goodbyes. First kissing the baby sister she carried, Beaumont ruffled the twelve-year-old's hair as he said to her mother, "I guess I'll take this one with me."

"All right," her mother retorted, "she is such a tomboy I can never make a girl of her, anyway." Bethenia ran off in tears. She wrote of the "many times afterward, when I was especially rebellious and wayward, which was not infrequently, I would be confronted with, 'I wish the teacher had taken you with him,' to which I never failed to answer promptly and fervently, 'I wish he had, too!'"

As Owens prospered and his herds increased, he needed more space. Moving his family that same year, Owens took up a larger homestead in the Umpqua Valley in southern Oregon, which lay across the river from the village of Roseburg. Here, for a year, Bethenia's life went along in a routine vein.

However, when a former farmhand of her father's asked for her hand in marriage, her parents gave their consent. In the mid-1800s, it was customary for girls to marry early. Her suitor's name was Legrand Hill, and he was in his early twenties. In her journal she wrote about their meetings in the offhand, unemotional way backwoods propriety demanded. "During that winter, Mr. Hill came to visit us. It was arranged that we should be married the next spring."

She mentioned nothing of how she felt about him or the forthcoming nuptials, but recorded in detail the preparations made with her mother's help throughout that winter and early spring. All her spare time was given to sewing her trousseau. From fabric her mother gave her, she wrote of having made four quilts, four muslin sheets, two pillow cases, two tablecloths, four towels, and several rugs braided from rags and cloth scraps. She also sewed herself two calico dresses and helped her mother with the finer work needed for her wedding dress, which she fondly described as "a pretty, sky-blue figured lawn."

Bethenia was fourteen on May 4, 1854, the day of the wedding. "I was still small for my age. My husband was five feet eleven inches in height, and I could stand under his outstretched arm. I grew very slowly, and did not reach my full stature until I was twenty-five years old, which is now five feet four inches."

At first the newlyweds lived with his parents in the Siskiyou Mountains south of Jacksonville, Oregon. Soon after, Legrand bought a farm property in Yreka, California, and began building a log cabin on it that measured twelve feet by fourteen feet. Sentimental because it was their first married home, Bethenia chinked the gaps between the logs herself, using grass mixed with mud to keep out venturing lizards and snakes.

The young couple owned no actual furniture, making do with a shelf nailed to the cabin sides for their bed, another for a table, and three shelves for a cupboard. Legrand's possessions consisted of "a horse and a saddle, a gun, and less than twenty dollars in money." In recalling, however, that her father had come to Oregon with only fifty cents in his pocket and gradually made it grow into twenty thousand dollars, Bethenia considered Legrand's meager assets an excellent start in life.

Just before the payment on the property was due, Legrand injured his hand and quit work, leaving their roof and floor unfinished. Because by then he had spent and sold nearly everything they had, even the cows her father had given Bethenia as a nest egg, Legrand decided it would be a good idea if they moved in with Bethenia's folks. To their dismay, her parents learned the young couple were broke when they overheard them fight over the fact that Legrand wanted to sell her horse Queen, another gift from her father. When Bethenia flatly refused, that became a bone of contention between them.

The fact remained that Legrand was not going to be able to meet the payment due on the farm. When the man who had sold him the property made an offer of sixty dollars to turn it back, Legrand was only too happy to accept.

In Bethenia's opinion, this was extremely poor business practice on her husband's part, as well as a want of industry and perseverance, all the more aggravating because she knew he was a skilled carpenter who could have been earning good money at his trade all along. But it seemed he would rather stop work early to go hunting, something at which he also excelled.

In her secret heart Bethenia began to disrespect him. When Legrand's parents wrote that they were doing well in Jackson County, Oregon, and why didn't Legrand bring his bride and settle near them, the young couple traveled south with a pack train, and stayed with them a couple of months.

His aunt, a Mrs. Kelly, with whom Legrand had spent eight or ten years of his boyhood, insisted they stay with her. "She thoroughly understood him," Bethenia later wrote, adding, "Had he followed her advice, he would have succeeded, instead of making a failure."

This time with his father's help, Legrand made a small down payment on a little house in Yreka township, with the rest owed. It was in that house on April 17, 1856, that Bethenia bore him a son. She named him George. Aunt Kelly immediately offered to adopt and raise the child.

"I will give him all I have," she promised, "and that is more than his father will ever do for him. I know very well that Legrand will just fool around all his life and never accomplish anything." She had lived with Legrand long enough to see that he "idled away his time, never continuing at anything." His penchant for trading and speculating made him a constant loser. Even though she knew Aunt Kelly spoke the truth, Bethenia found the idea of giving up her baby repugnant.

Yet living from hand to mouth as they were doing was equally upsetting to the young wife and new mother, so she was thrilled when her father intervened with an offer of "an acre of land and the material for a good house." She was ecstatic when Legrand agreed to accept his generous offer.

Her father and brothers had barely hauled the lumber to the site, however, when Legrand announced he was going into the brick business with a man he had just met. Despite Mr. Owens' advice to the contrary, Legrand moved his wife Bethenia and the baby to a tent in a low damp valley, and put his remaining money into the brick venture.

Heavy rains halted the work. Bethenia caught typhoid fever and was so sick that her parents had to come and take her and the baby back to their home to recover. Mr. Owens confronted Legrand with the unwelcome reality that, despite his having underwritten them initially to give them a decent start in life, three and a half years later all they had left was her horse. He would keep his word and give them that acre, but would put its deed in Bethenia's name. Affronted at what he perceived as a slight, Legrand declared he would never build a home on any lot he didn't own; the deed must be rewritten in his name. Bethenia's father gave in, and after sulking awhile, Legrand began the building of their house, while again living off his wife's parents.

Bethenia's recovery was slow. The baby, too, was ill and fretful. Unable any longer to hide her true feelings, Bethenia confided to her father and mother how unhappy she was with Legrand. Her mother said indignantly "Let him go. With his temper, he is liable to kill you at any time." But her father begged her to try again. She did try, bolstering her sagging spirits with the knowledge she could return to her old home if it didn't work out.

But they continued to quarrel, mostly about the baby. Legrand fell into the habit of spanking it unmercifully over the least little thing. One day, after throwing his infant son on the bed, he stormed out of the house in a rage. Bethenia dressed the boy and, packing only necessities, went home for good. And though her improvident husband begged her most piteously to come back, she said, "Legrand, I have told you many times that if we ever did separate, I would never go back, and I never will."

"And now," she confided to her journal, "at eighteen years of age I found myself broken in spirit and health, again in my father's house from which, only four short years before, I had gone with such a happy heart and such bright hopes for the future."

In 1859, in spite of the fact that divorce stigmatized women — even wives of ne'er-do-wells — Bethenia got a divorce. She was determined to make an independent life for herself and her boy, a life on her own terms. To do this, she realized, would require an education, something her son George would also need in time. Her mother encouraged her.

Chores done, Bethenia often sat in on classes in the same one-room schoolhouse as her son, beginning with kindergarten to refresh her memory. She was so intent on soaking up knowledge that she didn't mind being teased and seen as a figure of fun. Her time both before and after school and all her Saturdays were spent on the milking, laundry and ironing, her contribution to the family's well-being.

She never neglected her school work. She finished the third reader in four months, making good progress in spelling, geography, arithmetic and writing. The regimen she developed early on kept her constitutionally tough and healthy throughout her working life. She rose in the dark of early dawn and took an icy bath or shower, then exercised vigorously before breakfast. To earn the money for her own and her boy's clothes, she often worked past midnight on extra sewing or washing and ironing for their neighbors.

She also held short-term teaching posts like her former idol, Mr. Beaumont, staying at least a day ahead of her students in the subjects she taught. Any extra money she earned went into her savings jar. When discouraged, feeling she simply could not go on another moment, she would renew her vow of independence. Taking account of what she'd already achieved also helped to keep her resolve strong.

She recounted the details of one amusing job in her youth, long before she studied medicine. At nineteen, having already demonstrated her natural ability to care for the sick, Bethenia's services were much sought after. When she did accept pay, she was used to receiving the best wages any woman got at that time. But the following experience proved the exception to the rule.

A farmer named Kelly had employed Bethenia twice before to nurse his wife through her confinements. She was expected to take full charge of their household. As nurse, she was to attend the mother and newborn day and night; as housekeeper, she looked after both the older children and her own four-year-old George, as well as handling all the housework and cooking. This time the new baby arrived the day after Bethenia got there.

The family consisted of farmer Kelly, his wife and three children, herself and George, and because it was harvest time, four hired hands. She slept with the infant each night, to give the mother complete rest. She rose at four each morning after being kept awake by the baby who needed twice nightly feedings. She milked four cows, made butter from the cream, cleaned their house, cooked for eleven persons, fed the poultry, and carried wood upstairs to the attic for her own use.

After three weeks, when his wife was able to resume her own duties, Bethenia made ready to depart. Farmer Kelly, hand in his pocket, asked how much she was going to charge for her services.

"Five dollars a week," she replied timidly, knowing it was three dollars more than a hired hand usually got, but feeling she had earned that much.

"I didn't expect to be asked to pay over three dollars a week," he said in a surly voice," his face registering his disgust. "But if you will take it in an order on Heinerberg's store, I will pay your five dollars." Lacking the nerve to assert her rights, she accepted the order entitling her to exchange it for the poorest quality of goods.

She comforted herself, "The time will come when that man Kelly will be glad to acknowledge my superiority." But the experience rankled. Not because he was, in her words, "an ignorant foreigner," but because he had looked down on her and treated her as a servant.

Bethenia made up her mind that, in addition to employing her nursing skills, she would study medicine and gain a medical degree. To that end, she spent a part of every night with her nose buried in borrowed medical textbooks a doctor friend, sworn to secrecy, would loan her. Looking back on those difficult years she commented, "No more is it necessary for the student to pore over the old, thumb-worn books by the light of a pitch stick, or a tow string in a broken mug of refuse kitchen grease; and yet those times produced from and for this nation a Franklin, a Jefferson, a Greeley, a Clay, a Webster, and a Lincoln . . . who possessed the sterling qualities of intelligent, incorruptible citizenship. . . ."

When George was twelve, Bethenia moved with him to Roseburg, Oregon, the nearest town able to provide him an education. She depended on her talent for fine sewing to make their living. She leased a small store space and opened a modest milliner's shop. Within weeks she realized she was barely earning enough to pay their keep.

Swallowing her pride, she took to heart the words of an outspoken rival milliner who said she was "a rotten hat designer and an even worse businesswoman." Bethenia knew it was true, but that didn't make her give up her dream. Summoning all her courage, she talked a banker into loaning her two hundred and fifty dollars for a study course in professional millinery design. She temporarily closed her business in November of 1867, left her son in the care of the minister and his wife who shared the little home she rented and left for San Francisco.

When she returned to Roseburg, the course completed, Bethenia leased a new space directly across from her tactless rival. Now a competent mistress of the millinery arts, this time she prospered. Each day the women of Roseburg flocked to her for their hats, and each night she spent poring over medical text-books. The years passed while mother and son worked hard, scrimping and saving for college educations.

In those days the medical profession was less structured, with fewer legal restrictions. Beseeched by ill friends to attend them, Bethenia gladly worked her nursing magic. She even employed her minor surgery skills for friends who begged her. Their doctors' disapproval only made her more determined than ever to see an M.D. after her name.

After enrolling sixteen-year-old George as a student in the University of California at Berkeley, her passion to acquire a medical education overcame all other considerations. Entrusting her successful business to the hands of a younger sister she had taught the trade, Bethenia left again by stagecoach in 1872, this time headed East. Her family and many friends had voiced strong disapproval, but weighed against their doubts and fears she had the support of an attorney friend who urged, "Go ahead. It is in you; let it come out. You will win!"

Now thirty-two, Bethenia enrolled in the Philadelphia Eclectic School of Medicine. A superior student, she graduated in a year with the only certification granted women at the time, a quasi-medical degree as a "bath doctor." She chose a smaller Oregon community than Roseburg in which to hang out her hard-won shingle in 1873.

She recalled her first important week of doctoring. "A few days after, an old man without friends died, and the six physicians who had each attended the man at times, decided to hold an autopsy." One of the six, a Dr. Palmer, already disliked her because she had successfully performed a minor surgery on one of his patients after he failed to do so.

In pure spite, he suggested to his colleagues that the new "Philadelphia" doctor be present. "A messenger was dispatched to me with a written invitation. I knew this was no honor for me, but I said: 'Give the doctors my compliments, and say that I will be there in a few minutes.' The messenger left, and I followed close behind him. I waited outside until he went in and closed the door." Moments later she heard a roar of laughter. When she entered, a Dr. Hoover came forward to greet her and ask if she knew "the autopsy was to be performed on the man's genital organs."

"No," she answered, "but one part of the human body should be as sacred to the physician as another." At this point Dr. Palmer strenuously objected to her being present at the autopsy of a man, and declared that he would leave if she were allowed to remain. She reminded him she was there by written invitation. "I would like to ask Dr. Palmer what is the difference between the attendance of a woman at a male autopsy, and the attendance of a man at a female autopsy?" He had no answer for her. When five doctors stood by their vote to allow her to stay and cheered as Dr. Palmer left the room, one of them then handed Bethenia his well-worn medical bag.

"You do not want me to do the work, do you?" she asked in surprise, convinced there were already too many doctors in this one small village. "Oh, yes, yes, go ahead," he urged.

Word of the irregular proceedings filtered outside as she began the dissection "all atremble inside." Later, walking home, she reported, "The street was lined on both sides with men, women and children, all anxious to get a look at 'the woman who dared.' As soon as possible after that autopsy, I closed up my business and, taking my sister, and the remnant of my store goods, I removed to Portland, Oregon."

On the Willamette River, Portland was larger than Roseburg but still a very small city. However it was there that Bethenia seriously began to consider the ramifications of political questions like temperance and woman suffrage, as well as other matters. She wrote and sent thought-provoking articles to the Roseburg papers for the next three years, as well as to the feminist Abigail Duniway's paper, *The New Northwest*. These pieces began to make her name known, even, she feared, "perhaps somewhat damaged it," in years to come. "Notwithstanding occasional rebuffs here and there and frequent slights from my brother M.D.s," she reported that her Portland practice increased weekly.

Meanwhile George turned nineteen, and Bethenia entered him in the Medical Department at Willamette University, Oregon, determined that he too would become a physician. His graduation two years later, Bethenia wrote, "was one of the proudest days of my life."

One day, when she returned from making the rounds of her patients, Bethenia found a mortally ill woman on the couch in her office, attended by the woman's husband and two of their neighbors. Close to death, she was in the last stages of double pneumonia. She was so badly off that Bethenia could do nothing but offer comfort. With her dying breath, she begged Bethenia to take one of her three little girls to raise.

"Which I promised to do; and a few days later, her husband brought me the eldest, but smallest of the three sisters, a puny sickly looking little creature, and as she stood beside her father, who was also undersized, in her old, faded calico dress up to her knees, her stockings tied up with strings, her shoes out at the toes, and holding a bundle done up in an old red cotton handkerchief, with a scared look on her pinched little face, the pair made a forlorn picture that stamped itself indelibly on my memory.

"Taking the child by the hand, I said: 'So this is my little girl? Come with me. This is your home now.'"

Telling the father to return for some presents for the girls at home, she turned the child over to the woman who helped in her work, instructing her to give the girl a good bath. Then Bethenia and a friend went out to buy the child some decent clothes. Bethenia's friend asked, "What on earth are you going to do with that child?"

"Oh, she's mine now. Her mother gave her to me on her deathbed," Bethenia replied.

"Well, if I took a child, I would find a better looking one than that."

Years later, the same friend stopped by and inquired, "What did you ever do with that little girl you took, when I was here last?" Bethenia called the girl away from her desk, introducing her as Mattie Bell. Currently sixteen, grown and filled out, she was the picture of a happy teenager. She was so devoted to Bethenia that she never wanted to leave her. Even after she married, she remained a faithful loving daughter until an untimely death in her early thirties.

Bethenia's reputation grew with her patient roster. One day her old rival, the milliner from across the street in Roseburg, came to her Portland office. First apologizing abjectly for her former nastiness, she sought Bethenia's medical help. Bethenia had to suppress a smile.

"Once a friend told me," she said, "if I wished to increase your height, I'd attempt to press you down. You'd grow from sheer resentment. So I thank you for your rudeness." She smiled now, adding, "for it made me grow."

"I was successful and prosperous," she wrote, "but not yet satisfied." She wanted to know more. She had paid for her sister's attendance at Mills College, and her son's professional education and start. She felt justified in treating herself to further medical education, intending to take a trip abroad, a move she knew would "equip her for business on a grand scale."

First she settled her son in the pharmaceutical business in Goldendale, Washington. Next, at the age of thirty-eight Bethenia sold everything, including some properties, to realize the sum of eight thousand dollars, the amount she had decided would be sufficient for her needs over the next three years.

When they learned of her plans, her friends and family offered their usual strenuous objections. "You will soon be rich," they argued, "why spend all you have for nothing?" Deaf to their censure, on September 1, 1878 Bethenia left Portland once more for Philadelphia where she hoped to enter the renowned Jefferson Medical College. With that in mind, she armed herself with glowing letters of recommendation from influential senators, governors, doctors and professors.

In Philadelphia, Bethenia called on and was welcomed by Dr. Hannah Longshore, one of the first graduates of the Woman's Medical School of Philadelphia and a sister of the founder of the

Eclectic school Bethenia had attended. When Bethenia revealed her hope of entering Jefferson, Dr. Longshore replied, "I have no faith that you can get into Jefferson College, but I want to see you try it. I believe the time will come when the doors of every medical school in our land will be forced to open for women. . . ." She then suggested Bethenia see Professor Gross, saying if anyone could get her into that school, he would be the one.

That same day Bethenia marched herself over to the professor's home. The great man invited her in and read her letters. She watched in awe, reminding herself she was in the presence of the man considered to be the greatest surgeon in the United States. When he finished the letters he apologized, explaining that while he was powerless to grant her request, he did have a suggestion. She should apply to the University of Michigan.

"It is a long-term school, and a mixed school," he told her. "And it is second to none in America." Thanking him, Bethenia proceeded directly to the university at Ann Arbor where she was accepted. She spent the two next intense years in dedicated study, and earned her M.D. degree in June of 1880. Her spartan habits of cold baths, little sleep and regular exercise saw her through each obstacle she met, not the least of which was the constant ridicule and harassment of playful male classmates.

Attributing much of her success to this regimen, she wrote, "During all that time I had not suffered from a day's sickness, and had been present at every class lecture save one, my absence from it being due to my having been so deeply absorbed in my studies that I failed to hear the bell. This lapse almost broke my heart, which had been set on being able to say, at the end of the course, that I had not missed a single lecture."

After a year as an intern at a Chicago clinic, she returned to the university to complete post-graduate requirements. Her son joined her there to finish his post-graduate work. An honors graduate, Bethenia now was able to fulfill another ambition. She took a sabbatical to treat them both to a long-needed first vacation, an extended European tour that combined work and pleasure. First they traveled extensively in the East, then abroad. While there, Bethenia made it a point to visit as many hospitals as she could to meet their most famous physicians and surgeons; after, she was invited to watch their operating techniques.

Still in Europe, she received a praising letter from a long time friend and champion, Oregon's retired Governor Chadwick, an excerpt of which read:

> After all, I believe you are the first woman in the United States who studied medicine regularly. In this I may be mistaken, but I think not. When you borrowed the books of Dr. Hamilton so many years ago to read up in your profession, I wondered at the step you had taken. . . . Time rolled on, and you came out of the trial with honor. Who could have done more, or as much? All your life you have been marked for decision of character, excellence of purpose, and great ability in all you have undertaken, and today you have the respect, confidence and praise of all your acquaintances. . . . You broke down the barriers of predjudice, and said to the world: "This delicate and sympathetic office of a physician belongs more to my sex than to the other, and I will enter it, and make it an honor to women."

The Governor incorrectly called Bethenia the first woman doctor in the United States, for Dr. Elizabeth Blackwell preceded her, earning her medical degree in 1849, when the first courses of study were two sixteen-week terms. By Bethenia's day, graduates were required to study and train for at least three years to achieve a medical diploma. At the height of her success and professional fame, Bethenia specialized in diseases of the eye and ear.

One day Farmer Kelly approached her in a public restaurant, wanting to show off that he knew her. At first she didn't recognize him. When he told her who he was Bethenia was polite, but couldn't find it in her heart to be cordial. He soon went away, discomfited, leaving her to reflect on the irony that one who bends those in his power to his will, is always ready to kowtow to a higher power.

Bethenia was forty-four when she fell in love with widower Colonel John Adair, and he with her. After a brief courtship, the couple were married on July 24, 1884, in Portland's First Congregational Church. A West Point graduate, now a farmer and land developer, they had known each other as children.

Handsome and debonair, John Adair was a cultured and kind gentleman who adored her. But he had no real profession. Bethenia loved him dearly but soon learned she had to be the sensible one because he was attracted to "pie in the sky" schemes for making money. Throughout their life together, Bethenia would be the family breadwinner. Like so many really strong women, she attracted weaker men. She put up with his impractical schemes because she loved him.

Her joy was unbounded when, in the first year of their marriage, their union was blessed by a baby girl. Tragically, this cherished baby lived but three days. Her early death proved an irreparable blow to a woman of Bethenia's sensibilities and calling, one from which she never fully recovered.

Overcome with grief, to try to escape sad memories they left the city and moved to a remote farm area in backcountry Oregon near Astoria. There, for eleven years, Bethenia would serve the community, dividing her time between being a country doctor and helping her husband run the farm. She wasn't afraid to drive great distances alone in her carriage, day or night, fair weather or foul, to bring her considerable healing powers to suffering and grateful patients.

She and Adair adopted and raised two other children. Her daughter Mattie's son, Victor Adair Hill, came to live with them after his mother's death, and in 1891 they acquired the newborn son of a patient whom they named John Adair, Jr.

By 1899, threatened with crippling rheumatism, Dr. Adair and her husband relocated to the drier climate of North Yakima, Washington, where her son George practised medicine. There her health improved, allowing her to resume her medical practice; she also doctored summertimes at Seaside, Oregon.

She wrote for all her adult life. She called one piece written for *The New Northwest*, "The Influence of a Cord of Wood". Motivated by her strong conviction that women should have the vote, it began:

> A gentleman of this place some months since laughed in my face when I asked him to subscribe for the woman suffrage paper. Shortly afterward he attended Miss Anthony's lecture. The next day he met me and asked if we women dealt in wood; if so, he would give a cord of wood for a subscription to Abigail Duniway's publication, *The New Northwest*. I accepted the challenge, and before morning his name was on the way to your office.

Later in the same article, she recounted meeting a "motherly, generous-hearted, pure-minded but simple old lady" who asked her, "You are not in favor of women voting, are you?"

"Yes, indeed, I am," Bethenia replied. The old lady threw up her hands in shock.

"Oh, no, no, you cannot mean it!"

"Indeed," Bethenia answered, "there is not another principle in the wide world I so dearly cherish, for there is no other power that can be compared to the power of the ballot." The dear old lady sighed and her eyes filled with tears.

"Well, well," she said. "I know nothing about this woman's movement, but I am bitterly opposed to it." Bethenia commented on paper, "if she would only give a cord of wood for *The New Northwest* she would soon learn better than to be opposed to truth and justice."

Spirited, far-seeing and forthright, after her husband died in 1915, Bethenia devoted the rest of her life to fighting in print and in person for special reforms she felt would better her state and her nation. One of her essays to the editor of a Washington newspaper read:

> The greatest curse of the race comes through our vicious and criminal classes, and to my mind this is the element that should be dealt with . . . by the science of surgery, for if their power to reproduce themselves were rendered null, a tremendous important step in advance would have been taken.

And to a Portland paper:

> I believe it will not require more than one century to effectually close the doors of our penitentiaries, insane asylums, reform schools, and all like institutions, under whose burdens we are now groaning, mentally, physically and financially.

How disappointed she would have been to discover that, almost a hundred years later, these predictions have not yet been realized.

The *Yakima Daily Republic* reported in an issue, "Dr. Owens-Adair has informed the Republic that she will close her office and retire from business here October 10. Dr. Adair has been in active practice for over thirty years, having been the first woman graduate in medicine in both Oregon and Washington."

Her primary causes were woman suffrage, and the evil inherent in letting the feeble-minded and insane bring children into the world. She also stumped for temperance, having seen the effects of drinking on her own father. Ever a crusader, she worked for change and finally in 1925 knew the satisfaction of seeing two bills she authored — mandatory sterilization of the insane, and mandatory medical examinations prior to marriage — pass into Oregon law.

Bethenia died in 1926 at the age of 85, and was buried in Ocean View Cemetery, Astoria, having fully demonstrated with her life the truth of a neighbor's remark made when she was a child.

"The trouble with Bethy is, she thinks she can do anything a boy can . . . just as good as him . . . and maybe even a little better."

Owens-Adair, Dr Bethenia. *Dr. Bethenia Owens-Adair: Some of Her Life Experiences*. Portland, Oreg.: Mann & Beach, 1906.

Reiter, Joan Swallow. *The Old West*, Volume 23: "The Women." Alexandria, Va.: Time/Life Books, Inc., 1978.

Bingham, Edwin R. "Bethenia Angelina Owens-Adair," *Notable American Women*, Vol. 2, Edited by Edward T. & Janet W. James. Cambridge, Mass.: Harvard University Press, Bellknap Press, 1971.

Stephens, Autumn. *Wild Women*. Berkeley, Calif.: Conari Press, 1992.

Gray, Dorothy. *Women of the West*, Millbrae, Calif.: Les Femmes, 1996.

Ann Eliza W. Young: Rebel Wife

"Patience, Lenny," the young mother told the three-and-a-half-year-old in an exasperated tone as she anxiously glanced left, then to the right of the dark street." The movers are going as fast as they can."

Two muscular workmen strained under the weight of the big wardrobe they carried to the moving van. Two of the three vans were already loaded, their doors fastened shut.

"We've only got the dining table and chairs, Mrs. Young," the older man said as they hefted the heavy piece past her into the back of the horse-drawn van parked behind two other vans in the dusty street.

"But it's nearly dawn!" she exclaimed. "You promised me you'd be done before dawn if I gave you an extra two dollars."

"And so we will, ma'am. So we will. Maybe if you took your son for a bit of a walk. . ." A pretty young lady, he thought, nicely made, even if she seemed out of sorts. It was hard to determine the color of her eyes and hair in the dark. Although he couldn't see them, she had intense blue eyes and brown hair.

Ann Eliza Webb Young looked into the upturned face of her boy, now hanging on her hand. Poor thing, he looked as tired as she felt. Thank the Lord his big brother is safe with my parents, she thought gratefully as she again checked the pre-dawn sky. The air was already oppressively humid on this July Tuesday morning of 1873. Ann Eliza kept alert and listening as she continued to sweep her eyes over the dark reaches of the street, an almost frantic expression on her face.

"No, I mustn't leave. I can't. The sky is starting to lighten. You simply must hurry or it will all be for naught." Four moving men carried out six chairs while the boss and his helper struggled with an unwieldy buffet topped by a mirror. Once these were properly loaded, the third van's doors were locked. The boss tipped his cap. "All done now, Mrs. Young," he said in his Irish brogue. "And in plenty of time, you see. It's only now comin' on dawn."

"Yes, yes. Thank you," she replied curtly, handing him a sealed envelope. "Your money's inside. And something to spare." She looked most forlorn, he thought, standing there all dressed as if for a trip, her satchels at her feet. What was his holiness Brigham Young up to now, he wondered, turning his pretty young wife out of her house in the middle of the night, without so much as a fare-thee-well?

"You'll be all right?" he inquired gently. "Would you be needin' a ride somewheres now, Mrs. Young?"

"No, thank you. I'm being called for." The boss tipped his cap again in good-bye then climbed to a perch by the driver of the third van.

"Gid-dap!" the driver called, slapping the reins. The other vans followed. "Funny people, these Mormons," he commented as the three wagons slowly rumbled off through the still-sleeping streets.

Ann Eliza glanced about again. Hearing nothing, she turned for a last look at the small ugly house where she had endured four wretched years of wedlock with her seldom-seen husband, Brigham Young. She noticed the men had forgotten to shut the front door. Who cares, she thought, let it stay open. Its dreary furnishings were on their way to an auction house, their sale to finance the start of her scary new life. Ann Eliza had just embarked on an unthinkable course none of his other wives had ever dared to pursue. . . that of leaving the all-powerful Brigham Young, deserting him without his knowledge or his permission.

She kept watching the street. He was perfectly capable of sending a goon squad after her to bring her back, or worse. Her tired little boy started to sniffle, catching her fear. She was thankful to hear a carriage entering the block. True to their promise, the Strattons were coming to fetch her. If the sounds had presaged Brigham's hoodlums, it would have been men on horseback and the uneven clop-clop of horses' hooves she heard.

For the past six months Ann Eliza had been ill and nearly bedridden, and so poor she had been forced to take in boarders; so poor the doctor who attended her did so without asking a fee. What she required, he prescribed, was "nursing and sympathy."

She had met Reverend and Mrs. C. C. Stratton at a church social months before. Pastor of the First Methodist Church, his was the first non-Mormon faith permitted in Salt Lake City. He had told her he was impressed by her "honest replies to his questions." Reared to think of "Gentiles" — the Mormon term for those outside their faith — as the disciples of Satan, Ann Eliza had been pleasantly surprised to find him warm and kind, and without horns. She set down in her autobiography, *WIFE No. 19, or The Story Of A LIFE IN BONDAGE*, that she felt "very strongly drawn toward the world which he and Mr. Sawyer (another infidel she had met earlier) represented." Shortly after, as if in response to a prayer, thirty-year-old Judge Hagan and his wife became her boarders.

She was not really wife number nineteen, and she knew it, a fact she never bothered to explain. Possibly because neither she, nor anyone but Brigham himself, really knew how many women he had actually married. According to the files in the Archives Room in the Church of Jesus Christ of the Latter-Day Saints Genealogical Society in Salt Lake City, Brigham had fifty-two wives, and Ann Eliza is listed as the fiftieth. Of course many of those listed never lived with him or consummated their marriage. Spiritual wives only, they were joined to him to receive his support.

Ann Eliza maintained she married Brigham on April 7, 1869, at which time eighteen of his twenty-six actual wives were living, causing her to name herself the nineteenth.

Two Ward teachers had routinely called on Ann Eliza in her ugly little house asking, as they always did, "Sister Young, do you enjoy the spirit of our religion?"

They were alarmed the last time when she responded, "No, I do not." This provoked a lecture, after which they talked her into being rebaptised to help recover her faith. On that day, she reported, "The men officiating were talking and laughing as if engaged in an everyday affair, while I was trying to feel solemn and to exercise faith — a signal failure, I assure you." To her, the ceremony was a farce of mumbled words and ritual that left her "thoroughly disgusted."

She made one last attempt to be satisfied with her lot in life. Soon after the Hagans moved in, Ann Eliza arranged an audience with Brigham during which she asked him for a new stove in order to better serve her added roomers. He registered surprise.

"I believe you are keeping boarders."

"Yes, I am, and that is why I want the stove. I cannot do the necessary cooking on the one I have," Ann Eliza replied.

"If you want a cooking stove," he snapped brusquely, "you'll get it yourself. I've put you in a good house and you must see to the rest. I cannot afford to have so many people calling on me for every little thing they think they want." His cold tone settled her mind. She would never call on him again.

She couldn't hide her hurt feelings. When she confided them to Mrs. Hagan, the lady asked permission to tell her husband. He, in turn, after conferring with colleagues and hearing that she wanted out of her marriage, reported back that they agreed she must start a suit for divorce and alimony against Brigham.

But he made clear to her the difficulties he foresaw in so doing. There was a distinct possibility that the law of the United

States might not recognize her polygamous marriage. He sensibly reminded her that leaving Brigham would not only strip her of a home but whatever stipend he was providing. Hagan suggested a wiser course might be to stay in the marriage until Congress passed favorable laws to help her, or else wait until God took care of her problem. Ann Eliza tossed her head. She trusted neither Congress nor God. She wanted to be free now. In that case, he advised, she must engage competent attorneys. In an overly agitated voice, Ann Eliza declared that she "was resolved to overturn my whole life," and to that end wanted to try to get a divorce under United States, not Mormon, law.

The carriage did indeed hold Reverend and Mrs. Stratton. They brought her to their home, and under cover of darkness that evening transported her and her exhausted child to Walker House, a Gentile hotel. They bade her goodbye after helping her settle into a two-room suite on an upper floor. For safety's sake, they advised her not to leave the rooms but have her meals served upstairs. After they left Ann Eliza bravely wrote in her daily journal, "My plans were quickly laid and with the assistance of friends whom I found in this hour of trouble, were carried into instant execution, before they could be discovered by Mormon spies."

But later, facing an unfamiliar bed, she penned, "Imagine, if you can, my feelings, on being alone with my little child, in a strange place . . . I had abandoned my religion, left father, mother, home and friends — deliberately turned away from them all, knowing that the step I was taking could never be retraced."

Ann Eliza found the days endurable because she was busy conferring with her new friends and lawyers. But she dreaded the nights. Disoriented to begin with, she had never been inside a hotel before. In fact, she had never lived in any but the Mormon lifestyle. Despite reassurances that she and the child were safe, that no one would dare harm her there in a public hotel, Ann Eliza lived in fear. Footsteps in the hall made her hold her breath while her heart beat faster until the steps faded. She knew Brigham had only to learn of her defection, and where she was, to retaliate in some dire way against her or her family, or both. But she also knew there was no turning back. Lying awake night after night she trembled—remembering.

She remembered jolting West in the fine covered wagon her father made for his family, the excitement of the trip dulled because her mother, Eliza, cried all the time. Ann Eliza was too young to know her mother's grief was not caused by the rigorous journey, but rather because a child was soon to be born to Elizabeth, her father Chauncey Webb's second wife, who traveled with them.

It was not until 1852 that Brigham made the news public that Mormon men must take more than one wife. But long before that Chauncey gave Eliza the choice of leaving the church forever, or sharing him with another wife. An agonized Eliza wept and prayed for guidance. "I came to her," her daughter wrote, "when the greatest misery of her life was about to fall on her." It was apparent that this enforced polygamy was the most hateful thing in the world to her . . . but she was afraid to oppose it, lest she be found "fighting against the Lord." Pressed to decide, Eliza gave in. Independently, the couple picked out a young woman and found they had both chosen nineteen-year-old Elizabeth Lydia Taft, who boarded at their home along with her sister.

Not without some embarrassment, thirty-three-year-old Chauncey Webb proposed to the girl and was accepted. In January of 1846, Chauncey and Elizabeth were wed in the new Nauvoo temple, with red-eyed first wife Eliza in attendance. Now Ann Eliza had two mothers. Although her mother Eliza kept her peace

with the second Mrs. Webb, she could not totally hide her feelings
from Chauncey, who settled all too comfortably into this new
domestic arrangement. Once, seeing what a mood she was in and
knowing why, he shook his head and remarked, "You were willing
at first. What is the difficulty now? Don't you think Elizabeth a
good, true girl?"

"Yes, indeed," she said.

"Don't you believe in polygamy then?" he asked.

"I suppose so. I wish to live my religion."

"Well, what is to be done about it?"

"Oh, I don't know," replied Elizabeth, totally miserable, "but I
can't endure this life." Which was pretty much the way most plural wives felt in their secret hearts, but none dared go against their
husbands and the church elders to say so.

"It was a difficult task," Ann Eliza wrote, her mother having
to play midwife to her rival during childbirth, then care for her and
the baby until she was well again, "but then polygamy is made up
of difficult tasks and trying situations. . . ."

After the Mormon's extended and successful mission in
England that gained many converts to the faith, a weekly flood of
young girls arrived in Utah looking for husbands. To add to her
mother's misery, and because of Brigham's further prodding, in
1856 Chauncey wed wives number three, four and five. Hardened
by now, a disillusioned Eliza Webb declared, "A few wives, more
or less, would make little difference to me now, and I would be as
well satisfied with one-fourth of a husband as with one-half."

No question, being raised in this unusual family circle marked
Ann Eliza. Having one mother, then two, then five and finally
four, (Chauncey divorced number five) left her with an insecurity
she would never lose. Under the doctrine of plural wives, she
acquired a secret hostility toward all men, albeit unconscious,
which blighted her own history of matrimony.

She could still conjure up the smell of the olive oil with which they had coated her body during her confirmation. That, along with the enforced ritual, made her sick to her stomach. The ceremony ended with her indoctrination into their arcane rites, after which she was required to take the oath of secrecy and obedience. She recalled how exhausting it all was, and how disenchanted she had been. Perhaps, she told herself, that was the beginning of her disassociation with Mormon ways, although it took eight more years to happen.

A man named John Hyde, claiming he had been initiated into the wonders of the faith, wrote of it: "It is impossible to state all the licentiousness, under the name of religion, that these sealing ordinances have occasioned." Suspect across the country because its rites were kept so secret, the Federal District Attorney of Utah labeled it, "a sink-hole of iniquity," and the noted Captain Richard Burton reported: ". . . the result is that human sacrifices are said to be performed within its walls." In truth, those sacred rites were harmless acts derived from the Bible, John Milton and Masonry. But the uninformed American public chose to believe the worst.

She thought back to the day Brigham forbade her to see a boy she adored. When she told a girlfriend of this, the girl retorted, "Perhaps Brother Brigham means to marry you himself."

"But he won't," she remembered snapping back. "I wouldn't have him if he asked me a thousand times—hateful old thing." But someone told Brigham and soon after, when he came upon her walking home, he stopped his carriage and ordered her to get into it.

"I heard you said you wouldn't marry me if I wanted you to so much," he began. Embarrassed, her reply was evasive, but from then on she sensed his mind was set on that very eventuality. She had not objected when the Prophet steered her into his theater, "for he wished to make an actress of me." She had acted, and enjoyed it, for the next two years. She remembered how Brigham was fond of saying that "Placed on a cannibal island and given the task of civilizing its people, I should straightway build a theater for the purpose."

At nearly eighteen, Ann Eliza wed a handsome English philanderer, James Dee, bore him two sons, then divorced him three years later. Never prettier, after her divorce twenty-one-year old Ann Eliza called that Christmas the merriest she had known in years. Many suitors constantly vied for her hand but she rejected them all.

After six serene months at her parents' home in South Cottonwood, Utah, helping with the chores and enjoying her boys, Brigham descended on them.When he left, her parents confessed that he had verbally bludgeoned them into promising her to him in marriage. Afraid to deny him, they had actually accepted on her behalf. She recorded in her autobiography that this was:

> . . . the shock of my life. I was frightened. The thought of it (the marriage) was a perfect horror. I thought Father had gone crazy, and I would not believe his statement for hours. When I finally realized that it was a fact I could do nothing but cry. The idea of an old man, sixty-seven years of age, the husband of about twenty wives living, asking me, at twenty-two, to be added to the number filled me with the utmost abhorrence.

Several versions exist of the event other than Ann Eliza's; all but hers maintaining that it was she who chased after Brigham, not the reverse. The truth probably lies somewhere in between. The fact remains that she managed to resist Brigham's courtship from 1864 to 1866 — two long years. At that point, patience exhausted, Brigham carried out one of his threats. After arranging the failure of a dubious business he'd railroaded her brother

Gilbert into, with debts he couldn't possibly pay, Brigham held bankruptcy and excommunication over his head. He informed the family if Ann Eliza's mother would force her to accept his proposal, he would forgive the debt. Out and out blackmail. This led to a loud quarrel, during which Eliza Webb stood up for her daughter against her leader, to no avail. Ann Eliza even went to Salt Lake City to plead with the stern-faced Prophet, but face-to-face, she lost heart. Returning home to her distraught family, she admitted through tears that she had given in.

In the week before the wedding, she had nightmares about Brigham. Awake, she knew every good Mormon believed it a great honor to marry their Prophet. The most powerful figure in their universe, he was the leader of the Latter Day Saints, a trailblazer, colonist, and statesman. Fully aware of his own importance, Brigham once answered a daughter who asked if he had read a certain history book, "No, daughter. I am too busy making history to find any time to read history."

Apostle Heber Kimball who married them, had cautioned earlier, "Some day there'll be one new wife who will give you trouble, Brigham." At the end of his marriage to Ann Eliza, he had to admit Kimball was right. She certainly did give him trouble, a whole countryful of it.

But now, through closed eyes and sleepless nights, the image of his stony profile and the pasted longish hair that curled above his collar and around his ears came back to haunt her. During the ceremony she saw his large pudgy fingers clasping and unclasping over his paunch. Just thinking of those hands as they had clutched at her naked breasts in lusty passion still caused the bile to rise in her throat. She could smell his smell, part freshly washed and ironed linen, and part body odor. Dear God, help me, she had prayed so hard then. Don't give me to this graying, portly old man of sixty-seven! But God hadn't heard. As the confirming statements loomed close, she repeated under her breath, "I am the

twenty-seventh woman with whom Brigham has recited these
marriage vows, the twenty-seventh woman!" Though born and
reared a Mormon, she shuddered at the idea of twenty-seven
wives!

Brigham Young's first wife died shortly after they were wed.
His next legal wife was in charge of Lion House, meeting the
needs of the other wives, giving orders to the eighteen male labor-
ers who tended the orchard, and supervising production of the
gardens and flour mill to the rear. She happily turned over the job
to Brigham's third and first plural wife when she retired, about the
time Brigham married Ann Eliza. She set a precedent by moving
out of Lion House to the White House, a small two-story home
Brigham owned. Taking advantage of this independent act, other
wives began to dispose themselves in various properties Brigham
had acquired about the city.

Regardless of where they lived, however, they were expected to
be present daily for dinner and prayers with him; only those were
excused who lived too far from Lion House. Because of the wealth
he'd accumulated, Brigham was able to scatter a number of his
wives and children to different dwellings. Four miles outside the
city he owned a two-story place with extensive acreage called the
Farmhouse. Many wives, including Ann Eliza, occupied it over the
years, doing the grueling physical work it required.

Besides these domiciles, Brigham kept an elaborate winter
mansion in St. George, Utah, and a fine old colonial home in
Provo with the city's telegraph office set up in one room. Each of
these places was run by a wife. Once Brigham was overheard to say
that if he could do it all over again, he would give every wife her
own home, rendering plural marriage "less inhibiting and fric-
tionless," although he admitted that would be quite an expensive
undertaking and require a lot of leg-work on the part of the
husband.

The announcement of his marriage to Ann Eliza was greeted frostily at both the Lion House and next door Bee House. For one thing, she was nearly a year younger than the newest wife, six years younger than the reigning queen of the harem, and forty-one years younger than Brigham's legal wife. They feared her youth and beauty would eclipse them in their husband's affections, and the need to share food, clothes and furnishings with even one more wife would take much away from their own security and comfort. Ann Eliza was as reluctant to meet with them as they with her. She knew the Lion House. As a youngster, she had been there as a part-time boarder on several occasions, playing and romping with many of Brigham's progeny. If the world imagined Mormon homes as sybaritic oriental bordellos, how very disappointing the reality would have been. In Irving Wallace's *The Twenty-Seventh Wife*, he graphically dispels that idea. "By the nature of its organization, sexuality was only faintly implied. Religious duty pervaded every parlor, hall and bedroom, and somehow this made sex seem a procreative bodily function rather than a pleasurable secret sin."

Brigham, however kept a bedroom at the Lion House accessible only to him, entered from his office. Richly furnished, it held a canopied four-poster bed, oak chairs, polished carved tables, a sofa, a wardrobe, a wall mirror and a large fireplace, all set off by thick-napped carpet.

Across from it was a series of bedroom suites, twelve by sixteen feet in size — reserved for wives with children, each a reflection of its inhabitant's personality or her pecking order in the harem. The forty-foot dining room held three tables capable of seating fifty women and children at one meal.

The third story, not open to outsiders, contained twenty gabled bedrooms; tourists often stopped in the street to count the smoking chimneys, trying to calculate the number of wives in residence. These were rooms mostly occupied by Brigham's childless wives or his older children, assigned by sex and age.

Eliza Snow, a former wife of Joseph Smith, and the poet laureate of Deseret, had the best room and sitting room, as befit her high station. She was sixty-five when Brigham escorted Ann Eliza in to formally meet her. Ann Eliza came to feel that she—the mediator of rows between disgruntled wives—was "the most intellectual of all the wives."

Ann Eliza had her favorites among them, and was grateful to those wives who showed her kindness. They were often the wives who had long before lost Brigham's favor. One had brought the silkworm culture to the marriage—a business her former husband had imported from France—and she managed their large and successful cocoonery outside the city. Plain, very religious, and in awe of her spouse, she had respect and responsibility, but little love from Brigham. The official midwife, she delivered most of the babies born in Lion House. At the final count Brigham had sired fifty-six.

Some wives were at least civil to Ann Eliza, but the fifteenth wife, an ailing short-tempered forty-seven-year old, was not one of them. Fanny Stenhouse, an apostate from Mormonism, who wrote a revealing book on the practice of polygamy in Utah, had this to say about her, "Brother Brigham acts toward her as if he had quite forgotten that he has ever married her, and she lives in all the loneliness of married spinsterhood."

Two wives openly hated and snubbed her. In their eyes, Brigham was God on earth. "It is almost painful to see the dumb worship which they accord to their master," wrote Ann Eliza, "and the cavalier manner in which it is received." One of them was mortally offended each time Brigham added another wife. "She would go about, crying bitterly for days, and would sometimes shut herself up in her room, refusing to see anyone. Her sorrow was the joke of the family, since no member of it could see what reason she had for indulging in it. She had but just got over mourning his alliance with Mary Van Cott, when she was called upon to grieve over his union with me. She knew me perfectly well . . . but on the occasion of my first visit after my marriage, she utterly ignored my presence, and would neither look at me or speak to me."

In twenty-six years of marriage to Brigham Young, the other wife had developed a cynicism about their religion; she enjoyed startling friends by stating, "Mormonism, polygamy, and the whole of it, is humbug, and may go to the devil for all I care." Perhaps this was because Brigham tended to avoid her too, never speaking to her unless he had to, punishing her by not frequenting her bed, thus not allowing her any more children after their first son.

Two of his wives were away the day Brigham brought Ann Eliza. One of these, a modest and kind southern woman, had lived at the Farmhouse for eight years, supervising the production of butter and cheese for the huge Young family. Worn out, she had come back to Lion house an invalid. It was during her recovery that Ann Eliza came to know her and more fully understand the constraints Brigham placed on his brood.

Pleased to learn that Ann Eliza intended to go ahead with her decision to divorce Brigham, Judge Hagan enlisted the aid of two locally prominent attorneys. Because the case was unprecedented and possibly weak, he wanted to plug every loophole he could. One way was to gather friends as well as influential Mormon haters around her: the Federal judge who might be trying the case, a politician and former military man to act as her legal "next friend" in court and, finally, a newspaperman who was employed by *The Salt Lake City Tribune*, an anti-Mormon paper. They became Ann Eliza's close friends, the most valuable being the High Justice of Utah, Judge James B. McKean, who had set a record for belligerent prosecution of Latter-Day Saints.

Nightly overwhelmed by a sense of desolate hopelessness at

not knowing what her fate would be, at each footstep in the hall she asked herself if it was someone coming to take her back to a dreadful death? She often fretted that she had put herself in the power of strangers to do with as they pleased. A thousand doubts plagued her. She thought of running away, back to mother. But she knew no Mormon would dare to shelter her in open rebellion against their leader. Brigham had so often thundered threats from the pulpit about the day "when we shall take the old broadsword, and ask, 'Are you for God?' and if you are not heartily on the Lord's side, (the Mormon side) you will be hewn down."

Daytimes she knew it was unlikely that Brigham would dare send an assassin into a Gentile hotel like Walker House; yet there was much evidence pointing to a secret service he had formed in 1838, and perhaps still kept, to frighten away or dispose of enemies of the Church. Horace Greeley quoted some United States soldiers camped near the city who said there were "not less than seventy-five distinct instances of murder by Mormons because of apostasy . . . known to the authorities here."

Only two years before Ann Eliza's defection, she had heard repeated tales told by Mark Twain of how Rockwell and Hickman (Brigham's paid hit-men) assassinated "intractable Gentiles." In this way, "Brigham Young 'managed' a great many murders," Ann Eliza was to report in her expose, "of which he would probably avow himself entirely guiltless, since his hands did not perform the deed. . ." This, admittedly, from an angry wife.

When Brigham learned Ann Eliza's three lawyers had filed her civil divorce suit, in it naming each detail of her complaint against him, he was upset and angry. As in all divorce cases, a good part of the fight was about money. Ann Eliza claimed that Brigham was enormously wealthy, worth millions, and in receipt of a monthly income of at least forty thousand dollars. As she had realized a mere $380 from the sale of the furniture, she asked for a $1,000 a month until the divorce was granted, another $200,000 for herself and children, and $20,000 to pay her attorneys' fees.

The news hit the papers almost immediately. The deserter of her faith, apostate Ann Eliza Webb Young became famous or infamous overnight, depending on one's point of view. At first Brigham neither acknowledged her action, denied her story, nor tried to woo her back.

Her divorce was talked of from coast to coast. The world debated the rights and wrongs of the case, even the question of the legality of marriage under polygamy. Now that even the public knew, Brigham sent Sisters to talk sense into Ann Eliza; his son-in-law to persuade her with a bribe that what she was doing would irreparably damage their Church. If she consented to drop the suit, Brigham promised her a divorce, $15,000, and a guarantee of safe passage out of Utah for herself and her boys.

She was sorely tempted by the chance of being able to "avoid the notoriety which I so hated. If it had been my own individual case alone, I should have eagerly accepted the offer, and made the compromise. But when I thought how much was involved, how many other lives would be affected by the decision . . . I put all thought of settlement aside."

Next, through others, Brigham tried intimidation. Now Ann Eliza's new Gentile friends found themselves under fire, and her family in a most insecure position. The hardest plea to resist was her mother's letter, begging her to recant. "My heart is broken, my dear and much-loved child," she wrote, along with many words harder to withstand.

"I longed to fly to her," Ann Eliza confessed, "but even to make her happy I could not violate my conscience, and go back into the old bondage of darkness again." She gave interviews, one of which was to a reporter from the *San Francisco Chronicle*, answering candid questions like, "If Amelia was a favorite [wife] of twelve years' standing, why did Brigham want to marry you?"

"Well, we think it is vanity," she replied. "They like to show that [even] if they are old men, they can marry young women." Then, wondering if she had said too much, she added in a fearful low tone, "Would you think that they could abduct me from here?" The reporter was surprised at such an idea. "Ah, you don't know them," she said quickly. "I have taken this room as high up as possible to protect myself. I dare not let my little boy leave the room, and I eat all my meals here."

Every newspaper in the country had fought to interview Brigham without success. But at this point Brigham granted one to a reporter from the *San Francisco Chronicle*. The favored reporter later confessed he'd found the Prophet an intimidating figure. Most of the interview consisted of Brigham's tirade against his enemies. Prompted by the reporter, he admitted he felt Ann Eliza's divorce was another part of the conspiracy against him. He made those in the room laugh at his satirical representations of those who opposed him. In response to the question of what step he would take should the court allow her suit for divorce, he sat perfectly still for a long time staring out at the twelve-foot wall surrounding the Lion House. Then he turned back to face the reporter. "Adultery," was his pronouncement. He would charge her with adultery. No more serious charge could be made by the Prophet who regarded adultery as the ultimate crime. Now the world would know his side of the story.

She began to be bombarded with requests for appearances. Phineas T. Barnum offered Ann Eliza $100,000 a year to let herself be exhibited. He had made Brigham the same offer three years before. Lecture managers' offers were tempting because her savings were gone and her purse empty. The one she liked the best came from a James Redpath of the Boston Lyceum Bureau. He had formed the bureau and converted lecturing into a paying proposition with Ralph Waldo Emerson, Henry Ward Beecher and Mary E. Livermore as clients. By adding Ann Eliza Young to his stable he hoped to make lecturing more topical and exciting.

Ann Eliza wavered. It was the journalist on the *Salt Lake City Tribune*, Major James Burton Pond, who changed her mind in favor of Redpath when he suggested that by taking the lecture platform and telling her story, she could educate the public about Mormonism. Until then, she would be totally dependent on the divorce action to solve her financial problems.

"I shrank from the very mention of it, and replied to the friends who proposed it that I could not, and would not, do it."

But the divorce was long in coming. Sunk in legal technicalities, would it require a territorial, or a Federal court to hear her case? They even argued over who should serve Brigham with the divorce papers. Their decisions proved a setback for Ann Eliza. Always her attorneys tried to see that the developments would not be pro-Mormon. When it was certain their case would not even be heard for another eight months, she knew she must take some action. Major Pond proposed that he become her full-time lecture manager, helping them both to acquire fame and fortune. Ann Eliza listened, and fretted. Could she do such a thing?

"To parade myself and my troubles before the world seemed such an indelicate thing to do!" Her Gentile friends reminded her of Brigham's ill treatment, how he was even now scandalizing her name, and how the lectures would give her a public platform from which to rebut his claims and hit out at the system she hated so much. This argument convinced her. And time and again in later years, she would defend her decision.

The Woman's Journal, a Boston suffragette publication, accused her of exploiting the fact that she was Brigham's plural wife. She snapped, "Does any one think that, for the sake of emolument, I could thus open my heart to the rude gaze of a curious public, bear all the slurs, slights, jeers, and aspersions that are cast at me by malicious Mormon and thoughtless Gentile papers, be made a byword of, have my name on every vulgar lip? Never. My womanhood revolts at the idea. As a means of support, I would never have

undertaken it. When I saw it was a duty, I adopted it without hes-
itation. . . ."

She wrote three lectures, revised many times until they satisfied her. "The first," according to *The Tribune*, was "a personal
record, in which the circumstances of her marriage with the
Prophet are detailed, and many racy incidents of the royal household given. . . . The second lecture grapples with polygamy, and
presents to the hearer a woman's view of 'the divine ordinance.'. . .
The third lecture . . . deals in a very able manner with the political
condition of Mormondom. . . ." While Ann Eliza was composing
these lectures, Major Pond was setting lecture dates. But unsure of
Ann Eliza's professionalism, he suggested she first speak at the
Walker House. Expecting a few Gentile friends, she was stunned
to walk into the large hotel parlor and find it jammed to capacity.
Conquering her first impulse to run away, she read the lecture
from her papers, making strong men and the ladies present silent-
ly weep in sympathy. She was a huge success.

Secret conferences were held in Ann Eliza's room. How to get
her safely out of Utah? The only way East was via the Union
Pacific, its point of embarkation the city of Ogden. Ann Eliza
would have to travel to Ogden on the local spur owned by
Brigham, and this she feared to do. It was decided to divert any
possible pursuers by buying her a ticket for Ogden, then taking her
at night in a private carriage to Uintah, a brief stop the Union
Pacific made beyond Ogden. Pond found an ideal traveling companion for her, the apostate and President of the Women's
National Anti-Polygamy Society, Mrs. Sarah A. Cooke.

First placing her boys in her parents' care to join her later, she
left her trunk at Walker House. A friend bought a new trunk, and
kept it at his place. Piece by piece, her personal belongings were
spirited from the hotel and packed in the new trunk. When it was
full, it was shipped to Laramie, Wyoming, in another person's
name. Their plan let them escape the city with the dawn; after a

few wrong turns, their driver reached Uintah where they were helped onto the train seconds before it departed.

Their sleeping car appointments were a wonder. Wyoming and freedom lay ahead and for a while as the train sped along at twenty-two miles an hour, Ann Eliza was filled with a sense of exultation. But after an hour or so, her high spirits wore off, leaving her desperately low and lonely. "What shall I do?" she asked in a tremulous tone.

"Keep up a brave heart, and think of the work before you," Mrs. Cooke counseled. But all Ann Eliza could think of was the person who would surely try to stop her from doing that work. Certainly she worried about her two small sons' safety with her parents and about her defection redounding on them all in some terrible way. And when she had to take the lecture platform in Laramie to deliver her now-memorized talks, would she be seen as an immoral concubine, or a victim of polygamy? And would she really be safe from Brigham and his henchmen there?

Major Pond arrived in Laramie a day or two later, carrying the edition of *The Tribune* that had come out the day after her departure. The story about her read in part: "Mrs. Ann Eliza Young left town yesterday to start on her lecturing tour in the East. . . . The lady departed without announcement, as her friends had reason to believe that efforts would be made to prevent her carrying out her design. . . ." She was heartened by the last sentence, "We predict abundant success for this lady in her new field of labor, and do not hesitate to express our belief that she is deserving of all the kindnesses that may be bestowed upon her."

She attracted a standing-room-only audience, a fact that surprised Major Pond. He realized for the first time that in her he had found an attraction that appealed to both sexes in every walk of life. But Ann Eliza, looking at the huge hall filled with people, was filled with terror. Initially worried that no one would come, she now feared the huge crowd. Too many, she thought, and later wrote, "As I looked into the crowded house . . . my courage almost left me. . . . But the thought of the poor women whose cause I was to plead . . . with firm step, and beating heart, I walked onto the platform, and stood facing my first audience, who greeted me with tumultuous applause."

She began in her rich clear voice, "The nineteenth wife of a man living in the nineteenth century, in a heathen country, would perhaps be considered a curiosity. But in civilized Christian America, where the abomination of polygamy is permitted by the Government, she is, of course, no curiosity." First defining words they might be unfamiliar with, she launched into her talk. Her lecture was a total success. The papers praised her and news of her triumph spread through the land. Major Pond was swamped with requests for engagements.

Her fears lessened, Ann Eliza delivered her second lecture. It traced the start and growth of the plural-wife doctrine from Joseph Smith's first mention of polygamy to his closest followers in 1843 to Brigham's formal pronouncement in 1852. A less personal account, it was more provocative and more dramatic. She told of the stealing of Gentile wives, and the justifying of their burgeoning harems by quoting the scriptures. The audience sat aghast as they learned Joseph Smith's claim that "the pure and exalted love of Jesus for Martha and Mary, her sister, as well as Mary Magdelene, showed that they were his plural wives, and that the marriage at Cana of Galilee was one of his bridal feasts."

She apologized for omitting certain spicy details, saying ". . . much that might be said, under some circumstances, cannot be told in a promiscuous [sic] assembly." In the final moments of her address she said that outsiders could not truly understand plural marriage as it was practiced. She also revealed her doubts and fears at leaving everything she knew to venture into their world, all new to her. She was again an unqualified success.

Two days later she boarded a Union Pacific train, headed East toward her heavy schedule of lectures. After Denver her stops in Kansas were Topeka, Lawrence and Leavenworth; in Missouri, St.Louis; in Illinois, Springfield, Burlington, Bloomington. After Chicago came a series of smaller bookings in Wisconsin and Illinois, and a final lecture in Freeport, with Boston to come. At a hundred dollars a night, he had gotten her almost more engagements than she could fill. Although she didn't say so, Ann Eliza was secretly enjoying her acclaim and celebrity.

Interviewed constantly, she worried about the silence of her Utah enemies. Then the bomb fell. The day before her first lecture in Boston the evening papers carried a "shameful article" (her words), a muckraking expose purporting to tell of Ann Eliza's love life. She was stunned. When she could speak, she told Major Pond, "Brigham Young's money is at the bottom of this." It threatened the ruin of all they'd achieved. An interview in a Chicago paper with Victoria Woodhull, the notorious advocate of free love, was another disaster. Woodhull professed first-hand knowledge of an affair Ann Eliza had with Major Pond. And approved of it. After all, Woodhull said, Ann Eliza had done no wrong. Her confirmation of the mythical affair further damaged Ann Eliza's name. In a state of near collapse, she awaited her entrance feeling she was about to be scalped.

This was the first lecture where Redpath personally led her on stage. He explained, "I have stepped out of my usual course to introduce Mrs. Young, as I want to be a good Christian as well as a good lyceum manager." This would be the twenty-third time she would tell her story, and the 2,000 people present listened soundlessly, applauding her for many minutes at the end of her talk. She had conquered, but there would still be ugly newspaper articles, and libelous accusations to overcome, and weary miles of travel to endure over the next nine years.

Some of Ann Eliza's greatest successes occurred in Utah.

Traveling between Ophir and Stockton, she heard that her long-dormant divorce action was revived and Brigham Young was forced to respond. He filed a lengthy reply to her suit on August 25, 1874, causing a series of front page sensations. CELESTIAL MARRIAGE AND SOCIAL HARLOTRY IDENTICAL . . . THE KINGDOM OF GOD ON ITS LAST LEGS . . . A WIFE IN THE STATE AND CONCUBINES IN THE CHURCH . . . were but a few of the sensational headlines. Brigham hedged, aware of a pending bill against polygamy, saying that Ann Eliza was never his legal wife. Instead, he asserted "she was and still is, the lawful wife of the said James L. Dee, never, as this defendant is now advised and believes, having been divorced from the said James L. Dee." He claimed his first wife, Mary Ann Angell, as his only legal wife. Without denying the adultery, he said theirs had been "a celestial marriage, a kind of mutual arrangment according to faith." He flatly rejected the charge that he had mistreated or ignored her. He maintained her monetary demands for alimony, a settlement, and court costs, were extreme. He also denied her claim that he was a wealthy man worth millions.

There must have been repercussions in the Lion House, even though his wives had been informed by his five lawyers that for good reason their husband had to publicly disown them. Ann Eliza replied that Brigham committed perjury in swearing she had never divorced Dee. She told the court her first divorce had taken place in 1873, and where to find the decree. Brigham replied since the Supreme Court had recently ruled that no Probate Court could deal with a divorce, this nullified Ann Eliza's suit. Six weeks later, the hearing judge told both factions he would render his decision early in the following year. When one of Brigham's attorneys bragged of the brilliance of his brief, an elder of the Church snapped, "You have complied with the law — and knocked hell out of the Kingdom!"

Six weeks later, Ann Eliza was to give her first talk in San

Francisco. So popular had she become that she got a flat fee of $1,000 for the three lectures. Somewhere along the lecture circuit, she was shown an item in the *Salt Lake City Evening News*. Buried in a column was an announcement:

> To Whom It May Concern.
> This is to certify that Ann Eliza Webb Young was cut off from the Church of Jesus Christ of Latter-Day Saints by the High Council, October 10th, 1874.

It was signed not by Brigham, but by a "Clerk of the High Council." The church had excommunicated her. For the rest of her life she claimed that she had quit it. In the wake of her expulsion, her father and mother were also expelled. Her mother broke her last ties with Mormonism when Ann Eliza sent money to bring her boys and move to Lockport, New York, near her sister. Her new home gave Ann Eliza a resting place between lectures. Ann Eliza was thrilled with the situation, her mother less so. She saw little of her peripatetic girl, busy earning their living.

Although the popularity of other lady lecturers waned, Ann Eliza enjoyed the best of times. She was still a fresh personality, attractive at thirty-one, and her material was topical. She lectured eight months out of every twelve, giving between 160 and 180 lectures each year, her ability ever improving. Major Pond wrote of her, "I have never found so eloquent, so interesting, so earnest a talker. She could sway audiences with her eloquence."

Now she consented to supply eager Eastern book publishers with her story. It turned out to be a tome of 605 pages, half of it a diatribe against polygamy, half an autobiography, subtitled "A Full Expose of Mormonism," by Ann Eliza Young. Its full title was *WIFE No. 19, or The Story OF A LIFE IN BONDAGE.*

Her book was printed in time to help keep her in the public eye and renew interest in her story. The hearing judge found the marriage between Brigham and Ann Eliza "legal and binding according to the laws of the Territory and of the United States," in spite of the fact that the ceremony had been the one used by the Mormon Church. He awarded her $3,000 to cover the costs of her suit, payable in ten days, and $500 a month in alimony, retroactive to the date the suit was filed. In other words, a total of $9,500, payable in twenty days.

In additon to the uproar this caused in Salt lake City, it brought castigation upon the judge. President Grant had never recognized polygamy, calling such marriages "licensed prostitution." By validating her marriage as legal, he had in effect made polygamy legal. Brigham, delighted at the victory of polygamy, was incensed at what he considered Ann Eliza's "extortion." He paid $3,000 but refused the rest, and was summoned to court. The judge declared that his judgment was "not appealable," and after a lengthy speech, ordered Brigham to pay a fine of twenty-five dollars and spend a day in jail for contempt.

Brigham became a free man again, but that judge was relieved of his judiciary post. His successor reversed the decision, decreeing Ann Eliza's marriage to Brigham had not been a legal one, so she was entitled to no alimony. The Mormon press loved this new judge but their triumph was short-lived when he resigned and a third judge took on Ann Eliza's suit, directing that Brigham pay up or be imprisoned. Thus the Prophet was jailed in his own house.

If Ann Eliza thought the case was close to a solution, she was wrong. President Grant now appointed J. Alexander White, Chief Justice of Utah, in charge of her case. Brigham's writ of *habeas corpus* was granted and he was free after five months confinement. Three months later Judge White was off the bench, the Senate having failed to confirm his appointment. He was replaced by a Judge Michael Schaeffer, who directed that Brigham pay Ann Eliza, but reduced the monthly sum to $100 and the $18,000 he now owed to $3,600. Brigham resisted. Judge Schaefferconfiscated three span of his horses, three span of mules, three cows, three carriages, and three wagons and prepared to auction them off. A weary Brigham agreed to pay up.

It took four years of legal manuvers, before Judge Schaeffer handed down a final decision, one that could not be appealed when he came to the conclusion that Ann Eliza hadn't been legally wed to Brigham Young, therefore any alimony due her was annulled. Brigham need pay only her court costs, the suit would then be closed. Everyone seemed relieved to have it done with, including Ann Eliza. Brigham had won, but had given up his last chance to accord plural marriage legal status. Now, in the eyes of the law, all but his first wife were labeled concubines. If any one of them left him now, she could expect neither support nor social standing.

The legal fight against his rebellious nineteenth wife was Brigham's last. Although he did not show his seventy-six years, he was not well, and four months later he lay dying. In a matter of days his health worsened and on August 29, he met his maker calling out "Joseph" three times before he expired. Of his wives, only Ann Eliza was absent at his funeral. In his will Brigham provided for every wife but Ann Eliza. His loss left his flock saddened but still vigilant. They elected a new leader, John Taylor, an Englishman, who continued to defy the world of Gentiles.

Two hundred Gentile women of Salt Lake City met to draw up a petition to Mrs. Hayes, President Rutherford B. Hayes' wife, demanding that the outlawing of polygamy be the price of statehood. Impressed because Utah had granted its women the vote in 1870, two suffragettes ignored the polygamy aspect and arranged a meeting between two of the deceased prophet's wives and Mrs. Hayes, trying to persuade her of the virtues of plural marriage. Hearing of this, Ann Eliza sent a long impassioned letter of her own to the First Lady and then released it to the press.

It included a paragraph on voting. "I voted once — being compelled to do so by Brigham Young — and his coachman was deputized to take me to the polls and show me how to vote. His instructions consisted in telling me to write my name on a piece of paper which he handed to me, and to this day I remain in blissful ignorance of whom I cast my only vote for. This . . . is only one of the least of the outrageous absurdities perpetrated in Utah, in connection with the ballot. . . ." And it ended, "Polygamy desolates every home which it enters. Surely it will be neither improper nor unwise for you to exert your influence against that vast and increasing crime. . . ." At each lecture she was apt to implore her audiences, "Will you not do something? Year by year this evil is growing great and strong and dangerous. . . ."

It remained for Chester A. Arthur, successor to elected President Garfield after his murder, to do something. In a December message to Congress, he called plural marriage "this odious crime, so revolting to the moral and religious sense of Christendom." The Edmunds bill against polygamy had more stringent restrictions, but did stipulate amnesty to all who had been polygamous prior to the passage of the law, and legitimized children born before 1883. A bloc of Southern senators, still seething at the injustices they felt the South had suffered after the Civil War, balked against its passage. However, the Senate did pass the Edmunds Bill on February 12, 1882.

Ann Eliza was thrilled, but she was also unhappy at the strong-arm methods used by Federal agents who would break into Mormon homes while wives were in bed or dressing. "It must be admitted," she wrote, "that some officials took a malicious delight in harassing Mormon women as well as men."

The enemy was all but vanquished, she thought, and her long crusade nearly at an end. Besides, she was sick of uncomfortable trains, filthy flea-infested hotel beds, the constant exhibiting of herself. Her personal life had become complicated. Her mother's illness in 1880 had necessitated placing her in a sanitorium in Michigan. Trying to spread herself between East and Midwest was hard to arrange, and her poor health—bouts with fatigue and a nervous stomach—became more frequent.

Then occurred a series of events that changed everything. In 1881 she was introduced to an admirer named Moses R. Denning. A big, extroverted, middle-aged fellow with a crippled hand, Denning was charming and rich, and an important resident of Manistee, Michigan. He was twenty-five years married, with children, but when he invited Ann Eliza to be his house guest the next time she spoke in his town, she accepted. She arrived sometime late in 1881, and her visit shattered the Dennings' union. Fifty-three-year-old Moses and thirty-seven-year-old Ann Eliza fell madly in love. By the time she returned a year later, he had begun divorce proceedings. Moses' marriage was formally dissolved on February 7, 1883. Two and a half months later in May of 1883, he and Ann Eliza met in the town of Lodi, Ohio, where they had friends, to be joined in wedlock.

The news of their marriage caused excitement across the country. *The Daily Democrat* of Albuquerque summed it up as follows: "It affords us unusual pleasure to announce the recent marriage of Ann Eliza (Brigham Young's 19th flame) to an Ohio man. Not only does it relieve the country of a female lecturer, but at the same time a long suffering nation gets even with the irrepressible Ohio man." After honeymooning in Toledo, the couple returned to the groom's home in Manistee.

But the pleasures of domestic bliss eluded her. Instead of the welcome Ann Eliza hoped for, the society women of Manistee saw her "as someone notorious and something of a freak," and diligently snubbed her. In the decade that followed her life unravelled. Her mother, brought from the sanitorium to live with them, died "of paralysis." It proved futile to look to her husband for companionship, for Moses Denning traveled constantly—usually without

her — visiting his children by his first wife and attending to invest-
ments and his involvement in politics. For years she suffered from
a condition called "nervous dyspepsia" and sought various cures.
Her sons' health proved fragile. Both would eventually die of
tuberculosis. Denning turned out to be a womanizer who dallied
with servant girls before her eyes. By January 1893 she filed for
divorce. Her Manistee home was heavily mortgaged and she was
forced to sell it. She republished her book in 1908, but it failed —
by now its subject matter was merely a curiosity.

Ann Eliza died somewhere between 1909 and 1930. She was
reported to have died in New York City, Rochester, or Brooklyn,
New York, Arizona or California — no one seems to know for
sure. She almost certainly died in poverty. Facts aside, her years of
lecturing about the country bore fruit in the deeds of ladies like
Susan B. Anthony, who began the fight to give the women of
America the vote; and Mary Walker and Victoria Woodhull, who
opened the way for women to have careers. However it was Ann
Eliza Webb Young alone who courageously defied her church
in pleading for freedom and justice for the enslaved women of
her faith.

Young, Ann Eliza Webb. *WIFE No. 19, or The Story OF A LIFE IN BONDAGE.*
Hartford, Conn.: Dustin Gilman and Co., 1875, 1983.

Wallace, Irving. *The Twenty-Seventh Wife.* New York City: Simon & Schuster,
1961.

Seagraves, Anne. *High-Spirited Women of the West.* Hayden, Idaho: 1992.

Reiter, Joan Swallow. *The Old West,* Vol. 23: The Women. Alexandria, Va.,
Time/Life Books, 1978.

Brodie, Fawn M. "Ann Eliza Webb Young," *Notable American Women.* Vol.3. Edited
by Edward T. & Janet W. James. Cambridge, Mass.: Harvard University Press,
Bellknap Press, 1971.

Gray, Dorothy. *Women of the West,* Millbrae, Calif.: Les Femmes, 1976.

Mystic Mary Austin

From earliest childhood, Mary Austin practiced being two people. In her autobiography, *Earth Horizon*, published in 1932, she even spoke of herself in the third person. "Although she was highly competent in all subjects which required verbal facility," she wrote, "she had serious deficiencies in other skills. Her penmanship was atrocious, she had no real comprehension of arithmetic, and because she learned to read by the word method, she could not spell." It is sad that Mary's failings weren't recognized as dyslexia in those days and treated.

Perhaps she also struggled with dyslexia's frequent companion learning difficulty, attention deficit disorder. She knew she was bright, but not why she saw things so differently. "Why on earth or why in heaven for that matter," she wrote, "should anybody make a mind like mine and then not use it."

Mary spent a lot of time with Indians of the Southwest, and held their legends and traditions in great respect. She took her autobiography's title from the Sia tribe's "Rain Song," which meant "Earth Horizon is the incalculable blue ring of sky meeting earth, which is the source of experience." Writer, naturalist, feminist, mystic, Mary Hunter Austin often erred on the side of wordiness and dogmatism. But when ruled by the alter ego about which she wrote, her poetry and prose were incredibly lyrical and beautiful.

Born September 9, 1869, in the Hunter family home on Plum

Street in Carlinville, Illinois, Mary was the second girl and fourth of the Hunter's six living children; two others had died in infancy. Mary's parents were British-born George Hunter and American Susanna Savilla Graham. George Hunter had emigrated with his older brother in a company of Englishmen bound for the village of Alton, Illinois. Mary never tired of hearing her father's colorful anecdotes of the river trip he made into the American wilderness and the sights he saw. George settled in Carlinville after his brother moved on West. One of the small city's attractions for him was the number of English families already living there.

After completing law studies in 1855, George was admitted to the bar at the age of twenty-four. With the onset of the Civil War in 1861, however, George Hunter gave up his brand new law practice to enlist. Following the three months voluntary training, he earned a captain's rank by organizing his own company of Illinois volunteers. And in the week before going off to the war, he married Mary's mother, Susanna Savilla Graham.

She was descended from the prominent Dugger family (an Americanized version of the French *Daguerre*). Susanna's forebear, Pierre, came to America with the Marquis de Lafayette during the Revolutionary War and liked it so well that he stayed. She was also distantly related to the Louis Daguerre who invented the daguerreotype.

By age eighteen, Susanna had mastered the household arts required of young ladies of the day. In addition, she could do several kinds of needlework and concoct toilet waters, sachets, and cordials. When she turned "Temperance" shortly after marrying George, however, she had no further use for spirits or their recipes. Besides, her uncle's store stocked many alcoholic beverages by then as well as ready-made clothes, obviating the need even to spin and weave.

Mary's most vivid childhood memories were of being out of

doors, even at two and a half. For the rest of her life just being out in the fresh air wherever she lived inspired her and filled a need and deep yearning. Brother Jim was six and Mary barely four when "I-Mary" became a part of her consciousness.

> Mother was kneading the bread, she wrote, and Jim was studiously reciting his A B C's. At the other corner of the bread board, Mary was busy with a bit of pinched-off dough and looking over his shoulder. . . . Presently Jim pointed out an *I*.
> "Eye?" said Mary, plumping one floury finger on her own eye.
> "No," said Mother, "I, myself, I want a drink. I-Mary." She saw the room, her mother and brother, even the flannel dress and chambray pinafore she wore and the bit of dough she'd rolled into a grimy fat worm. And inside her, I-Mary, looking on. I-Mary, I-Mary, I-Mary!

At a remarkably tender age, Mary had made a discovery that would alter the course of her life.

In her "I-Mary" persona, she could escape the stresses of daily existence; her awareness of a reality other than the ordinary world around her gave her moments of pure exaltation.

At six, wandering off by herself one afternoon, Mary climbed a nearby knoll behind their orchard. Touched by a gentle breeze, she stood in the shade of a tall walnut tree, and had an experience she described a half century later:

> Earth and sky and tree and wind-blown grass and the child in the midst of them came alive together with a pulsing light of consciousness. There was a wild foxglove at the child's feet and a bee dozing about it and to this day I can recall the swift inclusive awareness of each for the

whole—I in them and they in me and all of us enclosed
in a warm lucent bubble of livingness. How long this inef-
fable moment lasted I never knew. It broke like a bubble at
the sudden singing of a bird, and the wind blew and the
world was the same as ever—only never quite the same.
The experience so initiated has been the one abiding reality of my life. . . .

She treasured the memory; in her mind it was synonymous
with "God." It was about this time that Mary began to notice her
mother's coolness toward her. She writes of a twilight hour when
her mother rocked the baby in front of the fire while telling her
and her brother stories of the war and old times. Brother Jim
leaned over Mother's shoulder. Mary gradually let herself snuggle
into Mother's knee, only to feel it moving subtly out from under
her.

"Hadn't you better get your stool, Mary?"

Mary got her stool. That was the day she learned that I-Mary
didn't need to be taken up and comforted, and to be I-Mary was
much more satisfying than being Mary-by-herself. She already
knew that only certain things could be said in front of Mother;
other private things you kept to share with Father.

She was between three and five when she began to get into
trouble over telling family stories, some she had heard and others
she had seen.

"You just imagined it," said Mother.

"What is 'magine, Mama?"

"Thinking you see things when you don't." She tried to make
Mary understand the difference between imagination and reality.
And storying—telling things as if she'd seen them when she had-
n't—was wicked. "But how did you know the difference between
seeing and thinking you had seen?" she begged to know. Her two-
years-older brother Jim, already a stern moralist, always told on

her. And her mother spoke of punishment to keep her, she said, from growing up to be a storyteller. "Well," Mary maintained, "she had seen them, and if she was punished for it, she'd simply have to stand it."

Mary was seven when she learned that live people wrote books and got paid for it. She not only loved handling books, the ones with nice paper, pictures, or gold edges to their pages, but quickly memorized and quoted from them. Her first writing efforts, her version of poetry which "neither jingled nor rhymed," brought shouts of laughter from her family.

Even as she grew, Mary had an embarrassing habit of speaking out. She couldn't stop, she said, because she never knew when it would happen. "She would blurt out things, inexcusable private things that offended visitors and mortified her mother. But she never knew until she saw their shocked faces that she had done it again. Nor did she understand why it was so annoying."

Constantly scolding and punishing her caused her mother to shed tears of vexation, crying "I think the child is possessed." She worried that people would suppose she'd been gossiping. Pressed for an explanation, Mary said, "It was like a little bird that hopped out of her mind, onto her tongue, before she could stop it." In older years she would blame it on something seen, a look, a tone, something so slight that she let the little bird out before she realized it. "To this day," she stated in her autobiography, "let her come into a room where there is a situation being saved, a secret antagonism guarded, and unless she is warned ... Mary in the first half-minute can quite innocently explode the whole works." Although she doesn't say so, her mother's subtle and constant rejections must have hurt her. Her close bonding with her beloved father was a much different story. Mary pictured her father as a man of medium height, his long brown hair with auburn tints worn brushed back in the fashion of the day. He affected a full mustache and beard but even those, she said, could not mask his handsome features and keen blue eyes.

Less evidently attractive, her mother Susanna's strong featured face, Scotch harebell blue eyes, pink and clear complexion, dimpled left cheek and the tiny cleft in her chin labeled her "sweetly pretty." Mary inherited her mother's unusually thick dark brown hair. Susanna wore hers parted in the middle and drawn severely back into a knot as befitted a proper Methodist lady. Mary let her hair hang loose about her head and shoulders whenever she could. It took so many hairpins to secure it to her head, and it was so heavy that it gave her a headache.

George Hunter always drew cartoons to make his children laugh, but he wanted them to be able to draw and paint better than that. To that end, he sent to London for a special art book. Mary copied its sketch of the church at Stratford-on-Avon so often that she recognized it immediately when she visited there years later. The only other thing she learned to draw by heart was her father's cartoon of Horace Greeley. She confessed that, whenever seated and waiting for a telephone call, she always drew Horace, instead of the doodles others made.

Her father delighted in Mary's intelligence and did what he could to challenge it. At eight she read a short-story version of *Ivanhoe*, which struck her as thrilling. "Said Father, 'I hope you will read all of Scott when you are older;' it was the sort of thing it was never safe to say to Mary unless you expected it to happen." She spotted a full set of Scott's works at Moran's, their local book store, and asked her father if they might borrow the volume of *Ivanhoe*. Father thought it far too old for her.

"I've already read *Lady of the Lake*", she announced. *Ivanhoe* was duly borrowed. Her father read much of it aloud, explaining as he went along. But Mary read it all, guessing at the words she couldn't pronounce, faithfully wading through even the footnotes and the dry appendix. She knew then, she wrote, that she wanted to write books like that, "books you could walk around in."

Even though, on Father's advice, Mary read no more Scott for several years, she now had a gauge by which to measure all books. They were either to be "walked about in" or "paper on the wall," wallpaper being a recent import to their city from the more genteel East. "A wall-paper book," Mary declared, "was one you couldn't walk around in, as you did in *Alice In Wonderland* or *Ivanhoe*, with notes."

She said of herself, "It was only in the matter of moral attitudes that Mary came into anything like conflict with her time." Taking it for granted that everyone felt about everything as she did, "Mary was convinced there shouldn't be any such thing as moral attitudes. Morals, yes! Things you should or shouldn't do on sufficient reason; but why take up attitudes about it?"

It was during his army service that her father contracted malarial fevers which, aggravated by severe asthma attacks, would plague him the rest of his life. Very worrisome to Susanna was the health of their succession of babies, several of whom carried incipient signs of a lameness due, it was believed, to their father's poor health.

From *Earth Horizon* again, Mary relates the changes that began in 1877 when she was nine. "The children had grown up accustomed to the labored, strangling rhythm of their father's asthma, the odor of burning pastilles, the night alarms, and their own helplessness about it, but this new illness came on so insidiously and intermittently...." She never knew what it was that her father suffered from, but only that it was excruciating. He underwent an operation that did not cure the problem.

"The end came on October 29, 1878.... For once Mary had nothing to say; she laid herself dumbly against the sharp edge of sorrow, fearful that she would miss, as she thought she had missed her father's last moments, the least aching instant of loss."

This marked the end of that life style, those friends, the house and orchard, the freedoms of Plum Street. Two months later, in a cramped little house in town—all they could afford—Mary had barely recovered from a bad sore throat when her younger sister Jennie came down with a worse case of it. Jennie's soon developed into a fatal diptheria which caused her sudden death. "I remember in the bleak little burying ground looking up at my mother in her weeds and making toward her for the last time in my life the child's instinctive gesture for comfort, and being thrust off in so wild a renewal of Susie's own sense of loss. . . ." Mary referred to her mother as Susie in seeming empathy, for nowhere in her writings does she blame the grief-stricken harried woman who loved her so little.

After her husband's death, Susanna went out nursing to earn the family's keep. "A woman who has had seven children in fifteen years, and an invalid husband, should know how to do that," Mary commented. For her part, as elder sister, "She would hurry home from school, collect baby Georgie from the woman who took care of him for a pittance during the day, clean up, cook supper, sleep with one ear awake toward the child who became the very apple of her eye, scramble through breakfast, put up lunch for herself and Jim, deliver her young charge and, if anything went wrong, be held responsible."

There is no question that Mary's "differentness," and the loss of ". . .all those luminous contacts with beauty in the brook, in the bird, in the flower, from which Mary's spiritual life had sprung," caused problems in her school years. A quick trip to Kansas with Mother and George to visit Aunt Mary and Uncle Peter on their farm, paid for by Grandfather, where she was able to run and play outdoors with a dozen cousins, acted as a refresher. The following summer a check came from Uncle Charlie and Aunt Mary Lane, along with an invitation to spend six weeks with them in Boston. Boston and its environs struck Mary as familiar; having met the look and history of New England in so many books.

Mary was a voracious reader by then. But her quick mind, her need to explore and question, didn't suit most of her teachers who wanted their pupils to be agreeable, well-mannered little robots. Of the times, Mary wrote, "There was still, in the late seventies, a general notion that book learning wasn't directly applicable to daily life. . . ."

At eighteen Mary felt unattractive. A student at Blackburn College, Mary described herself as ". . .rather under the average height, not well filled out, with the slightly sallow pallor of the malarial country, with a tendency to bluish shadows under the eyes, and made to look older than she was by the mass of tawny hair, brown with coppery glints, thick and springy, falling below her knees when loosed, and difficult to get under any sort of hat suitable to her years." Bangs were in fashion that winter, but by the time Mary graduated bangs had been replaced by a high pompadour. Regarding the clothes of the day, Mary described them as dresses with plain "basque" fronts and heavily draped skirts, puffed out in the back over huge bustles of wire and buckram, and drawn in at the waist with the popular tight-as-a-glove corset. Mary damned them as "probably the worst ever designed for the immature girlish figure."

Trying to prepare her for future social interaction with boys, her mother took great pains to impress upon Mary that one didn't talk to males of the beauties of nature, or her fossil collection, or quote poetry. "A very little experience demonstrated that Susie was right. You gathered that outdoors as a subject of conversation was boring to most people."

Elaborating on that theme, she added, "I suspect that Mary's mother was more than a little troubled by Mary's interest in men older than herself. Moreover, Mary had a way of talking to men more directly, more disputatiously, than was usual for young girls."

According to books on the subject, "The Lady must be sufficiently well read to be able to introduce aptly the most fruitful topics, but she was not to express an opinion on them. The gentleman will tell the lady what to think." One can only imagine how poorly this advice sat with Mary! She disdained the use of wiles on boys. As for "post-office," she hated such games. If she wanted to kiss a boy, she would; she saw no sense in working up to it. In keeping with the morality of the times, she reported, in some homes they still modestly cloaked their piano's legs in chintz ruffles.

Mary wrote of longing for something she didn't find in her Methodist faith. Later they would "read" her out of the church because she organized a community theater movement, one sin among many she committed against the faith. Mary did not care. She observed that Protestant sects were more easily abandoned than religions whose hold was stronger.

By then, due to selling the farm, Susanna was able to move the family to a better house and neighborhood. But Mary found life there so dull that one day, disguised as a poor Irish widow, she went begging about the neighborhood with great success; she kept the bread and old clothes given her, but returned Lawyer Burton's gift of money. Susie told her that was what came of reading strange books.

In 1885, in the middle of her second semester at the State Normal School, Mary suffered a nervous breakdown. They blamed it on overwork but Mary knew better. It was due to being bored, nagged and regimented. It was "their repetitive pedagogic methods," she said, and being forced to creep at their intellectual pace "with the least allowance for individual variation." It violated "the natural motions of the mind."

She couldn't explain her ailments to the doctor — a man who depended heavily on quinine and calomel, convinced as he was that every woman's ailment was due to being a female. He claimed the fastest cure was "severe doses of housework and child-bearing," adding, "The only work a female should do is beside her own fireside."

Bloomington got arc lights about this time, and Carlinville

had them a year or two later. Telephones were in the offing, but none of this altered the male conviction that whatever was the matter with women was the direct result of their gender. Pregnancy, despite their participation in it, was also classified as an illness. Worse, in a topflight magazine, a young male writer theorized that women were a subspecies, intended only for propagation.

Mary stoutly resisted the ideal foisted upon the American woman, best summed up in a verse by one Mattie Lumpkin, quoted verbatim in Mary's autobiography, complete with the author's exclamation marks:

> *Be a woman! On to duty!*
> *Raise the world from all that's low!*
> *Place high in the social heaven*
> *Virtue's fair and radiant bow!*
> *Lend they Influence to each effort*
> *That will raise our nature human!*
> *Be not Fashion's gilded lady,*
> *Be a brave, whole-souled, true woman!*

Mary returned to Blackburn College in 1884, studied art, then switched to a science major, graduating with a B.S. degree in 1888. Following after brother Jim, the family moved West that same year to a desert homestead in Tejon, California, at the edge of the San Joaquin Valley. As usual, nobody asked Mary's opinion. It was just assumed they must all live together on Jim's land. In Tejon, during the hot summer, they had a stretch of near starvation. In near-failing health, Mary ate the grapes growing wild in the canyons, and recovered.

"Plagued with an anxiety to know," she sat outside on moonlit nights listening to the little owls on the roof of Susie's hut, the calls of the coyotes, the shuffling gait of starving cattle, the patter of little field mice and the kangaroo rat. Once, in daylight, she followed a bobcat to its den, and lay down before it to gaze at the wild creature, eye to eye, for several hours.

In January of 1889 the Tejon Ranch's owner, General Edward Fitzgerald Beale, arrived and settled in. This was the Beale who, as a young lieutenant, went with General Kearny to parley with Pio Pico, the last Mexican governor. He was the Beale who carried the official evidence of the 1848 gold discovery back to the president in Washington. And the same Beale who was appointed the Commissioner of Indian Affairs, and who gathered into the Tejon area the remnants of the Central California tribes. He knew everything and everyone of importance in his day and Mary was thrilled to make his acquaintance.

He took her with him to the Indian Village; she sat and heard their stories. He arranged for her to get government documents, reports of military explorations, agricultural reports, geological and botanical surveys. Her health improved rapidly. She spent each day on horseback, attending round-ups, shearings, brandings, observing animals and Indians in their habits and customs, taking notes. It was a mind-shattering, glorious period.

The family moved again, courtesy of General Beale, this time to Rose Station, a stagecoach stop on his land just below the Tejon Pass. Unlike Jim's arid land with no water source, this was farm land with water of its own. Having water allowed Mary's family to furnish travelers with meals and hay, thus affording them a living. Just when Mary decided she needed an income she was hired to live at Mountain View Farm and teach neighboring ranchers' children, whom she reached by cart and horse.

It was there she met her husband-to-be, Stafford Wallace Austin, son of a Hawaiian missionary family. After a stilted, rather unromantic courtship, they married in 1891 when Mary was twenty-three. Something of a homegrown aristocrat, Austin seemed doomed to fail at everything he tried except teaching. He failed first as a wine grape grower, next as the on-site manager of an irrigation project his brother promoted for Owens Valley. When that project died aborning, Austin went to San Francisco to confer with his brother.

Mary joined him there late in the spring of 1892. Her personal mission: to meet with Ina Coolbrith, first librarian of the Oakland Free Library, for advice on her writing. Coolbrith was a published poet whose work often appeared in the *Overland Monthly*. She explained to Mary how professional writers submitted their manuscripts and sent her off with a recommendation to see the editor of that popular publication. To Mary's delight, he accepted two of her stories, only later defaulting on the second when the publication folded. By then, Mary was preoccupied with more urgent matters than her stories or her husband's occupation. She had discovered she was pregnant.

The Austin brothers' company failed in 1892. Ruth, Mary's beautiful child, was born retarded on October 30 of that same year. Life was now doubly hard for Mary; suspecting her marriage was a failure, she had to resume teaching to support the family, with no time to write or relax.

After several years, she separated from Austin to accept a teaching post at Inyo Academy in Bishop, California, where she and the child lived in a small room above the cellar of the Drake Hotel. Returning at the end of the school day she was apt to find the room a shambles, dishes broken, food spilled, the child wailing and filthy from her own feces. Neighbors criticized her severely for leaving the girl alone, calling her a bad mother. Admitting she could not look after Ruth properly and teach at the same time, Mary searched for a boarding situation, and found a childless couple who were happy to take the child.

Able to breathe again, Mary felt inspired. A new friend, a Miss Williams who taught at the Indian School a few miles away, also aspired to be a writer. The two women spent many pleasant evenings together, reading and critiquing each other's efforts. One of Miss Williams' grave concerns was the practice of *mahala*-chasing, the pastime of carousing Anglo youths of the town. It was a game of running down and harrassing Indian girls on their way home from working all day as servants in the town's more affluent homes. One girl who resisted was kicked to death, and two others who were raped committed suicide. This was so detestable to Mary that she was forever after a staunch advocate for Indian rights.

At this point her husband gained a teaching job in her district. At last they were together and for once all was going well. Two salaries allowed for the paying off of old debts. Mary sold another story. Austin was a fine teacher, but he acutely disliked the work and refused every lucrative offer he got from other parts of the state. Mary was distressed by his seeming lack of the will to succeed.

Her mother's sudden death and her deep sorrow over Ruth's condition combined to make her ill. During a brief stay in Los Angeles for treatment, she contacted Charles Lummis, editor of the magazine *Land of Sunshine*. He and his wife befriended Mary and he bought the poem she sent him. Her pleasure in this was short-lived, however. Upon her return she found Austin had resigned his post as Superintendent of County Schools only months after taking it, and had applied for the job as Registrar of the Desert Land Office at Inyo's county seat, Independence. He took it for granted that Mary would fill out the rest of his term in addition to her own teaching chores, then join him at the new location. She was furious. Another small town!

Again overwork and aggravation forced her to seek medical help, this time in Oakland. While there, she attended a lecture entitled "Relaxation," based on Annie Payson Call's current book *Power Through Repose*. It changed her thinking. From then on she tried to apply the principles of relaxation and psychic energy to her work, the latter aspect taught her by a Paiute shaman.

Her move to Independence, California to join her husband actually proved a blessing in disguise, for near the base of the mountains was an Indian campsite. There Mary spent many hours learning Indian ways. But after nearly a year, she felt the need for the stimulus of people involved in the arts. Remembering editor Lummis' reputation for encouraging new talent, she resolved to move back to Los Angeles. Austin had only mild objections. She took seven-year-old Ruth with her, hoping to find a medical solution to the child's problems.

Lummis, an authority on Mexican-Indian culture, called himself Don Carlos and affected Mexican dress. His home was noted for being a waystation for the famous of stage and print, as well as for new talents like Mary. The friendships she made there would, in future, help to open doors. David Starr Jordan, president of Stanford University, shared her passion for the study of plant and animal species; another, Frederick Webb Hodge, was a famous anthropologist and specialist in Indian ethnology; Charlotte Perkins Gilman was a well-known lecturer and writer who was fighting for social and economic freedom for women. She and Mary found they had many life experiences in common.

Mary accidentally walked into a teaching assignment at Los Angeles' Normal School by taking over a class in wildlife from a young woman who patently knew little about her subject. With that as a base of income, Mary began to write intensively. She was offered a good post in the fall at a school in northern California. Still thinking of herself as part of a couple she wrote to Austin, asking him to join her, saying her salary would support them both until he could find a job. Offended, he refused. She even went to see him, hoping to talk him into changing his mind, but he said she should go it alone for another year.

During that year she received a note from her sister-in-law that drove her wild. It told that, because of other relatives with similar disorders, she believed that Ruth's mental retardation was congenital. Mary was so furious with Austin she almost couldn't speak. Why, she cried, hadn't he let her know this before they had a child? Austin replied that he thought it improper to divulge family secrets like that. Mary felt betrayed beyond forbearance. This was the emotional end of their marriage for her.

Mary sold a few stories during this lean period, enough to encourage her to determine that writing would be her career. She and Austin moved from one arid desert town to another, and while he fell in and out of intermittent jobs, Mary spent off-hours writing studies of the land and the Indians she met. In her book, *The Land of Journeys' Ending*, she included this charming legend:

> Still, among the tribes nearest, by their mode of life, to the people of the pits, lingers a myth of the Pleiades as little lost children, who, because their mothers gave them no meat for the play cooking pots around which they danced in the long Southern twilights, grew light and lighter, drifting skyward till only the vault stayed them. That is why, as Papago mothers will explain to you, Papago babies are kept as fat as pin-cushions; and ever after, the Pithouse mothers, as the constellation of the starry dance rose over the hyacinthine ranges, came hurrying up the hatchways to stay the feet of some little brown ghost with the comforting flame and the smell of savory dishes.

Finally Mary's dedicated efforts paid off. In 1903, fourteen of her written sketches were published as *The Land of Little Rain*. Even as her marriage failed, this first slender volume brought her fame. Mary held very strong beliefs about writing and writers.

> To take the measure of his own subconscious capacity, to control and direct it, to take advantage of its sudden spurts of superiority and restrict its lapses into infantilism, is the

first business of the practising novelist. It becomes—the deep self of the creative writer—another entity almost, with which he learns to live and never be surprised at, an entity so much more than his immediate sensory self. . . . Many novelists do accept mediumistic phenomena as evidential. Others discover the capacity of this subliminal self for something that I have called . . . sleight of mind, since psychologists have so far failed to name it. It is so quick, this other entity—as much quicker than the intellect as the cat is quicker than the mouse—so inherently anxious to arrive at the given point before the intelligence can forestall it, that it performs tricks equivalent to sleight of hand, tricks that occasionally deceive its host.

She left Austin, this time for good. She spent the ensuing years in Carmel, California, and New York City as an accepted member of the inner circle in politics, society and the arts . Her friends were Jack London, Bret Harte, Mark Twain, Ina Coolbrith, George Bernard Shaw, the Joseph Conrads, Hilaire Belloc, William Butler Yeats, H. G. Wells, and Lou and Herbert Hoover.

Once, before returning to Carmel, Mary happened to attend a lecture in San Diego given by a woman who provided a partial explanation as to why her mother treated Mary with such disaffection. She said that in her youth she "had been more than a friend to your father." On the heels of this confidence, she added, "I didn't know your mother, but I know she didn't want you." This confirmed her sense of her mother's rejection of her.

Mary wrote of this era: "I had already put my marriage aside. When I came home from Europe the first time, I knew that I could never take it up again. . . . The proposal of divorce came from me. I thought there was still a chance that if he were free he might make a more satisfactory marriage." Mary obtained her divorce in 1918, the year their institutionalized daughter Ruth died at the age of twenty-two. It was a further heartbreak Mary kept buried deep in memory. It was also the year she moved to Santa Fe.

While she never married again, Mary thought she was in love several times. A woman of considerable passion and unconventional convictions, she was past mid-life when she had her most serious love affair with a man named Dr. Daniel T. MacDougal who was the curator of the Carnegie Botanical Laboratory at Tucson, Arizona. Their shared interest in the Pima and Papago Indians and in all plant life and the outdoors gave them a meeting of the minds, but not of intentions. When MacDougal was willing to do anything to be with Mary, she would be ill, or prevented from joining him by the press of her work commitments. Despondent, in one of her letters to him she wrote:

> . . . All my life I have lived with the idea that I had gifts that would justify me in trying for success on a large scale; and I don't just mean the fruits of success. I could have put up with poverty and with the lack of public acclaim if I had been able to do the work that I felt that with moderate good luck I might have done. And now I find myself at the time when I ought to be doing that work, a hack writer, sick and hurried and overworked. . . . And the one thing I can't bear is that there doesn't seem to be anybody who cares enough about it to lift a finger in my behalf. . . . In order to be allowed to go on making a living, I have to pretend that this is the thing I want most to do. But I simply can't bear to pretend to you. . . . If I must take failure I will take it straight, and not sweetened with compliments and consolations. . . . If I have been, as most people think, a conceited pompous fool, then I must find it out.

In her later years, she had to admit to herself that all her attempts to manipulate her life and to call on the higher entity, I-

Mary, which she had been so sure of—all that mystical know-how—had somehow failed her. She returned to the property she had bought long before in Santa Fe, and built a small attractive adobe house on it of her own design. She loved Santa Fe. It was her home for the rest of her life.

She was active in community affairs, joining her voice to rallies for suffrage and Prohibition; she also kept busy with speech-making, traveling, putting on plays and sponsoring exhibitions of Indian arts and crafts. But for her living, she wrote the things her publisher wanted that she so loathed doing. And all the time her health was declining. She would be laid low for several days by abdominal pains, get better, then have another attack. But no set-back, physical or otherwise, kept her from her political and charitable endeavors, her friends, her lectures, or work in progress and planned. She kept writing, traveling and renewing old acquaintances. When she met H. G. Wells, he called her "the most intelligent woman in America."

Returned from a final trip, she suffered a heart attack that kept her an inactive invalid for the remainder of the year. The unhappy news that her younger brother George—the baby she had cared for—had been shot to death by one of his psychiatric patients was a blow almost too awful to bear. They had had a falling out over Mary's attempts to direct the education of his daughter and Mary suffered from guilt at not having made up their differences before he died.

There were rumors that Mary's illness was stomach cancer, but Mary denied this. "You know," she told friends, "I have never been afraid of death. I've always thought of it as a great adventure. . . ."

In her final year it was her sister Jennie, dead years before at age nine, whom Mary missed most. She claimed to be able to feel her presence and clearly recall her face and form at will. "Still in the night—such times as when I have written a book and see it for the first time in the cold obscenity of print and know without opening the pages that I have failed . . . she comes in the first sleep and strokes my cheek with her soft hands. The loss of her is never cold in me, tears start freshly at the mere mention of her name. And I would not have it otherwise She was the only one who ever unselflessly loved me. She is the only one who stays."

Following a final heart attack on August 12, 1934, Mary Austin died quietly in her sleep. Quoting from *I-Mary*, Augusta Fink's brilliant biography:

> To the east of Casa Querida, on the edge of the Sangre de Cristo Mountains, stands a great pyramid of sand and rock called Mount Picacho. Below its lofty eminence, the valley of Santa Fe spreads in a luminous checkerboard of green and gold, and on the far horizon, multi-layered mountains meet the sky. Near the summit of Picacho, sealed in the crevice of a cairn amid rough granite boulders, are the ashes of Mary Austin. There they remain forever at one with the earth.

Mary would have been completely happy with that final resting place, chosen with sensitivity and care by friends who loved her well. She even seemed to have foreknowledge of it in these lines:

Some day I shall go West,
Having won all time to love it in, at last
Too still to boast,
But when I smell the sage,
When the long, marching landscape line
Melts into wreathing mountains,
And the dust cones dance
Something in me that is of them shall stir. . . .

Always that recurring theme, a oneness with Nature. She wrote of it over and over in so many ways.

"Her words live on," Augusta Fink wrote in *I-Mary*, "a testament to the undying quality of her country and her spirit." Not long before her death, she reiterated her uncompromising belief:

I will be Mary. I will be forever Mary. And others will be themselves, those who have contributed something by the individuality of their lives and thought.

Her beloved Santa Fe home was bought privately and turned into an art gallery featuring western paintings. That would have pleased Mary. It is now also a part of the School of American Research, underwritten by the copyrights to all of her writings. That also would have pleased her. Mary Austin published thirty-one books and two anthologies; over one hundred twenty-five of her articles, stories and poems have appeared in more than sixty periodicals.

Austin, Mary Hunter. *Earth Horizon*. Cambridge, Mass.: Houghton Mifflin Co., 1932. Albuquerque, N.M.: University of New Mexico Press, 1977.

Experiences Facing Death. Brooklyn, New York City: Bobbs-Merrill Co., 1931. Ayer Co., 1977.

The Land of Little Rain. Garden City, N. Y.: Doubleday & Co., Inc., 1961.

The Land of Journeys Ending. New York City: AMS Press, 1969.

Fink, Augusta. *I-Mary*. Tucson, Ariz.: University of Arizona Press, 1983.

Pearce, T. M. *Mary Austin*. New York City: Twayne Publishers, Inc., 1965.

Wilkins, Thurman. "Mary Hunter Austin," *Notable American Women*, Vol. 1. Edited by Edward T. & Janet W. James, Cambridge, Mass. Harvard University Press, Bellknap Press, 1971.

CHAPTER 12

Intrepid Nellie Bly

The men in the cluttered, noisy newsroom of *The Pittsburg Dispatch* looked up and saw a teenager standing in their midst, breathless from rushing up three flights of stairs. Her outlandish costume—a floor-length black silk Russian cloak and an odd little fur turban calculated to make her look older—caused them to break into smiles.

Aware all eyes were upon her, she whispered hoarsely to the equally young office boy in her path, "Pardon me. My name is Elizabeth Cochrane. Can you tell me where I might find the editor?" The boy jerked his thumb in the direction of the managing editor, George Madden, seated within earshot.

The girl's face brightened in a smile that revealed perfect teeth. "Oh!" she cried, "I expected to see an old, cross man." Later, she claimed she had pictured Madden as a "great big man with a bushy beard who would look over the top of his specs and snap, 'What do you want?'" Instead, she saw a "mild-mannered, pleasant-faced boy."

Even Erasmus Wilson, whose "Quiet Observer" columns were Pittsburg's favorites, and who bore the nickname "Q. O." after his column headline, turned out—in her words—to be a "great big good-natured fellow who wouldn't even kill the nasty roaches that crawled over his desk. There wasn't an old cross man about the place."

A half-year into 1885, Wilson wrote a satirical column excoriating, "those restless dissatisfied females who think they are out of their spheres and go around giving everybody the fits for not helping them." He had ended it by listing cultures that routinely killed off girl children or sold them as slaves, an eventuality he claimed America might have to adopt in a matter of a thousand years or so. It evoked angry protests from female readers.

An especially passionate rebuttal, signed "Lonely Orphan Girl," caught Editor Madden's eye. Although such replies usually wound up in the trash, this one pleased him with its verve and sincerity. "She isn't much for style," he told Wilson, "but what she has to say she says it right out regardless of paragraphs or punctuation. She knocks it off and it is just right, too." He wanted to locate this "lonely orphan." Wilson suggested placing an item in their Mail Pouch column. The next day the following item appeared:

Lonely Orphan Girl

If the writer of the communication signed "Lonely Orphan Girl" will send her name and address to this office, merely as a guarantee of good faith, she will confer a favor and receive the information she desires.

Instead of writing, the letter's teenaged author presented herself the next day in person. After talking with her, Madden suggested she try a piece for them on "the woman's sphere." Thrilled, she wrote and turned it in promptly. Requesting a follow-up article, Madden paid her and edited her piece himself. Wilson recalled that her grammar was "rocky," but her facts were straight.

In school hateful boys had dubbed her Lizzie, a name she detested, and called her a skinny, sickly, plain brunette. Such jibes only hardened her resolve to be self-reliant, and helped develop her ready tongue.

Elizabeth was nine when her twice-widowed mother married John Jackson Ford, a man who became vicious when he drank. In a final scrap he sprang at her mother with a loaded pistol. Only his poor marksmanship saved her. Elizabeth and her brother blocked his way, letting their mother escape to the safety of a neighbor's home.

Her mother won a divorce, family members, neighbors and friends joining to testify to his cruelty. Elizabeth later referred to that time as a brutish education, teaching her that marriages weren't made in heaven and didn't always last "till death do us part." It was the main reason why she determined to be her mother's devoted champion as well as her support.

As Elizabeth neared fifteen, she and her mother decided she would become a teacher, and chose Pennsylvania's Normal School for her training. When she enrolled in 1879 she added a final *e* to her name; already she was beginning to reinvent herself. Her formal schooling was doomed, however, when she learned that Colonel Samuel Jackson, administrator of a small trust that should have covered her tuition costs, had mismanaged her money and lost it. Later, she would sue him for malfeasance. Her hopes of teaching crushed, she sought other ways to earn a living for herself and her mother.

At sixteen, the age when most girls married, she was violently opposed to the idea for herself. Her siblings had found themselves mates and white-collar jobs; for the next four years she supplemented her newspaper earnings by working as a nanny, by tutoring, perhaps even by housekeeping, and stewed at the injustice of being unable to secure equal employment, although she was better educated than her step-brothers.

Meanwhile, her secret desire was to be a reporter. It was inevitable that she would jump at the invitation the Mail Pouch column proffered, and Madden kept his word. Her first published work, "The Girl Puzzle," appeared prominently at the top of page eleven in the paper's successful new Sunday edition. Detailed and emotional, her article blamed the rich for doing nothing but criticize the many women unable to find work.

They read of what your last pug dog cost and think of what that vast sum would have done for them — paid father's doctor bill, bought mother a new dress, shoes for the little ones, and imagine how nice it would be could baby have the beef tea that is made for your favorite pug, or the care and kindness that is bestowed upon it.

She also had strong words for the leaders of the women's rights movement:

Let them forego their lecturing and writing and go to work; more work and less talk. And why not let ambitious young girls start as messengers or errand boys and work their way up to good positions like young boys could? Let them also be hired as messengers or 'office boys' instead of slaving in airless factories. Even let them become conductors on Pullman Palace cars. Take some girls that have the ability, procure for them situations, start them on their way and by so doing accomplish more than by years of talking.

Madden assigned "Orphan Girl" as the byline for her first polemic. Her next effort dealt with divorce. She claimed the laws needed rewriting to ensure that men and women, unprepared by experience, would not marry until they first confided their faults. To lie, she wrote, should be a crime. In her words:

Let the young girl know that her intended is cross, surly, uncouth; let the young man know that his affianced is anything that is directly opposite to an angel. Tell all their faults, then if they marry, so be it; they cannot say, "I did not know," but the world can say, "I told you so."

Her suggestion of a series on the factory girls of Pittsburg suited Madden, who put her on staff at five dollars weekly, a salary only slightly more than the girls earned whom she would interview.

In those days lady writers never used their own names. Madden asked his reporters to come up with a name for her byline. They chose Nelly Bly, after a Stephen Foster song, but changed the spelling to *ie*. And newly created Nellie knew just how she wanted to tell the factory women's story. Instead of describing the hardships of workdays, Nellie elected to tell what they did after hours.

She asked direct questions, and their responses both shocked and titillated her readers. One segment told of a woman who, contrary to the accepted code of female behavior, regularly met men, went with them to bars, got drunk and — as they said in her day — "fell." Nellie asked why she would risk her reputation that way. The woman laughed.

> Risk my reputation! I don't think I ever had one to risk. I work hard all day, week after week, for a mere pittance. I go home at night tired of labor and longing for something new, anything good or bad to break the monotony of my existence. I have no pleasure, no books to read. I cannot go to places of amusement for want of clothes and money, and no one cares what becomes of me.

Nellie's exposure to the working poor kept her from being judgmental. "If no amusement is offered them," she wrote, "they will seek it and accept the first presented. . . . Who shall condemn and who shall defend?"

The column of city vignettes she created, her byline in large type above it, brought in fan mail and offers of assistance with suggested projects.

When Madden ordered Nellie to write an article about rubber raincoats and she refused, the unwitting public had seen the last of the "Nellie Bly" column. Furious at the loss of her column, realizing at last that Madden wasn't about to let her cover real news, Nellie quit her job at *The Dispatch*. But she was careful to keep on the good side of both Madden and her friend Erasmus Wilson.

With a mere nine months as a newspaperwoman under her belt, she decided to appoint herself a foreign correspondent, hoping it would pressure Madden into giving back her byline. She and her mother went south of the border into Mexico, a foreign and possibly unsafe country. Notebook always at hand, Nellie immediately began making her first observations from the train windows and wired them back to Madden. In February, he authorized a new byline — "Nellie in Mexico."

Nellie knew no Spanish, yet was critical of others preceding her for the same reason. "No less than six widows of the crankiest type are writing up Mexico, each expecting to become a second Humboldt and have their statues erected on the public square." She felt her goals were higher. She wanted to tell stories of the country in a graphic and truthful way about families and customs and, as she grew more familiar, even politics. The year was 1877, during the second term of Presidente Porfirio Diaz, who ruled for thirty years until the country's collapse in 1910.

For Nellie, Mexico was an exercise in "working as an expatriate in a dictatorship with a gagged press." She learned to censor her own writings using bits of truth in her articles whenever she could get away with them, selecting items to interest Americans. One was a bit about the president and his very young wife watching a controversial French performer night after night despite talk that the show was licentious.

Nellie enjoyed finding ways to shock, even repel readers. She told of workmen digging holes for new trees before a church, and turning up great heaps of human bones. "Some claim the bones are of priests or victims of the Inquisition," she reported, " while others say they are of a more ancient origin. They would certainly have furnished a study for Eastern people but they caused hardly a second thought to the Mexicans."

She went into gory detail over the death of a poor Indian fireman and engineer. The interment was so long delayed that — while a leak in the coffin was being sealed — the body swelled; it was too big to fit inside. "So the arms and legs were cut off and the breast split open so it could be doubled up," a nonchalant Nellie wrote.

Back on the job at *The Dispatch*, Nellie again found herself stuck with dull topics such as the history of visiting cards, and marriage rituals in various cultures. Such *minutiae*, she felt, were beneath her abilities. Restive and frustrated, she again tried to generate her own columns. One she called "Footlight Gossip" and the other "Among the Artists," but both were soon cancelled. Wilson reported that she and Madden wrangled over subjects for her to write about. Nell stopped coming in not long after her last piece on March 20, 1887. After a few days of wondering at her absence, someone found her note. "Dear Q.O." it said simply, "I am off for New York. Look out for me. Bly."

After arriving in May, Nellie spent the next four months trying to see editors on Newspaper Row (Park Row's nickname). It was a blow to find she couldn't get past the front door desk of *The Sun, The World, The Herald, The Tribune, The Times* or *The Mail and Express*. Now living with her mother in a dingy little room in a dark back alley on West Ninety-Sixth Street, she began to despair of ever achieving her dream.

She would take any work, but it was Joseph Pulitzer's *The World*, with its high standards in reporting news, along with contests and crusades and plentiful illustrations to boost circulation, that Nellie wanted to work for.

The paper announced it would sponsor a hot-air balloon flight on May 1 in St. Louis, home of *The St. Louis Post-Dispatch*, Pulitzer's flagship newspaper. Nellie quickly sent a note of introduction and an offer to be the reporter on board. The reply was a polite rejection; such a trip was much too dangerous for a lady.

To keep money coming in, Nellie sent features on New York women and fashions back to Pittsburg. When a young woman asked if New York was the best place to begin a journalism career, she set forth the pros and cons for Pittsburg readers. Then she got the brilliant idea of interviewing "the newspaper gods of Gotham" on the topic.

This time her *Dispatch* credentials provided entree to them all. Her article detailed each chief editor's reactions, noting that the hardest problem for any female writer would be to overcome the prevailing editorial mindset. All professed to be in favor of the notion of a woman reporter, but all said it was futile to send a female to cover police or criminal news—not because the crime world was sordid, but because court officials would just try to get rid of her without telling her anything.

Nell's article was published complete with the editors' quotes. She also included a list of the few women in the country already working on papers. It not only served as a useful introduction to New York, but caused much talk when it was picked up by papers and magazines about the country. Excerpts from those interviews were included in *The Mail and Express* at the end of August, describing Nellie as a "bright and talented young woman who had done a great deal of good writing for the newspapers."

However, all that was small consolation to Nellie, who lost a purse with all her money in it. A year later she revealed, "I was penniless. I was too proud to return to the position I had left in search of new worlds to conquer. Indeed, I cannot say the thought ever presented itself to me, for I never in my life turned back from a course I had started upon."

Borrowing carfare from her landlady, she brazened her way

into the office of *The New York World*'s managing editor, John Cockerill, claiming she had an important piece to propose. If the editor-in-chief would not see her, she would take her subject somewhere else. She was so persuasive and had such interesting ideas that Cockerill slipped her twenty-five dollars to keep her from applying elsewhere until he could get a decision from his boss.

She called back a week later, as agreed, and was told her main idea was too involved for a newcomer. However, her idea to pretend insanity to get admitted to the Women's Lunatic Asylum on Blackwell's Island in the East River in order to write the inside story was an idea that took Cockerill's fancy.

"You can try," he said, "But if you can do it, it's more than anyone would believe." He told her to use the name Nellie Brown, to stop smiling so much, and promised to extricate her when she asked. She got in, then requested rescue ten days later. Her two-part series "Behind Asylum Bars" proved timely, as several newspapers were currently running pieces on the alleged mistreatment of inmates and cruelty of keepers. Her reward was a job on the staff of *The New York World*. Nellie's temperament jibed perfectly with that of her new boss's policies. She was a girl who thrived on taking risks.

By the time the second segment appeared, her name was a part of the headline. And Nellie was already famous when her book, *Ten Days in a Madhouse*, came out two months later. Her article caused a stir and some social change. She wrote Erasmus she had been offered lecture tours and a chance at an acting career, both of which she refused.

From then on, she specialized in exposé pieces: Nellie posed as a maid to disclose unethical practices in employment agencies, as a factory girl to divulge the cruel work required of the women (she dubbed them white slaves) who worked in paper box factories.

A job with Pulitzer was never smooth sailing. He loved to set one talented reporter against another. After hiring Nellie, he engaged three other females to fight her for feature space. It made his paper a nerve-racking place to work. Normally kind staff members were driven to dirty tricks in self-defense. The level of disgust, rivalry and mistrust grew so intense that, in the words of one reporter, it drove "at least two editors to drink, one into suicide, a fourth into insanity and another into banking."

Backed by a regular income, in 1888 Nellie and her mother moved into a nicer apartment on West Seventy-fourth Street. In February and March she posed as a sinner desiring to reform, and reported that the mandatory six-month stay in the Magdalen Home for Unfortunate Women was a pointless effort, equal to the futility of trying to reform criminals. She spent one night as a chorus girl and wrote about it. She took a fencing lesson and wrote about it. She unmasked a certain mesmerist as a fake. She exposed lobbyist Edward R. Phelps of Albany, New York, as the "briber and boodler" she called him in her piece. It did not bring about his formal indictment, but did force him to leave town permanently.

Constantly seeking odd and interesting people to write about, she did a piece on the wives of President Harrison's cabinet members. She exposed washing machine swindlers. She described the life of a female medical student. She discussed the capabilities of private detectives. Desperate, she even wrote of a charitable Harlem hotel that served free dinners. She ended 1888 with her report on a week spent at "Dr. Cooley's Cure Factory." She wrote for three weeks on whether women were entitled to propose to men. Her piece on passing herself off as a charity patient in the Throat, Skin and Ear Infirmaries carried the headline, "Nellie Bly Narrowly Escapes Having Her Tonsils Amputated." She got herself arrested and strip-searched on a grand larceny charge in order to spend the night in a co-ed jail. Her article dwelt on wrongs she felt needed righting, and limned by name both the lawyer who tried to bully her into hiring him and the detective who made sexual advances while detaining her. After her piece on the fighter John L. Sullivan appeared, he reportedly told her, "You are the first woman who ever interviewed me, and I have given you more than I ever gave any reporter in my life." The fifty-year-old experimental Oneida Community used her article as a pamphlet to explain their way of life.

By mid-1889, turning out nearly an article a week on one stunt after another, Nellie managed to outdistance her competition and make enough money to move again, this time to modish Murray Hill.

She published her first novel, *The Mystery of Central Park*. Despite its cool reception, her fame as a reporter had reached such a pitch that many women now used her name for their own nefarious purposes. While her stories got *The World* new readers, they also brought Nellie much envy. As usual, she shared this fact with her readers:

> I have no way to protect myself or the public against such people. I would only say to too confiding business people that I never run up bills, that I never under any circumstances use the name of "Nellie Bly" outside of print.

Troubled by migraines, Nellie consulted seven different distinguished New York doctors, each of whom diagnosed her ailment differently, and wrote different prescriptions. They were embarrassed by Nellie's tell-all article which sold a good many papers.

With a drop in *The World's* circulation, it was time to find a new stunt or contest to increase circulation. Many newsmen claimed credit for proposing a trip like the one in Jules Verne's popular novel, *Around The World In Eighty Days*; all wanted to better the time of Verne's fictional hero, Phileas Fogg. But it was Nellie Bly who won the prize. A reporter recalled how she badgered Cockerill. "Send me! Please send me, Cockerill. Think what a publicity splash that'd make!"

"Are you crazy?" he had retorted in irritation. "I can't send you."

"Why not?" Nellie snapped back, eyes shining.

Cockerill counted off the reasons on his fingers. "First, you're a woman. Second, you're a young woman. Third, there's the matter of a chaperone. Fourth, arrangements would have to be made for someone to meet you at every stop and make your connections. Fifth, all women carry too much luggage, and sixth. . . Well, the whole idea's preposterous! Too dangerous, too expensive!"

Nellie's hands flew to her hips. In her best confrontational stance, her chin out in defiance, she retorted, "I'll buy my own tickets and make my own travel arrangements. I'll plot my itinerary. In fact, I already have. Here it is." She extracted a paper from her skirt pocket, unfolded and spread it on the desk under his nose. He glanced at it, then at her, too surprised to speak.

"What if I take a single piece of luggage?" she persisted.

"Impossible," he muttered.

"I don't need a chaperone. Or a lot of money. Please, Mr. Cockerill. Choose me!"

He gazed, helpless, into her brimming eyes. She was so young, so self-confident, so endearingly pretty. "I guess I'm the one who's crazy," he said. "Okay." Nellie jumped on his lap, embarrassing him with a hug and a kiss.

Once the date was set, Nellie swept into a fashionable dressmaker's establishment at ten on a Tuesday morning to order a traveling dress. "It must be able to withstand three months of constant wear," she decreed, "and be ready in twelve hours." She left, ignoring all talk of needing more time. Five hours later she was back for the first fitting, and the dress was in her hands early Wednesday morning. She ordered a dress for warm weather from her personal dressmaker and went out to purchase the things she needed for the trip, namely:

An Ulster overcoat in a Scotch plaid for cold; a "water-proof" coat for rain, an "English" cap with a double peak, and no umbrella. For her jewelry, she took some heirloom earrings, a silver chain bracelet, a twisted gold ring, and a wristwatch on a leather band.

The paper gave her two hundred pounds in English money. The coins she would carry in her pockets, and wear the notes in a chamois skin bag tied about her neck. She also took some American money, in case of emergencies. She kept her word and took only one piece of luggage. It measured sixteen inches wide by seven inches tall. In it, she managed to pack:

> two traveling caps, three veils, a pair of slippers, toilet articles, inkstand, pens, pencils, and copy paper, pins, needles and thread, a dressing gown, a tennis blazer, a drinking cup and small flask, changes of underwear, handkerchiefs, extra ruchings, a big jar of cold cream, and a twenty-four hour watch to register the time at the start and end of her journey.

Because the hot weather dress crowded the little suitcase, she left it home, substituting a silk bodice she already owned. For luck, she also wore the thumb ring she'd worn the day *The World* hired her. She packed no medicines, maintaining, "I never was very sick in my life and I don't expect to be now." She also refused the advice that she carry a revolver.

The newspaper's half-hearted attempt to arrange an itinerary provided her with a ticket as far as London, and a confusing set of schedules. On the morning of November 14, 1889, while three official timekeepers activated their stopwatches, Nellie and her headache waved goodbye as her ship nosed from its Hoboken pier at 9:40 and thirty seconds. It hadn't yet made the open sea when a busybody on deck asked Nellie if she ever suffered from *mal de mer?* For answer, she made a sudden dash for the ship's rail. At dinner the Captain's guest excused herself three times, but returned "to cheers and Bravos" from all but a critic who remarked unkindly, "And she's going around the world!" But Nell recovered after napping the next day, and proved a good sailor from then on.

Met at Southampton by Tracey Greaves, her paper's London correspondent, Nellie was thrilled to learn that the famous Jules Verne had invited her to visit him at his home in Amiens, France. This treat required the trade-off of giving up two nights of sleep to make very tight connections. Nellie willingly agreed.

After a brief stop at *The World* office, Nellie and Greaves hurried to the American Legation office for a proper passport. Filling out her application, the Legation Secretary inquired Nellie's age. "The one question," she wrote later, "all women dread to answer." She cut three years off her age, knowing the true date had never been registered, and she looked even younger. She gave her birth as May 5, 1867 and her age as 22. Later, recording the incident as an amusing memory of the trip, she asked her readers, "Who did the deception hurt?" It was Nellie's way to arrange facts and present herself as she wished to be seen.

Met by Jules Verne and his wife, Nellie and Greaves and a Parisian journalist named Sherard were taken to their home. Verne confided that the idea for *Around the World in Eighty Days* came from a French newspaper piece which detailed calculations of such a trip. He wanted to know her travel route. She recited:

> New York to London, with stops in France, Italy, Egypt; down the Suez Canal to French Somaliland, across the Indian Ocean to Ceylon, stopping at Sumatra, Singapore, China, Japan, San Francisco and back to New York.

Would she stop in Bombay as his hero had done? Nell said she could not, "Because I am more anxious to save time than a young widow." She was referring to the seductive Aouda, the fictional girl Fogg rescued while circumnavigating the globe. Delighted with Nellie, Madame Verne kissed her on each cheek in parting. Of their farewell Nellie wrote that she was tempted to return her goodbye with a kiss on the mouth, American style. "My mischievousness often plays havoc with my dignity, but for once I was able to restrain myself and kissed her softly after her own fashion."

France was so stimulated by the proposed journey that Verne's book was reissued in ten new editions, and a stage play based on it was produced. Verne later described Nellie as "the prettiest young girl imaginable... and what took the hearts of myself and Madame Verne was the complete modesty of the young person. Nobody, to look at the quiet ladylike little thing, would have thought for a moment that she was what she is and that she was going to do what she is doing."

At *The World*, marriage proposals poured in daily for Nellie, along with letters of praise. The day she sailed her paper carried the headline:

AROUND THE WORLD

in their largest type. Under two smaller lines a final huge headline read:

A VERITABLE PHINEAS FOGG
(an inadvertent misspelling of Verne's hero's name)

The owner of *Cosmopolitan Magazine*, John Brisben Walker, bet Cockerill $1,000 to $500 that his contender, Elizabeth Bisland, would beat Nellie's time going around the world the opposite way. A columnist mused in print that both young women were the best-known women reporters of their day and that it made no difference to anyone but their newpapers who arrived first back home. Bisland was representing *The Journalist*.

Nellie, dashing from place to place, knew nothing of this. Greaves, referring to what she had not seen of England and France, and would not see of any of the other countries she passed through, commented: "It will be much the same as a man describing Broadway if he were shot through a pneumatic tube from the Western Union Building to the 23rd Street Uptown office."

The World did not expect Nellie's trip to contribute any real knowledge, but felt any advice she might bring back on the facilities for world travel and communication could be of value. In an effort to hold the public's interest, the paper ran a contest called "The Nellie Bly Guessing Match." The prize was a free trip to Europe. Over 100,000 entries were submitted.

Meanwhile Nellie, riding across France and Italy on the mail train from Calais to Brindisi, chatted with a young English woman who shared the compartment. In her piece, Nellie called her a zealot "of the uncompromising kind, that condemns everything, forgives nothing, and swears the heathen is forever damned because he was not born to know the religion of her belief." Following India's conquest, many Englishmen held this view.

By the time Nellie boarded the *Victoria*, a British ship bound for Port Said, Egypt, she had acquired a lifelong distaste for the British "and their much-talked-about prejudices." Her cables had nothing good to say about the food either, or the "rude" English captain and his crew. Despite her antipathy for things British, she gave them credit for their devotion to their monarch. Each ship's entertainment ended with a chorus of "God Save The Queen" when the royal image was thrown on a white sheet during a lantern show, the passengers' applause was warm and genuine. Nellie was ashamed not to feel the same degree of respect for America's leaders. "I could not in honesty speak proudly of the rulers of my land, unless I went back to those two kings of manhood, George Washington and Abraham Lincoln."

Word about the ship was that Nellie was "an eccentric

American heiress, traveling about with a hairbrush and a bank book." Two fellow travelers sought her hand in marriage; one, smitten because she got along with only one satchel, while he needed nineteen trunks.

The *Victoria* reached Aden two weeks later on December 2. Nellie mentioned the Adenites' beautiful teeth, which she attributed to their use of a toothpick made from soft, fibrous tree twigs. She wrote of their lime-bleached yellow hair, striking against black skin. She found the jewelry-laden women exotically beautiful except for the earrings that split their earlobes and reached their shoulders.

Arriving in Colombo, Ceylon (now Sri Lanka), two days early, Nellie endured an anxious five-day wait for her next ship, the *Oriental*. When Nellie wired that news, everyone held their breath. She needed that week to reach Hong Kong from Singapore and catch the *Oceanic* on December 28 to San Francisco. The loss of even a day along the way would set her behind as much as ten days, causing her to arrive in New York two days too late.

Nellie used the time in Colombo to sight-see. She described her embarrassment at having a man pull her on her first jinricksha ride; changing her mind, she wrote, "It was so comforting to have a horse that was able to take care of itself. . ." Frustrated by the delay, she pictured herself as "creeping back to New York ten days behind time, with a shamed look on her face and afraid to hear her name spoken." Then amused "at my own unenviable position" she resigned herself to her fate.

Her next ship, the *Nepaul*, took six days to reach Penang, Malaya, two days to Singapore, and another week to Hong Kong. Instead of making Singapore on the second day from Penang as expected, the captain laid over to land a complement of coolies; It stayed a night to drop off mail. Nellie was fit to be tied. "These few hours might mean the loss of my ship at Hong Kong; they might mean days added to my record. What agony of suspense and impatience I suffered that night!"

In Singapore, she was denied entry into a Hindu temple because of her gender. Back aboard the ship, she wrote of a detour they took to meet their driver's pretty Malay wife. Nellie remarked on her large gold nose ring, the rings on her toes and about her ankles, and the edges of her ears. She was fascinated by the tiny babies and a monkey that squatted in her doorway nearby.

"I did resist the temptation to buy a boy at Port Said, and also smothered the desire to buy a Singhalese girl at Colombo, but when I saw the monkey my willpower melted and I began straightway to bargain for it." She named it Mr. McGinty.

Nellie described a monsoon in crossing the Indian Ocean as "the most beautiful thing I ever saw." An odd fellow passenger, after vomiting at her feet, engaged her in a conversation about life and death. He wanted her to let him jump overboard with her in his arms so "we would be at rest. Death by drowning is a peaceful slumber, a quiet drifting away." Nellie was greatly relieved when the ship's chief officer happened by and rescued her.

Despite the monsoon, her ship docked at Hong Kong two days early. Nellie rushed to the offices of the Oriental and Occidental Steamship Company to arrange her departure for Japan. When she gave her name, the man in the office invited her in and said without preamble that she would be beaten.

"What? I think not. I have made up my delay," she retorted. He repeated that she would lose it. "Lose it?" she replied. "I don't understand. What do you mean?" It was the first she knew of Elizabeth Bisland who had left Hong Kong three days before, traveling the other way.

"And you will be delayed here five days," he added. Nellie refused to believe him. Recovering from the shock, she retorted that she had only promised to go around the world in seventy-five days, "and if I accomplish that I shall be satisfied. I am not racing with anyone. I would not race. If someone else wants to do the trip in less time, that is their concern."

Because of her meager wardrobe, she said no to all social invitations in Hong Kong. She did sail to Canton on Christmas eve to see a "Simon-pure Chinese city," and stood in grisly fascination before lime-filled jars displaying heads of executed criminals; she was rendered speechless with horror at the sight of tied-down prisoners, their legs spread above sturdy bamboo shoots which, Nellie was assured, would—within thirty days—grow right through their bodies.

Nellie left Hong Kong for Yokohama, Japan, on December 28, a trip of five days. By now crew and passengers rooted for her success. The chief engineer's couplet was painted on the ship's engines:

> For Nellie Bly
> We'll win or die
> January 20, 1890

The third day out they ran into a violent storm that lasted twenty-four hours. Feeling hopeless, Nellie vowed, "If I fail, I will never return to New York. I would rather go in dead and successful, than alive and behind time." She clung to the chief engineer's prediction that she would be in New York with three days to spare, and prayed a lot.

Back in New York, Nellie's circling of the globe gave *The World* its biggest circulation in history. Coupons for the guessing game came in by the thousands, even one in verse that went:

> *Nellie Bly is flying high*
> *On the China Sea*
> *With her goes the hope of one*
> *Who wants to see Paree*
> *She'll get here in '74*
> *Sure as she's alive*
> *Hours 12, minutes 10, and seconds 25.*

As her ship neared San Francisco there was a positive furor of copy about Nellie, but her paper's rewrite men grew ever more fervent in their praise.

"She is coming home to dear old America," one wrote, "with the scalps of the carpers and critics strung on her slender girdle, and about her head a monster wreath of laurel and forget-me-nots, as a tribute to American pluck, American womanhood and American perseverance."

The paper added perks to the prize package, more spending money, and the services of Low's Exchange, a London travel bureau. A comedy duo wrote a song, "Globe-Trotting Nellie Bly." Across the United States, all sorts of organizations made ready to give her lavish receptions. Nellie was due to dock in San Francisco on January 20th. Her bosses, aware that the toughest leg of the journey might yet be ahead, due to the worst winter in memory, arranged a southern route. Nellie had covered more than 21,000 miles in sixty-eight days, yet the 3,000 miles ahead could prove her undoing.

As the *Oceanic* sailed into San Francisco harbor, Nellie's heart beat "with a hopefulness that had not known me for many days." Suddenly the ship's purser rushed up to her, his face pale with despair.

"My God," he all but sobbed. "The bill of health was left behind in Yokohama!" He explained the ship would not be allowed to dock without it. That meant a wait of two whole weeks until the next ship from Japan could bring it! Nellie threatened to cut her throat. Luckily, a better search turned up the document in the ship's doctor's desk.

A rumor of smallpox on board raised a second groundless alarm. The quarantine doctor yelled down at Nellie as a special tug raced her toward Oakland, saying he could not permit her to land without seeing her tongue. She stuck it out. "All right," he yelled again and watched her sail out of earshot.

Twenty minutes later Nellie was on the special train that would carry her to Chicago by a southerly route. She had traveled all that way without a mishap, but three miles from Gallup, New Mexico, she faced real danger. Workmen were repairing a bridge that spanned a deep gorge. The span was temporarily held together by jackscrews. The men heard the train approaching too late to flag it down. While they agonized, the train whipped across the rickety construction at a smart fifty miles an hour. The rest of the run across country was accomplished without a problem.

It was a thrill for the happy crowds that met her wherever the train stopped. There were telegrams, people wishing her well who kept her car filled with flowers. Calling it a queen's ride, Nellie rejoiced with all America "that it was an American girl" who had accomplished the feat.

Nellie replied to *The San Francisco Chronicle* newsman who praised her for her extraordinary achievement, "Oh, I don't know. It's not so very much for a woman to do who has the pluck, energy and independence which characterize many women in this day of push and get-there." Nellie began writing her version of her trip as the special train sped east. Characteristically omitting mention of her illness aboard ship or her migraines, she wrote that nothing pleased her more than the "violent rocking of the ship, so long as it didn't endanger the success of my trip," and that she had known only "good health ever since I left New York."

At a stopover in Topeka, Kansas, Nellie told the *The Topeka Daily Capital*'s reporter that anyone could make a trip like hers in seventy-five days at a cost of about $1,500; even an unchaperoned woman need not fear a circumnavigation like hers. "There is really not much for Americans to see in foreign lands," she remarked, having seen nothing. "We've got the best of everything here; we lack in nothing . . . they are so very slow in Europe and to my mind are behind America in almost everything."

After a nap, Nellie greeted her Pittsburgh relatives and friends, and a crowd of about 5,000 Philadelphia people at 3:10 a.m. All had waited nearly ten hours to meet the train. Jules Verne cabled his congratulations. Not only France, he said, but England and Germany were equally enthusiastic about her achievement. Nellie detrained at Jersey City, New Jersey, at 3:51 p.m. on Saturday, January 25, 1890, as the three timekeepers pressed the stops on their watches. She had circled the globe in exactly seventy-two days, six hours, eleven minutes and fourteen seconds— almost eight days less than her fictional rival. (*The Journalist's* representative, Elisabeth Bisland, had missed a key connection.) F. W. Stevens of New York City won the newspaper's contest, correctly guessing her travel time within an astounding two-fifths of a second. *The World's* lead editorial that day stated that the uproarious receptions she received everywhere were a fitting tribute to Nellie, who had that "combination of superb qualities which all sound-hearted men and women admire."

As for Nellie, she was only sorry the journey was over. She wanted to go back to work. "You know I must do something for a living," she said. "And I expect to work until I fall in love and get married." The paper, terming it Nellie's "authentic biography," printed her travelog in installments. This recital in print, much of it supplied by Nellie, told of her entry into the newspaper world, and her "many and brilliant" attainments in the brief two and a half years since. It ended with the trip, which had made her "the best known and most widely talked-of young woman on earth today. She has worked hard," it concluded, "and deserves all her success."

Within days Nellie stood at the foot of Fifth Avenue, selling a hundred photographs of herself for five dollars apiece to help raise funds to build the Washington Memorial Arch. Her name and image appeared on all sorts of products, and she did a brisk business in trading cards with smart little poems and caricatures of her in color wearing her checked traveling coat. She gave a successful hour and a half lecture at the Union Square Theatre on Sunday, February 9. Her performance a week later had a soldout house. Suddenly Nellie was famous for being famous. In an unfortunate way, she fell victim to her own celebrity. *The World* made a terrible mistake. It featured a paragraph about Nellie that made it sound as if she was on a well-earned vacation and no longer working for them. Insulted and irate, Nellie left *The World* offices swearing she would never return. She made a public statement: she had not gotten so much as a thank-you from the editors, much less been offered a bonus, or a salary increase, or other meaningful compensation for her efforts. "Pulitzer cabled his congratulations," she stated, "and begged me to accept a gift he was sending from India; I accepted the congratulations but have never seen the present." Of the medal supposedly struck in her honor, she wrote, "I have it on good authority that the medal was given as a prize in a telegrapher's contest."

Nellie realized $9,500 from a lecture tour, and was gifted with some properties worth about $1,500 by two real estate men enchanted with her feat. She signed a three-year contract with a publisher named N.L. Munro to write fiction in installments for his weekly, *New York Family Story Paper*, for which she would be paid the munificent salary of $10,000 the first year, and $15,000 for the next two years. Unhappily for Nellie, she was no good at this kind of writing. Walt McDougall, a contemporary of hers, tried to help her. In his memoirs, written after her death, he recalled his amazement that she had undertaken such an offer when she had "no plot, characters or ability to write dialogue." But his description of her, quoting from Brooke Kroeger's 1994 fine biography, *Nellie Bly*, was fond:

> . . . a shapely young woman with gray-blue eyes in a pointed eager face, her voice with that indescribable rising inflection peculiar to West Pennsylvanians. . . Her sole

assets were courage, persistance and a modest unassuming self confidence. She was sprightly, yet not frivolous; like [Bill] Nye, everybody knew her but she had few familiars. Not a deep mind but a warm and sensitive heart.

Because she undertook a lecture tour and was preoccupied with the preparation of *Nellie Bly's Book: Around the World in Seventy-Two Days*, Nellie was out of touch with the public for six months. The book did well. Its first edition of 10,000 copies sold out and went into a second printing.

During that time her beloved twenty-eight-year-old brother died, and she took on the responsibility of looking after his widow and two small children. Six months into her "Story" contract, she was confined to her home on crutches, suffering from an unnamed illness, with McGinty the monkey, a parrot, and her dog as her only companions.

She wrote her old friend, Q.O. that she suffered from "the most frightening depression that can beset mortal." And again, "You can imagine how severe it is when I tell you I have not done a stroke of work for four weeks."

The letdown was certainly predictable. After having been the toast of the world, she was suddenly old news And although she couldn't imagine such an eventuality, at twenty-five she had reached the zenith of her life. Her next thirty years would unfold in a sort of slow decline.

But she had accomplished one thing. She had paved the way for women reporters. Not on a par with men in salary or assignments because editors were wary of entrusting them with hard news like disasters or crime, yet now women worked in newspapers across the country.

In December of 1891, Pulitzer hired young Arthur Brisbane away from *The New York Sun*. For the rest of her life, Brisbane would be Nellie's good friend and sometime rescuer, the one she turned to when all else failed.

Two years of interviews and routine covering of special events followed. Perhaps it was the impersonal heading of, "Special Correspondence of the World," on her columns that caused her to jump at an offer from the merged *Chicago Times-Herald*, with the promise that she would excite its readers. Even Walt McDougall gave her that accolade, calling her the lady reporter with "fire and flame." She wrote only two articles, the last she would write for them.

Footloose a month before her thirty-first birthday, Nellie stunned her friends by marrying an attractive wealthy sixty-nine-year-old bachelor named Robert L. Seaman, president and owner of The Iron Clad Company, a manufacturer of many metal items. Ill-starred from the first, theirs was an up-and-down union beset by complications and problems, not the least of which was a series of lawsuits. Seaman's younger brother, an immediate enemy, did everything he could to ruin the marriage. In addition, Seaman reneged on his promise to support Nellie's mother and sister.

When Nellie learned his 1895 will would leave her only $300 beyond her widow's dower right, she got Brisbane, now Sunday editor of *The World*, to assign her interviews with men and women of stature, one of which was a prized in-depth interview with the National American Woman Suffrage Association President Susan B. Anthony.

Nellie gave up reporting when her penitent spouse whisked her off to Europe, this time with her mother, sister and niece in tow. Much of their time abroad was spent in consulting eye specialists for Seaman's failing sight. Nellie got Seaman to draft yet another will. Handwritten, it was two sentences long and gave Nellie total control. A coda, a long letter, written or at least motivated by her, sought to justify this version and defend against the inevitable contesting of the will by his heirs.

They had planned to stay abroad four years, but trouble in the company and her sister's death in July of 1899 brought them back to New York. They still had business problems, but for a brief and magic time their home was a welcoming place for Nellie's friends in the literary and artistic fields.

In February of 1904 Seaman was struck by a horse and wagon while crossing the street. His fractured rib healed well, but on March 10th he collapsed. Despite the efforts of the three physicians in attendance, he died two hours past midnight.

Nellie bravely took over Seaman's company, determined that her factory would treat its employees well. She learned to operate each machine, even designed new ones; by 1905, twenty-five patents were issued in her own name. Her employees got weekly wages, a recreation centre, and other exceptional benefits for leisure time, all under the care of her general manager, Edward R. Gilman.

But Gilman died in 1914, leaving the company plagued by lawsuits. Her new firm of auditors discovered that Gilman and others had been forging checks to the tune of an incredible $1.6 million. Banks sued Nellie, asking to be reimbursed for the $500,000 worth of checks they'd cashed with her signature, even though it was proven that she not only hadn't written them, she'd never seen them.

"I cannot blame myself enough for not having learned banking methods and commercial accounting when I first went into the Iron Clad," she said. Everything seemed to go against Nellie. The forgers, with no sentence rendered, were set free. To add insult to injury, her former lawyer sued her for nonpayment of a legal bill in the amount of $25,143.

Leaving her affairs in the hands of her octogenarian mother, Nellie went abroad. In Vienna she hoped a friend would help solve her financial problems. Four days before her ship left, Austria declared war on Serbia and Germany invaded Luxembourg. It was the beginning of World War I. Nellie sailed anyway, assuming she would be back in three weeks.

Once in Vienna, when she discovered she could not leave Austria, she used the clout of new acquaintances to become one of four accredited correspondents covering the war. This time it was for *The New York Journal*, a paper which had delighted in taunting her in the past. Now it was happy to print anything she wrote. As always, her reporting was an amalgam of fact and her own perceptions.

From the front she wrote many moving accounts of soldiers, both the well and wounded. Nellie went from war reporting to working for Austrian War Relief. Due to news blackouts, in four years the only news she sent favored the Austrians and Germans. Once the war ended, fancying herself an intermediary between the U.S. and Austria, she illegally made her way back to Paris. Intending to interview Wilson, she was armed with letters from Austria's new chancellor and Foreign Minister.

Refused access to the busy president, she in turn refused to give her "information" to save the world from "creeping Bolshevism" to anyone but him. Questioned by various intelligence people, she hinted at knowing plots important to America, saying she could even name names. After talking to her at length, they were satisfied she was no threat. However, her pro-German sentiments were potentially embarrassing during the peace process, so she was issued a passport for America and kept under surveillance until she left.

Nellie found herself unwelcome in her brothers' homes. Her ungrateful mother actually testified against her in a final law suit which she lost over the ownership of the all-but-defunct Steel Barrel branch of the old Iron Clad Company.

Only able to feel desolate for so long, Nellie moved into the McAlpin Hotel and took Brisbane's pittance as an editorial page columnist on *The New York Journal*. It paid $100 a week, half of what she had earned thirty years before. The lead sentence of her first column could have been Nellie's creed: "A man may be down but he's never out." By 1920 her column had become a clearing house for the destitute, the abandoned and the abused. She finally had her long desired column and was turning out more copy at fifty-seven than she had written in her most productive years. Hundreds of letters crossed her desk asking for help and advice, and this involvement with others' miseries helped her to rise above the anger she must have felt at hearing of the fine new three-story home her mother bought. But her mother didn't live to enjoy it. She died that year at ninety-four.

Nellie wrote her last column in January, spinning a tale of two lifelong friends and their disparate fortunes. She was taken to St. Mark's Hospital that same day, suffering from a severe case of bronchopneumonia and heart disease. She lay in her hospital bed penning her will, delegating personal gifts of jewelry, furs, her dog, and the bit of stock she still owned to friends. She left nothing to fight over.

Nellie died on January 27, 1922. The newspapers recognized her with many encomiums, but the most meaningful to her would have been Brisbane's eulogy the day after. The capitals are his.

Nellie Bly was THE BEST REPORTER IN AMERICA and that is saying a good deal. Reporting requires intelligence, precision, honesty of purpose, courage and accuracy. Nellie Bly died too young, cheated of the fortune that should have been her own, suffering for years from ill health that could not diminish her courage or her kindness of heart.

But her life was useful and she takes with her from this earth all that she cared for, an honorable name, the respect and affection of her fellow workers, the memory of good fights well fought and of many good deeds never to be forgotten by those that had no friend but Nellie Bly.

Happy the man or woman that can leave as good a record.

Bly, Nellie. *Around The World In Seventy-Two Days*. New York City: Pictorial Weeklies Co., 1890.

   Ten Days in a Madhouse. New York City: N. L. Munro, 1887.

   Six Months in Mexico. New York City: J. W. Lovell, 1888.

Kroeger, Brooke. *Nellie Bly*. New York City: Random House, Times Books, 1994.

Stephens, Autumn. *Wild Women*. Berkeley, Calif.: Conari Press, 1992.

Weisberger, Bernard A. "Elizabeth Cochrane Seaman," (Nellie Bly) *Notable American Women*, Vol. 3. Edited by Edward T. & Janet W. James. Cambridge, Mass.: Harvard University Press, Bellknap Press, 1971.

CHAPTER 13

Carrie Chapman Catt: General

She liked to joke of herself, "I have a voice like a foghorn that can reach out of doors." Perhaps she did project more forcefully before the invention of the microphone, but she was credited with a beautifully modulated and nicely pitched speaking voice. Carrie was a tall woman, well formed, with beautiful pensive eyes, gently wavy brown hair and a strong chin finishing off an oval face.

Never the radical she was constantly accused of being, Carrie Catt's only crime was dedicating all her time and energy over twenty-five years to better the lot of America's women. How? By teaching them basic politics, then helping them gain the right to vote. A mesmerizing public speaker, she educated and inspired millions of women in pursuit of that goal.

"The common law in Great Britain and the United States," she told them, "held husband and wife to be one, and that one the husband. The legal existence of the wife was so merged in that of her husband that she was said to be 'dead in law'." Comparing the freedom women of other countries already enjoyed to that of the women of North America, she said all of them could vote by acts of their parliaments, ". . . while we alone, excepting two Canadian provinces, have to go to each state on referendum!"

The financial powers of the United States greatly feared the impact of suffrage and were determined to block its passage at any cost. Their efforts became so transparent that in 1918 a senate committee was formed to investigate their propaganda against

NAWSA (the National American Woman Suffrage Association) in general and its president and leader, Carrie Chapman Catt, in particular. The prevailing sentiment of the day was that any females who espoused the cause of suffrage were "militants and non-women." The three primary founders of the movement, Elizabeth Cady Stanton, Lucretia Mott and Susan B. Anthony, and every woman after them who worked for suffrage—women like Carrie Catt, Dr. Anna Shaw, and Maude Park—were labeled "rebels and lunatics," and accused of trying to lure America's women into a state of perdition. In truth, the religious community hated the idea of suffrage so much that one impassioned minister pronounced from the sanctity of his pulpit:

> The woman who undertakes to put her sex in an adversary position to man, to contend and fight against man, displays a spirit which would—if able—convert all the harmonious elements of society into a state of war, and make every home a battleground, a hell on earth.

The struggle for suffrage began in 1848, eleven years before Carrie Catt was born, when Elizabeth Cady Stanton's close friends met over tea one afternoon in her Seneca Falls, New York, parlor. They spent the afternoon drafting a Declaration of Principles modeled closely after the Declaration of Independence. Later that year these rebels dared to hold the first woman's rights convention in Seneca Falls. First reading their Principles from the podium, Stanton addressed the audience. A clergyman of her acquaintance, father to several children, got up with the intention of shaming her for speaking in public.

"The apostle Paul enjoined silence upon women," he pronounced grandiloquently. "Why don't you mind him?"

Stanton was quick-witted. "The apostle Paul also enjoined celibacy upon the clergy. Why don't you mind him?" Stanton, like

Carrie Catt, loved to bait chauvinistic men; among many salty remarks she said, "The idea of masculine grace has long been a thorn in my flesh." Even before the cause became widespread, Stanton urged women whose husbands held them in check by intimidation—dubbing them "spaniel wives"—to speak out against the idea of male supremacy. Stanton offended with another remark that wrote *finis* to any possibility of financial help from any religious group when she declared, "The Bible and the church have been the greatest stumbling blocks in the way of woman's emancipation." By 1859, the year of Carrie Chapman Catt's birth, the fight to win the right to vote had been under way for eleven years.

Carrie, born on the family farm in Ripon, Wisconsin, was the middle child of Lucius and Maria Lane's three children. Her great grandparents on both sides were New Englanders dating back to the mid-1700s. Carrie was a bright child who grew into a brilliant and attractive woman. Destined to lead the suffrage movement to its ultimate victory, her ordinary childhood gave no hint of the extraordinary role she would later play on the world's stage.

Schooled in northeastern Iowa, where her family moved, her early loves were reading and horseback-riding. She loved cantering over the miles of virgin unploughed prairie lands around their farm, the wind blowing her hair. Even as a child, she resisted stereotypes that classified women as weak and inferior to men. When she finished high school in three years, her father refused to pay for college, feeling more education was wasted on a girl. She defied him by earning a credential and teaching for a year to save the money for college herself.

At eighteen she was able to enroll at Iowa State College as a sophomore, washing dishes and working in the library to support herself for the three years it took her to graduate. Avid about natural sciences, she ate up Darwin and Spencer, and called her belief in the evolutionary process "the chief control of my life."

Next she obtained a clerk's job in a law office where she spent a year in preparation for law school. However, when offered the principalship at nearby Mason City high school the following year, she accepted. Carrie proved so capable over the next two years that at age twenty-five she was promoted to the post of school administrator.

However, Carrie's academic career was short-lived. When she was twenty-six and he was thirty, she was courted by Leo Chapman, owner and editor of the *Mason City Republican*. They were married on February 12, 1885. Leo put her to work as his assistant editor. Because the paper was doing so well, a year later Leo went to San Francisco to buy a second paper. Tragically, while there he contracted a fatal case of typhoid fever which progressed so rapidly that, even though Carrie was immediately notified, he died before she could arrive. Heartbroken, adrift and unready to face family and former colleagues,Carrie spent the next year as a copywriter on a San Francisco daily. At her boss's request, early one morning she stopped on the way to work to collect payment for a bill owed the paper. It was a blustery rainy day and Carrie entered the business office clad in a raincoat and rubbers. Alone in his shop, the boss wrote out a check on the spot, then requested a receipt.

Carrie sat down to sign and date it while he stood behind her. Suddenly she felt her raincoat thrust aside and his hands roughly cupping her breasts as he murmured endearments. A proper Victorian girl, she was outraged. Jumping up, she turned on him with all the invective at her command. His ardor quickly cooling, he hustled her out the door. She left in tears, not because the man was an insensitive lout, but because she knew that many women, in fear of losing their jobs, had to put up with that sort of daily harassment. She promised herself that one day she would do something to alleviate such indignities. But what, she didn't know. Within the year Carrie moved back to Charles City, Iowa, where she began lecturing on women's issues. At the end of 1887, she joined Iowa's Woman Suffrage Association. An attractive, well-dressed young woman, Carrie was a commanding presence on stage, and so effective a speaker that her state leaders soon asked her to lecture on suffrage; it was a cause she would eloquently espouse for the next three years.When she married again in 1890, Carrie was thirty-one. Her husband was an uncommonly liberal-minded engineer named George Catt, who not only agreed with her that suffrage was important, but went so far as to sign and have officially notarized a prenuptial agreement promising to earn their living if she would handle all public service activities. The agreement also allowed Carrie two months in spring and fall to devote to suffrage.

This was most unusual for at the beginning, when the push for suffrage began, women had no legal rights, whether single or wedded. Any assets, financial or otherwise, a woman might bring to her marriage were automatically taken over and managed by her husband, regardless of his ability or character. A wife or daughter had no recourse even if her husband or father beat or otherwise abused her. In Carrie Catt's era, most men tended to view their wives as an extension of themselves, a kind of exalted but necessary chattel, even if the union was a happy one.

So for years suffrage simply was another lost cause. The kindest thing said of it was, "We know suffrage is just, and that it will come, but this is not the time."

Men clung tenaciously to the idea of their perceived superiority over women and detested the idea of women voting. The premise of female inferiority was so widespread that when a man named H. K. Root published his opinion on why women could not, and should not, be allowed to have the vote, the male population was very much in accord. His three given reasons were:

1) God had laid down that man should rule, and if men gave up their rights to women, some great calamity would befall them.

2) Law of Physical Force: Man's strength was greater than
woman's.

3) If woman says, "We shall vote," and man says "She shan't," that
is reason enough why she shan't!

All Susan B. Anthony had to do was meet Carrie and hear her
well-thought-out opinions to know she had found a woman of
rare talent and organizational ability, an aptitude the cause sadly
lacked. Bundling Carrie up, she took her along on the grueling
South Dakota campaign of 1890 where suffrage lost miserably.
Afterward, Carrie Catt wrote, "I formulated my future creed that
day. I realized we needed four things to win a referendum
at the polls: a) Endorsement by a great citizen's organization,
b) Endorsement by political parties, c) Adequate campaign fund,
d) A well organized and energetic campaign force."

"Never again," she vowed, "would I go into a campaign with all
the cards stacked against me!"

Although Mississippi had been the first state in 1839 to pass
a "Ladies Bill" that gave women permission to own property and
Wyoming was first to ratify a bill for women's rights, their women
were not allowed to vote until 1890, nearly thirty years later. Over
time, other Western states extended a like privilege, but Eastern
and Southern states were holdouts to the bitter end.

Disillusioned despite a victory finally gained in Wyoming,
when Carrie Catt spoke at suffrage's annual convention in 1895, it
was to scold the members for the omissions and shortcomings she
had observed. The convention immediately voted themselves an
Organization Committee, and made Carrie its chairman. She
would spend the next number of years planning and honing skills
for gathering information and verifying details, all the while
searching for new and capable women to train as leaders. In fact,

creating a strong and effective foundation was the purpose under-lying all she did for the next twenty-five years.

When Miss Anthony gave up the leadership of NAWSA in 1904, she picked Carrie to succeed her over Dr. Anna Howard Shaw. It was a painful decision, for Dr Shaw had been Susan B. Anthony's confidante and closest friend for more than twenty years. Dr. Shaw was a brilliant woman and an electric speaker, but Anthony realized she would not make the best administrator.

George Catt had started a company of his own which quickly prospered. But he fell ill within the first year of its operation. After her four year term, when Carrie saw how his health was declining, she resigned in 1904 in order to give all her time to nursing her sick husband. Dr. Shaw took on the job of president of NAWSA and ruled it for eleven rocky years. For Carrie Catt, it was a blessing to be able to stay home with George, for they would have only one more year together. George Catt died prematurely at the age of forty-five in 1905.

Shortly after his death a grieving Carrie Catt moved in with Mary Garrett Hay, a close friend and fellow suffragist. After four years in New York City they bought a farm in Ossining, up the Hudson River from New York. Only a few months before Miss Hay's death in 1928, they moved to New Rochelle. Carrie Catt made New Rochelle her permanent home, traveling from it to her various assignments. Fortunately for Carrie, her husband had pro-vided her with financial security for the rest of her life.

At first nearly undone at losing him, she soon realized she must be constantly active to rise above her grief, and began to devote all her time to suffrage. An ancillary effort, she helped to form the International Woman Suffrage Alliance.

Drafted by popular vote in December of 1915, Carrie suc-ceeded Dr. Shaw as president of NAWSA. Fifty-six-year-old Carrie Catt's deeper involvement was timely, because seventy-three-year-old Susan B. Anthony was literally near exhaustion.

Lucy Stone and Elizabeth Cady Stanton, the other two ladies who had bravely spearheaded the movement by her side, were also well into their seventies.

Carrie Catt had spent her years before resuming the presidency in inventing and testing strategies to be taught to their volunteers. An avid believer in public relations and advertising, each Fourth of July she directed that the women's Declaration be read aloud from fifty courthouse steps to gather new initiates. Each of the twenty-six English and foreign language papers in New York state carried articles about it. A genius at promoting their cause in colorful ways, in readying for each campaign Carrie would tell her workers in her winning manner, "This time no voter must escape our notice. We will have barber's days, street cleaner's days, banker's and broker's days, student's, factory worker's, ticketseller's days, ditch digger's days, longshoremen's days, streetcarmen's days, butcher's days, baseball player's days . . . and tell me if I've overlooked anyone."

She set bonfires on hills, flew advertising balloons, arranged tableaux and musicals to illustrate the progress of women from primitive campfires to the council of state, held torchlight processions with Chinese lanterns and banners. Each occasion ended in a street dance the women hosted in the Irish, German, Italian, Polish, Syrian and Chinese quarters of New York, and each either began or ended with speeches on the subject of suffrage delivered in their own languages.

Carrie never ceased to caution her recruits:

> Bear in mind that we have no vested or real power. We have only ourselves, our eloquence and sense of rightness to persuade new men and women alike to join our fight, brave men able to steel themselves to the ridicule they will endure. And if you feel discouraged, remember those first brave women who saw the need seventy years ago, and all those who have worked unsung all these difficult years.

Then she always added, to buck them up:

And we are close to victory now. Closer than we have ever been before. Now we are informed, better organized, less vulnerable, able to digest and use political information, able to talk to political figures and assess their worth to us. Now we are a genuine force to be reckoned with at last!

After yet another defeat she would say, "A battle has been lost. Forget it. Others lie ahead." No wonder her women fondly called her "The General." Carrie seldom complained of their lack of success. Only after they had finally won did she admit, "Not only was the battle for woman suffrage fought longer in the United States, it was fought harder."

It took years for Mrs. Catt and her followers to be able to call themselves a force to be reckoned with, years in which Carrie drew up specific plans for each local group to follow. She opened headquarters in each state; she created studies in political science and economics to ensure that every worker grasped the process and what they were trying to achieve; she devised a Manual of Organization, a method for accurately keeping track of their membership, and a way to get soundly based national association financing. However, it took twenty years to achieve this latter goal.

As women about the country heard their sisters speak their minds, they were imbued with a new restlessness and sense of potential power. They were the untapped pool of able, energetic women from which Carrie Catt would draw her team. By actual count it took her nine long years just to build a sound organization and inspire its disparate members to exert efforts equal to hers. She invented what had to be done as she came to it, but it was killing work. Possibly no other woman would have persisted in the face of so resistant a climate, so unrewarding a job. She later admitted to having gone through on-the-job training as she taught herself to employ the diplomacy, tact, patience, judgment, and human understanding she claimed she lacked when she first took on the monumental task.

The Senate Committees' 1918 investigation disclosed powerful machinations among the enemies of woman suffrage which Carrie Catt and her ladies often suspected but never could prove. It revealed an unholy alliance existing between the brewing industry and a dummy corporation called National Farmers Union, a front through which they channeled funds for years. A secret coalition bonded several railroads engaged in the same kind of undercover activities. Whether they were institutions, oil companies, ship lines or wealthy contributors, all regularly paid into a slush fund set up for the sole purpose of defeating the passage of suffrage. And as if they were not formidable enough foes, a confidential marriage between liquor interests, hotel-owners' associations and the National Association of Manufacturers also paid undercover agents to harrass suffrage workers, and regularly sent heated articles against suffrage to newspapers around the country. Business had every reason to fear women getting the vote. Women were for Prohibition; they wanted to revoke the Poll Tax that had denied Blacks the right to vote for so long; they wanted an investigation into many illegal Wall Street practices. They would certainly use the vote to improve working conditions and salaries for women at every social level, raising the costs of all businesses. They would demand a reduction in the tariff schedule. Last, and most dire, should these demands become law, men with high incomes currently enjoying an oligarchy of the rich would find their power and money measurably curtailed.

A New York senator expressed the fear that, if women were given the vote, they would lose their femininity. Rose Schneiderman, a noted pro-union garment worker, gave the following impassioned speech at a suffrage rally:

We have women working in foundries, stripped to the

waist, if you please, because of the intense heat. Yet the Senator says nothing about these women losing their charm. They have got to retain their charm and delicacy, and work in foundries. Of course you know the reason they are employed in foundries is that they are cheaper and work longer hours than men. Women in the laundries, for instance, [who] stand for thirteen or fourteen hours in the terrible steam and heat with their hands in hot starch. Surely these women won't lose any more of their beauty and charm by putting a ballot in a ballot box once a year than they are likely to lose standing in foundries and laundries all year round.

Nobody dared to contest that speech.

When Carrie again took on the burden of the presidency, Dr. Anna Shaw gallantly resumed exhorting the public on behalf of suffrage; in the process she became the most acclaimed and sought-after speaker wherever the aim was the women's vote. With great insight, a few months prior to her death, Shaw would prophesy:

You younger women will have a harder task than ours. You will want equality in business and it will be even harder to get than the vote, for you will have to fight for it as individuals and that will not get you far. Women will not unite, since they will be competitors with each other. As soon as a woman has it for herself she will have entered the man's world and cease to fight as a woman for other women.

The vision of an international alliance was sparked by Mrs. Stanton's and Miss Anthony's 1884 visit to Great Britain, where the intention was born to form an International Council. Subsequent congresses of 1888, 1893, and 1902 made it a reality.

Once Carrie Catt had spent two years reorganizing it, the International Woman Suffrage Alliance was formally launched in 1904 at a Berlin Congress. It already had affiliates in Denmark, Norway, Australia, Germany, Great Britain, the Netherlands, Sweden and the United States. In addition to her work in the United States, Carrie Catt remained at the helm of the international organization until 1923.

After suffrage's 1893 victory in Colorado, Miss Anthony was enthusiastic; "The mandate from the country to the Congress is given, the way opened after years of wandering in the wilderness. Now we can submit a Federal amendment." She was premature. Today we call that simple measure the ill-fated Equal Rights Amendment. It failed to pass for all those years, then at last the 1983 Congress made it law. It was never ratified by the required number of states, but no fair-minded citizen could fault Miss Anthony's even-handed statement:

> Equality of rights under the law shall not be denied or abridged by the United States or by any state on account of sex. The Congress shall have the power to enforce, by appropriate legislation, the provisions of this article.

Susan B. Anthony was still the heart and soul of the movement, actively involved as long as she lived. Despite failing health, during the 1906 suffrage convention, held in Baltimore, Susan B. Anthony stood center stage and raised her arm, asking the audience, "Remember the old Jewish oath? 'If I turn traitor to the cause I now pledge, may this hand wither from the arm I now raise!'"

The entire audience stood, raised their arms, and took the oath with her.

Anticipating her death, Anthony exacted a promise from two of her friends to raise a fund of at least sixty thousand dollars to support Dr. Shaw for the next five years, ensuring her ability to lecture and not be forced to earn her own living. Anthony died a month later. A giant among women, she had labored long and well, undeterred by the calumny and vilification often heaped upon her in a seemingly hopeless cause.

Carrie Catt proved equally steadfast. NAWSA was badly in need of direction when she resumed its leadership. She always reminded the women, "It isn't the vote you were after all those years, it is the vote that would give women the chance to improve their lot in life."

Women were living by a double standard. "Men still regard, or would like to regard woman as he has seen her in the past, and hence considers eternal," said Carrie Catt. In men's eyes, women were delicate flowers, to be protected.

But in reality, women capably filled men's jobs during World War I. They manufactured steel plate, high explosives, electrical apparatus, armaments, machine tools, agricultural implements, and railway, automobile and airplane parts. They smelted and refined copper and brass, refined oil, produced chemical fertilizers and leather. Thousands of women labored in textile mills, turning out uniforms for the armed forces and transport services. And yet, men kept blindly insisting that women were too fragile to endure "the rowdyness of the polls!" Once the polls closed in 1916, following another crushing defeat in New York, Mrs. Catt faced her dispirited workers from her headquarters podium. Though her face was lined with fatigue, she stood tall and proud as a queen, the radiance of her spirit blessing them all.

"Yes, we went down!" she cried. "But we went down with our colors flying!" Once the applause abated, she said, "On our way here this evening a man shouted at us, 'Don't give up, ladies! Win or lose, don't give up!'" She gestured toward the painting on their headquarters wall. "Elizabeth Cady Stanton, Amelia Bloomer, my dear mentor Susan B. Anthony, and all the rest who began our fight in 1848. . . they too lost, again and again. But did they give up?"

The crowd roared back a resounding "NO."

"Remember when Susan Anthony told us the story of young Clara Lemlich, the shirtwaist maker, who braved strikes and suffered broken ribs when the police attacked the picket line?"

Cries of "Yes, we remember."

"She didn't desist when things got rough. She only became more determined. So will we! If it takes another sixty-seven years!" Again cheers and applause. "I now declare this night of defeat the opening of our next campaign! You all know your assignments, so just keep to them. We will meet tomorrow at nine sharp to make new plans. I thank you all from the bottom of my heart for your hard work. Good night."

Carrie Catt would never concede failure. "Sex-prejudice," she said, "has been the chief hindrance in the rapid advance of the women's rights movement to its present status, and it is still a stupendous obstacle to be overcome." And in yet another lecture:

When a great church official exclaims petulantly, that if women are no more modest in their demands men may be obliged to take to drowning female infants again; when a renowned United States senator declares no human being can find an answer to the arguments for woman suffrage, but with all the force of his position and influence he will oppose it; when a popular woman novelist speaks of the advocates of the movement as the "shrieking sisterhood;" when a prominent politician says "to argue against woman suffrage is to repudiate the Declaration of Independence, yet he hopes it may never come. . ." The fate of the woman question turns upon the truth or falsity of the premise from which the world has reasoned throughout the ages past. . . Women are either inferior to men, or they are not.

Finally, in May of 1919, after many more parades and congresses and lectures and money-raising schemes, their hard work paid off. In a special session the Sixty-sixth Congress of the United States passed the Nineteenth Amendment. Mrs. Emily Pankhurst, spearhead of Great Britain's earlier and successful campaign for woman suffrage, was visiting Carrie Catt at the time.

"I wonder if your senators realize they are less progressive than our House of Lords," she said.

Carrie Catt made a wry face. "I know," she replied. "I get a hot flash every time I think of it!"

Once the measure passed, Mrs. Catt instantly launched their drive for ratification, sending reminder telegrams to the governors of every state needing special sessions of its legislature. The first eleven ratified barely a month after the measure was submitted. By the summer of 1920, thirty-five had ratified. Only one more state was needed to make the measure into law.

But the remaining states were either neutral or irrevocably opposed to suffrage, each of their governors loathe to call the needed sessions. When Delaware held its session, its legislature was locked in heated debate for over two months. Mississippi's session also ended in a stand-off, the same number of legislators voting for ratification as voted against it. One very distraught senator literally howled, his words immortalized in his state's congressional record, "Why I'd rather die and go to Hell than vote for woman suffrage!"

Connecticut's governor delayed scheduling its session so long that, by the time he did, the amendment was already law; at which point his legislators ratified the amendment twice. Vermont's governor also put off scheduling, which left only Florida, the Carolinas and Tennessee to decide the outcome of ratification.

Of the states remaining, Mrs. Catt felt Tennessee would provide their best chance to win. Its governor was up for re-election and its state parties were divided on every issue except his nomi-

nation. The NAWSA ladies' toughest job would be talking
Tennessee's disinclined politicians into disregarding party lines
and voting for the amendment.

Aware of how difficult the path before them would be, Mrs.
Catt cautioned, "In trying to change the minds of influential men,
don't stay too long, don't nag, don't threaten, don't talk about your
work where you can be overheard. Above all, don't do anything to
close the door on the next advocate of suffrage."

Tennessee's governor finally set his special session for August,
an August that would turn out to be the hottest one ever recorded.

Without the information networks of today, people could only
be reached by newspaper or direct contact. The legislators Carrie
Catt's ladies hoped to persuade had rarely, if ever, heard their
speeches or attended a NAWSA convention. In their view, suffrage was either a woman's thing or an unexplored embarrassment,
an excuse for derision. Most men held that "Woman's work is to
have and train children, to make their husbands a good home."

"Give women the vote and you will promote divorce," they
declared. Or "Someone should start a rat and mouse farm, to sell
them to people desirous of breaking up suffrage meetings."

A most convincing speaker herself, Mrs. Catt rehearsed and
sent her best speakers to Tennessee before leaving for an international conference in Germany. On her return she was met by a
frantic plea from the women already at work in Nashville.

"Please come down, Mrs. Catt. These politicos are doing
everything in their power, including staying drunk, to keep the
special session from convening. We don't know what more to do.
Can you come?"

Though exhausted, she arrived, bringing several of her ablest
lieutenants. Instead of the few days she expected to spend master-
minding their efforts and helping them organize the campaign,
she stayed for two of the most grueling months of her life.

Once the session was underway, she warned her women, "We believe they are buying votes. We have a poll of the House, showing victory, but they are trying to break a quorum, and God only knows the outcome." At the same time, in a letter to a friend she wrote:

> We are terribly worried, and so is the other side. We hope our fate is decided this week, but God only knows that. I've been here a month. It's hot, muggy, nasty, and this last battle is desperate. . . . We are low in our minds. . . . Even if we win, we who have been here will never remember it with anything but a shudder.

The Speaker of the House had secretly rigged the House vote, arranging for suffrage to lose by a respectable margin. Twenty-four-year-old Harry Burn, a new legislator, had gone along for two tallies, meekly voting "Nay" as he'd been told.

He suddenly threw the proverbial monkey wrench into the works. First ceremoniously unfolding a letter he said he'd received that morning from his mother, he requested and was given permission to read its contents into the record. He loudly proclaimed its final line, "Be a good boy and help Mrs. Catt put the 'rat' in ratification. Signed, Your Mother."

On the third tally, young Harry Burn switched his vote from "Nay" to "Aye." The chamber erupted in pandemonium, for his was the deciding vote. Suffrage had been ratified and passed by a single vote. The legislators either laughed and hugged each other for joy, or angrily shouted for a new count.

A dismayed Governor Roberts signed the Certificate of Passage, and sent it on to Washington by special courier. Once it was registered, it went to the Solicitor General, who had been waiting up all night to attest to its validity. It was next hand-carried to the State Department where, at eight o'clock on the morning of August 26, 1920, Secretary of State Colby signed it into law.

Mrs. Catt and two of her lieutenants followed it to the capitol posthaste. Once arrived, she telephoned Secretary Colby, who told her, "Yes, the Nineteenth Amendment is now truly law. Would you ladies like to come over and see the document for yourselves?"

After accepting his invitation, Carrie Catt let herself sag against the wall. She had fronted the battle for twenty-five years as its general, and longer as a worker in the ranks. And one vote had kept them from another defeat.

The passage of this measure made the United States, not the first, but the thirty-first nation in the world to grant its women the right to vote.

Carrie Chapman Catt's stellar life ended in 1947 at the age of eighty-eight when she died of a heart attack and was buried in New York City's Woodlawn Cemetery. But by then she had founded The League of Women Voters, written her autobiography and co-authored with Nettie Rogers Shuler a detailed account of their long and hard fight. Setting down the true costs of the hard-won victory, she wrote:

> To get that word "male" out of the Constitution cost the women of this country fifty-two years of pauseless campaign: Fifty-six state referendum-campaigns; Four hundred and eighty legislative campaigns to get the state suffrage amendments submitted; Forty-seven state constitutional convention campaigns; Two hundred and seventy-seven state party convention campaigns; Thirty campaigns; Thirty national party convention campaigns to get suffrage planks in the party platforms; Nineteen campaigns with nineteen successive congresses to get the federal amendment submitted; and the final ratification campaign.

> Millions of dollars were raised, mostly in small sums, and spent with economic care. Hundreds of women gave the

accumulated possibilities of an entire lifetime, thousands gave years of their lives, hundreds of thousands gave constant interest and such aid as they could. It was a continuous and seemingly endless chain of activity. Young suffragists who helped forge the last links in the chain were not born when it began. Old suffragists who helped forge the first links were dead when it ended.

Carrie Chapman Catt received many honors, including the first honorary degree awarded by the University of Wyoming (appropriately, the state which was first to give its women the vote), followed by similar awards from her alma mater, Iowa State College, Smith College, and Moravian College for Women. She was awarded the American Hebrew Medal for her work on behalf of German Jewish refugees, a citation of honor from President Franklin Roosevelt, and the gold medal of the National Institute of Social Sciences.

It was not overmuch in the way of recognition, considering that her efforts, more than those of any other single person (with the exception of Susan B. Anthony) brought women the privilege of having a say in their government. If she hadn't come to the fore, the women of America might still be waiting around, being lorded over by their men. But there was a Carrie Catt—wise, witty and sanguine as well as pragmatic.

Shortly before the Tennessee ratification in 1920, bracing herself for the possibility of yet another defeat but ever resilient, Carrie Catt wrote to Maude Park, one of her oldest friends;

If our familiar experience is repeated, I want you to know that I am resigned. Those who will eventually triumph can afford to be patient and forgiving. . . . Nothing has been left undone, except the Lord's creation of certain creatures who pass for statesmen. He might have done a better job! Yours for victory, Yours for defeat, Carrie.

Flexner, Eleanor. *A Century of Struggle*. Cambridge, Mass.: Harvard University Press, 1959.

"Carrie Clinton Lane Chapman," *Notable American Women*, Vol. 1. Edited by Edward T. & Janet W. James. Cambridge, Mass.: Harvard University Press, Bellknap Press, 1971.

Frost, Elizabeth Knappman- and Cullen-Dupont, Kathryn. *Woman Suffrage In America*. New York City: Facts on File, 1992.

Rogers, Agnes. *Women Are Here To Stay*. New York City: Harper & Bros., 1949.

Order of Countries giving their women the vote:

1881 - Isle of Man	1918 - Canada, England, Scotland, Wales, Germany,
1893 - New Zealand	Austria, Hungary
1902 - Australia	1919 - British East Africa, Holland, Poland. Serbia,
1906 - Finland	Rhodesia, Sweden, Roumania, Belgium, Latvia,
1907 - Norway	Luxembourg, Burma, Littonia, Estonia,
1913 - Iceland	CzechoSlovakia
1915 - Denmark	
1917 - Russia	and finally in
	1920 - The United States

ADDITIONAL SOURCES

Beckwourth, James P. *Life and Adventures of James P. Beckwourth.* New York City: MacMillan & Co., 1891.

Botkin, B. A., editor. *A Treasury of Werstern Folklore.* New York City: Crown Publishers, Inc., 1951.

Caughey, John W. *The California Gold Rush.* Berkeley, Calif.: University of California Press, 1948.

Marryatt, Frank. *Mountains and Molehills.* 1855. Facsimile: Palo Alto, Calif.: Stanford Press. 1952.

Miller, Ronald D. *Shady Ladies of the West.* Los Angeles, Calif.:Westernlore Press, 1964

Noble, Iris. *Nellie Bly, First Woman Reporter.* New York City: Julian Messner, 1956.

O'Meara, Walter. *Daughters of the Country.* New York City: Harcourt, Brace & World, 1968.

Shinn, Charles H. *Mining Camps: A Study of American Frontier Government.* New York City, 1885: Peter Smith Publishers, 1984.

Shirley, Glenn. *Law West of Fort Smith.* New York City: Henry Holt & Co., 1957.

Stevens, Doris. *Jailed for Freedom.* New York City: Boni & Liverwright, 1920.

Taylor, Bayard. *Eldorado.* New York City: Alfred A. Knopf, Inc., 1949.

Wellman, Paul I. *A Dynasty of Western Outlaws.* New York City: Crown Publishers, Bonanaza Books, 1961.

Glory, God and Gold. New York City: Doubleday & Co., 1954.

Frances Laurence was born in Pittsburgh, Pennsylvania, where her inventor father, M.C. Rypinski, an electrical engineer with the  Westinghouse Company, got the job of launching KDKA — the world's first commercial radio station. She met husband Douglas in New York in 1945. When they relocated in Los Angeles, he managed and produced live comedy and musical acts; she named one The Continentals, and created their stage costumes. When he produced 400 fifteen minute transcribed radio shows with The Riders Of The Purple Sage, she wrote the lead-in and exit dialog for every song. The show won an award.

While Douglas moved from live to filmed entertainment at MGM, she raised three children, sewed, sculpted, painted, decorated movie stars' homes, designed products and began writing. Frances and Douglas recently celebrated their fiftieth wedding anniversary.

Her profiles and articles have been published in magazines and newspapers in the U.S. and abroad, and she has written two historical novels. This is her first non-fiction book.

ALSO FROM MANIFEST PUBLICATIONS:

Books by Virginia Cornell:

*Doc Susie: The True Story of a Country Physician in the
    Colorado Rockies*
She was beautiful, she was smart, she was dying —
When Susan anderson, M.D., stepped from the train into frigid Fraser,
Colorado — "Icebox of the Nation" — she had everything to die for and
nothing to live for. This is the true story of how Doc Susie recovered her
health, then ventured forth to save the lives of lumberjacks, miners, ranch-
ers, railroaders and their families. Over 100,000 copies of the biography of
Susan Anderson, M.D., have been sold to people who love a good story.
ISBN 0-9627896-5-8, quality paperback $14.95

Ski Lodge — Millers Idlewild Inn — Adventures in Snow Business
High in the mountains, there once was a rustic, homemade ski lodge — pop-
ulated by reluctant honeymooners, errant husbands, truant plumbers, youth-
ful ski bums . . . plus one naive innkeeper. With humor and insight the
author remembers when, as a single mother, she struggled to fill the gigan-
tic footprints vacated by her frenetically energetic father.
ISBN 0-9627896-6-6, hardcover $12.95

The Latest Wrinkle — and other Signs of Aging
If you want to slam on the brakes at the first Signs of Aging, this book offers
some original thoughts about how to smooth out the wrinkles caused by:
fractured families, family reunions, curmudgeonly husbands, grafts on the
family tree, pets that kill, obituaries, gum disease, burial plans, Chia Pets.
ISBN 0-9627896-3-1, quality paperback $9.95

ORDER FORM

The following titles are available from Manifest Publications:
Indicate number of copies ordered.

Maverick Women	$ 18.50
The Latest Wrinkle	9.95
Doc Susie	14.95
Ski Lodge	12.95
Shipping and handling per order Book rate, U.S. Post Office	3.00
California residents add 7.75% tax	_____
Total Amount Enclosed	$ _____

Send to:

Name _____

Street Address/P.O. Box _____

City _____ State _____ Zip _____

Daytime Phone Number (____)_____

Phone orders encouraged. (805) 684-4905

Or mail to:
Manifest Publications
P.O. Box 429
Carpinteria, CA 93014-0429